Italian Signs, American Streets

New Americanists

A Series Edited by Donald E. Pease

ITALIAN SIGNS, AMERICAN STREETS

STREETS

The Evolution of Italian

American Narrative FRED L. GARDAPHÉ

Duke University Press Durham and London 1996

© 1996 Duke University Press
All rights reserved
Printed in the United States of America on acid-free paper ∞
Typeset in Galliard by Keystone Typesetting, Inc.

Library of Congress Cataloging-in-Publication Data appear on
the last printed page of this book.

Contents

Acknowledgments

This book grew out of my dissertation, and so I owe much to my committee, Christian Messenger, A. LaVonne Brown Ruoff, Michael Anania, Marion Miller, and Rebecca West, for their support and criticism during the course of my graduate study. That dissertation was awarded a 1994 prize for doctoral theses on Italian emigration by the Fondazione Giovanni Agnelli in association with the Italian Ministry of Foreign Affairs, an honor for which I am extremely grateful.

To Clark and Carolyn Hulse I owe my appreciation for convincing me that the University of Illinois at Chicago was the right place to do that work. My thanks to Professor Bernard Kogan and Mrs. Kogan and the American Italian Historical Association for financial support through the Irene Kogan and AIHA Memorial Fellowships.

I thank the friends and colleagues who provided me with the most help throughout this work. Anthony J. Tamburri who was always there when I needed a critical eye or ear. Mary Jo Bona, Tina DeRosa, Thomas J. Ferraro, Paul Giordano, and Giose Rimanelli (this work's godfather) all helped me better understand both the subject matter and my self. Philip Klukoff, chairman of the English Department of Columbia College, offered encouragement and support at the right times. To Rudolph Vecoli and the Immigration History Research Center, *tante grazie* for providing me with support and the place at which this project was conceived and initial research was conducted.

Support from Columbia College came at crucial times during my work. A sabbatical enabled me to complete my dissertation, and a Faculty Development Award enabled me to rewrite it and prepare it for submission.

Frank Lentricchia's guidance and support was crucial in directing me to Donald Pease's New Americanists series at Duke University Press. The editorial direction of Donald Pease and Reynolds Smith helped turn a hope into a reality. Thanks to Sharon E. Parks, Pam Morrison, and Mindy Conner of Duke University Press, I was able to survive the often tedious, but rewarding, production and editorial processes.

To my wife Susan, I owe my greatest debt. Without her support and love this project would neither have happened nor mattered.

Introduction

The starting point of critical elaboration is the consciousness of what
one really is, and is "knowing thyself" as a product of the historical
process to date, which has deposited in you an infinity of traces, without leaving an inventory; therefore it is imperative at the outset to
compile such an inventory.
Antonio Gramsci, *Quaderni del carcere*

Breaking and Entering: Reading *The Godfather*
and Other Cultural Crimes

What I have to say about Italian American narrative is best introduced
through a brief personal account of the role that reading and writing have played in the development of my own ethnic identity. Through
this development I have come to see my life's reading and writing as entries
onto a historical rap sheet of the cultural crimes of breaking and entering
mainstream America. The study of ethnic literature is more than reading
and responding to the literary products created by minority cultures; it is a
process that, for its advocate, necessarily involves a self-politicization that
requires placing a personal item onto a public agenda.

I grew up in a little Italy in which not even the contagiously sick were
left alone. The self-isolation that reading requires was rarely possible and
was even considered a dangerous invitation to blindness and insanity (this
was evidenced by my being the first American born in the family to need
glasses before the age of ten). There was no space in my home set aside for
isolated study. We were expected to come home from school, drop our
books on the kitchen table, and begin our homework. It was difficult to
concentrate with four children at the table, all subjected to countless interruptions from the family and friends who passed through the house regularly. We returned home from school every day to scenes that most of our
classmates knew only on weekends or holidays. The only books that entered my home were those we smuggled in from public institutions. Reading anything beyond newspapers and the mail required escaping from my
family. My chronic reading was seen as a problem and quickly identified
me as the "'merican," or rebel. It betrayed my willingness to enter main-

stream American culture, and while my family tolerated this, they did little to make that move an easy one. In spite of such obstacles I managed to become a reader. For a long time it did not occur to me that what I read was something that could or even should speak to me of my ethnicity. The books I read were written by others about experiences that were not mine.

Since books were nonnegotiable in my community, the giving of them was considered not only impractical but taboo. One day—a day of no special occasion—one of my aunts broke this book-as-gift taboo by giving my mother a copy of Mario Puzo's *The Godfather.* She told my mother that if her nephew was so intent on reading, he might as well read a book about Italians (neither of them had read it). The title of the book was quite appropriate since, after my father's early death, I had taken his place, at the age of ten, as godfather to one of my cousins. Perhaps my aunt thought the book would make an appropriate handbook for my new role in the extended family.

The Godfather was the first book with which I could completely identify, and it inspired my choice of the Mafia as a topic for the dreaded senior thesis that my Irish Catholic prep school required. One way or another I had been connected to the Mafia since I left my Italian neighborhood to attend high school, so I decided it was time to find out what this thing called Mafia was. This was the first writing project to excite me, and when I completed it I was certain of receiving an excellent grade. But the grading committee decided that the thesis, although well written, depended too much on Italian sources, and that because I was of Italian descent, I had not achieved the objectivity essential to all serious scholarship. I read the "C" grade as punishment for my cultural transgression and decided to stay away from anything but English and American literature in my future formal studies.

I continued to search for and read books by Italian Americans—outside my formal classes, of course—but I never considered them in the same light as the literature that I studied in my undergraduate courses and went on to teach to high school students. Not until I began to submit my own writing to publications did I realize that disseminating my work would demand political action. My first attempt at a novel received mixed reactions from a number of editors. One suggested that I follow in Puzo's footsteps and heighten the Mafia material he was certain was lurking under the surface of my story. Another suggested that I change the characters' ethnicity because Italian Americans do not read and so could not be counted on to buy the book, and because Italian American characters could alienate even those who did buy books — unless, of course, I was willing to tell more about the many murders that had occurred in my family's past. Not willing to follow any of these suggestions, I put aside my novels, thinking that before I could do anything with my own fiction, I had to change the mistaken notions of those editors. I believed that if I could prove that there was Italian American literature beyond Mafia stories, and that it did not depend on a distinctive Italian American audience, then my own writing would have a tradition and I a place in it. I began relentlessly pursuing writers I had identified as Italian American, even those who did not see themselves as "ethnic." I interviewed them, reviewed their books, held public forums, and did all I could to promote the reading and criticism of their work. Some people even suggested that I was fabricating this notion of the Italian American writer in order to jump into the new fad of ethnic studies that was hitting the universities. The result of all my efforts was a strong personal intraethnic identity, which I subsequently stabilized by studying the Italian language and traveling to Italy whenever possible.

In order to gain a sense of how to critically approach Italian American writers, I began reading criticism of other minority literatures. In "Criticism in the Jungle," Henry Louis Gates, Jr., provided exactly what I was looking for when he said: "W. E. B. DuBois argued that evidence of critical activity is a sign of a tradition's sophistication, since criticism implies an awareness of the process of art itself and is a second-order reflection upon those primary texts that define a tradition and its canon. . . . All great writers demand great critics" (8). These ideas soon led me to the scene of my next cultural crime: graduate school.

After completing my master's degree with a thesis on Walt Whitman, I decided to turn my attention to Italian American writers, who had so far earned only one book-length study. I found a professor who agreed to be my accomplice; after polling the other faculty, he suggested that I bail out of academia and do the work on my own. Breaking in, he suggested, would be impossible. The only alternative would be to strike a compromise by working on Henry James, who had, after all, used Italian settings and characters in his fiction. I followed his first suggestion and escaped. Six years later I found a graduate program that allowed me to incorporate ethnic literatures into my required studies. Beyond the courses on the traditional Anglo-American mainstream writers, the University of Illinois at Chicago offered courses in Jewish American, Native American, and African American literatures. I also benefited from courses in history, linguistics, and ethnography. There were no courses in Italian American literature at the graduate level, but reading the critics of minority American literatures enabled me to gain insights to approaches I could use to create a viable criticism of Italian American texts.

This book is the result of my nearly twenty years of reading, thinking, interviewing, and writing about Italian American literature. It represents my attempt to categorize the diverse texts created by American writers of Italian descent and to form a critical approach to these texts that identifies and analyzes the Italian signs present in these American artifacts. This book also attempts to explain the place of writing in the process of cultural transmission, which for southern Italians less than a century ago was primarily through oral tradition. The context for the oral transmission of cultural messages has changed during the movement from Italian to American culture. The writers have become the witnesses of this movement and the recorders of the lives and stories of those people who initiated the process of change. As the primary oral culture disappears, we must depend on the writers for access to the past. Through their writing they preserve the memory, the history, the meaning, and the truths of their ancestors' lives, but in order to understand the Italian American narrative, one needs to understand the complexity of the signs these writers use and the figures they create inside their narratives.

It is the job of the critic, the scholar, and the teacher to make sure that the cultural crimes of the past do no increase others' ignorance of Italian American culture — not only the ignorance of those my grandfather used to call "merdicans," but of those the merdicans used to call guineas and wops. It is in this spirit that I offer the following historical survey of key figures who have contributed to the establishment and evolution of a critical discourse of Italian American literature. I do so with the hope that my work, along with the work of the critics I discuss next, will take its proper place in the history of American literature.

Making History: Creating a Culture-Specific Criticism

There is, of course, an ethnic story to tell, but the ethnic subject must
first learn to be at ease among signs. And given the history of American ethnogenesis, the world of signs — the world of absence — should
be the ethnic subject's natural place.
William Boelhower, *Through a Glass Darkly*

If Italian America is to regain the power of effective speech, it must
work to conquer a language for itself.
Robert Viscusi, "Breaking the Silence"

The history of the Italian American intellectual is yet to be written, but
when it is, one of the stories it will tell is of the tension between what
Antonio Gramsci has identified as the organic and the traditional intellectual. It will present a gallery of rogue scholars whose voices are sometimes vulgar and always vital, and whose place in American culture has
never been stabilized by political lobbies, cultural foundations, or endowed chairs. It will tell the tale of the pre-Christian paganism of Italian
culture that has resurfaced in popular culture through the antics of Madonna and the controversial cultural analyses of Camille Paglia. While
both of these American women of Italian descent seem to be innovators in
interpretation, they are in fact popularizers of ideas that have long remained submerged in the shadows of Italian American culture. One need
only look to Diane di Prima's *Memoirs of a Beatnik* or the cultural criticism
of Luigi Fraina and Robert Viscusi to find their antecedents. The major
problem facing Italian American intellectuals is not a lack of preparation
for producing cultural criticism or a lack of sophistication in their critical
methods, rather it is a lack of self-confidence that they can use the culture
from which they come to express themselves to the American mainstream
audience. The lack of this self-confidence is one result of the immigrant
experience.

What was referred to as "the southern problem" in Italy, a problem that
even today is raised by Italians in northern Italy, became the "Italian
problem" in America. Gramsci analyzes this problem in "The Southern
Question." Written in 1927, this essay identifies the activity of southern

intellectuals as the link binding southern peasants to the big property owners. In effect, the activity of such representative southern intellectuals as Benedetto Croce and Giustino Fortunato kept the southern bloc from becoming a revolutionary element. Without hope for change, many southerners decided that an uncertain future through emigration was a better option than the future they would have if they stayed. For many of those southerners, the solution to the southern problem was to leave Italy. This fate seems doomed to be repeated today; without a strong show of leadership by Italian American intellectuals, Italian Americans will opt to assimilate into mainstream American culture at the expense of losing contact with both the past and the present of Italian culture.

The vast majority of American writers of Italian descent can trace their ancestors back to those who left Italy during the late nineteenth and early twentieth centuries. The earliest voices of Italian Americans heard publicly were those of political and labor activists such as poet-organizer Arturo Giovanitti, Frances Winwar, journalist-organizer Carlo Tresca, and Luigi Fraina. Luigi Fraina, who later changed his name to Lewis Corey, was one of the first to publish Marxist literary criticism in America in the early 1900s.[1] Fraina was born in Italy and came to America with his mother at the age of three to join his father, a republican exile. An early participant in the DeLeon socialist labor movement, Fraina was involved in the founding of the American Communist Party. By the age of thirty Fraina had disconnected himself from all political groups and had become a leader of the anticommunist liberal movement.[2] During this period he was a union activist and a prolific Marxist critic and journalist. Early on, Fraina investigated the clash between paganism and the Christian culture that attempted to annihilate it. While he paid no attention to the cultural products produced by his fellow Italian Americans, Fraina's work represents the preoccupation of Italian American intellectuals with the obstacles they encountered in adapting to life in America.[3]

Without scholarly societies or formal programs dedicated to the study of Italian American culture, American intellectuals of Italian descent who were intent on defining and developing Italian American culture had to do so independently, and more often than not such work was considered an adjunct to their "real" work. While there were many Italian American newspapers that carried creative and critical work by Italian American writers, it was not until the children of Italian immigrants came of age in the 1930s that an articulate voice of Italian Americana was heard in the mainstream media.[4]

One of the earliest acts of indigenous Italian American criticism is Jerre Mangione's 1935 *New Republic* review of Garibaldi Lapolla's *The Grand Gennaro*. In it, Mangione introduces the rarity of meeting Italian Americans in American literature and credits Lapolla for "creating Italo-Americans who are vivid and alive and probably a novelty to the average person who, not knowing them intimately, is likely to draw his conclusions about them from the gangster movies" (Review, 313). A few years later, Mangione reviewed Pietro di Donato's *Christ in Concrete* in the *New Republic*. While he praises the beginning writer's rendition of the Italian American life, he does not hesitate to point out the novel's roughness and "minor deficiencies" ("Little Italy," 111). During this early stage of his writing career, Mangione took on the task of interpreting Italian culture and life under Mussolini. He reviewed translations of Pirandello's books *Better Think Twice about It* and *The Outcast* in the August 28, 1935, issue of the *New Republic*. During the same year, Mangione reviewed *Mr. Aristotle*, a translation of Ignazio Silone's collection of short stories. He wrote articles and short sketches for national publications such as the *Nation* and the *New Masses* and went on to be a spokesman for Italian and Italian American culture through his many books. His critical analysis of the dual identity in urban ethnic writing, his many reviews of books by Italian American writers, and, most recently, his survey of literary history in *La Storia* have all helped to establish Italian American literature and criticism as a serious presence in American culture.[5]

Over the past eighty years American writers of Italian descent have created a significant body of literary texts that have received little, if any, serious critical attention. While recent attempts to refigure the American literary canon recognize texts produced by minority cultures, nearly all fail to include recognition, let alone discussions, of contributions by Italian American writers. The word *Italian-American* appears only once in *Redefining American Literary History* (1990), and it shows up in a sentence that all but dismisses the need for any critical consideration of Italian American literature. The sentence is in Harold H. Kolb's essay "Defining the Canon": "Americans of Italian descent, who move easily between assimilation and ethnic preservation, seem not to have a particular need for courses in the Italian American novel" (38). A number of unsupported assumptions are put forth in Kolb's statement, assumptions that are characteristic of American critics and the literary industry at large, who ignore, if they do not dismiss, Italian American literature on the grounds that there is an absence of perceivable interest on the part of what such American critics have designated as its intended audience. One assumption is that Italian Americans, like chameleons, can assimilate or not at will. Another is that because they have not exhibited a desire for courses in the Italian American novel, Italian Americans must not need such courses. One explanation for statements such as Kolb's is that until recently the critical work necessary to bring this literature to the attention of the canon makers and breakers has been, at best, minimal. More often than not, when criticism of Italian American cultural products appears, it is produced by critics who are at best sympathetic to the Italian American writer. Critics who belong to the Anglo-American culture tend to speak for the Italian American writer and to restrict their interpretations to the mimetic functions of the Italian American narratives they discuss.[6] This criticism generally neglects to read the diegesis produced by the Italian signs that signify the Italian half of the adjective *Italian American*. Critics of Italian literature, who view Italian American literature as an inferior second cousin to Italian literature, are also guilty of neglect. Thus, it is no wonder that Italian American literature, which is neither "American" nor "Italian" in the traditional cultural sense (abandoned by its two parent cultures), is relegated to the *vicoli*, or "side streets," of literary discourse. In spite of the fact that Italian Americans have established a significant presence in American culture, an active community of scholars has only recently begun serious inquiry into the idea of Italian American culture. This has been the case with nearly all non-Anglo-American literature: a significant cultural presence emerges only with the development of an indigenous critical voice able to enter into a dialogue with canonical critics of the dominant culture.[7] The establishment of a critical dialectic is thus the first step toward validating the contribution that Italian American authors have made to American literature.

Rose Basile Green's *The Italian-American Novel* (1974) is the first major work that attempts to identify and critically examine the contributions of

American writers of Italian descent to American culture.[8] This work, typical of the ethnic revival period in which it was written, reflects an early stage of cultural examination, one that invites critics to consider the fiction of Italian American writers through an essentially universal sociological paradigm related to understanding the process of Americanization through the experience of immigration.[9] An observation by Giambattista Vico, one of the earliest cultural critics of Western civilization, points to the pitfalls inherent in such attempts to create universal methodologies: "When men are ignorant of the natural causes producing things, and cannot even explain them by analogy with similar things, they attribute their own nature to them. The vulgar, for example, say the magnet loves the iron. This axiom is a piece of the first namely, that the human mind, because of its indefinite nature, wherever it is lost in ignorance makes itself the rule of the universe in respect of everything it does not know" (*New Science*, 70). Vico's observation suggests that there exists a dominant tendency in human beings to define the unknown (which often can be read as "other") in terms of the known (which can be read as "self"). This tendency is the same notion set forth in many of the theories proposed by literary critics and scholars through the first half of the twentieth century; that is, the dominant trend until recently has been to create universal categories and criteria by which the literature under consideration is categorized and criticized. This sense of unity versus diversity can also be seen as the basis of the battle that has been waged over expanding the American canon. While Green's efforts have greatly assisted critics and scholars in locating Italian American literature on the map of American culture, we must avoid falling into the same monologistic, methodological trap that reads Italian American texts through critical paradigms created by the dominant culture. It is time to move into new dimensions of critical examination of the Italian American contribution to American literature.

While a number of challenges to New Critical methodologies have been created, the most interesting and relevant work is being done in "culture-specific" criticism.[10] The culture-specific approach examines the multicultural contexts out of which emerges the "other" American text and relates texts to indigenous cultural histories and philosophies. Essentially, the culture-specific approach employs what Houston Baker calls "an anthropology of art." Alan Wald suggests that the theorizing of cultural difference needs to proceed from the ground up: "Our primary task now is not to declare by fiat a precise 'universal' methodology, but to deepen our familiarity with the distinctive features of the texts themselves" ("Theorizing Culture Difference," 31).

Following Wald's suggestion, I present a way of identifying the distinctive features of the writing of Italian Americans which when compiled will form a cultural self-inventory. In essence, this self-inventory will contain the Italian signs generated through codes specific to Italian and Italian American cultures. Subsequent chapters will present readings of the Italian American signs that result from attempts to represent Americans of Italian descent in writing. By first developing and then applying this aesthetic to representative works, and through examining the historical and ideological contexts out of which they emerge, I hope to present a new perspective by which these writers can be read, and therefore to increase the discursive power of this ethnic group.

In a recent essay entitled "Breaking the Silence: Strategic Imperatives for Italian American Culture," Robert Viscusi sets forth a program designed to realize a distinct discursive power that would allow "its possessors to grapple directly with the problems that confront them" (3) through the development of three possessions that discursive power requires: *the creation of a language* (for, as Viscusi says, "to be Italian American we must speak the diglot" [5]); *the creation of a narrative*, the articulation of a history or "collective purpose"; and *the creation of a dialectics*, which would "proceed from a double tongue and a double narrative of passage." Such a narrative would enable the deconstruction of "the monotone discourse of weakness that has led us to repose so much tacit faith in the forms of ethnic self-enclosure" (9); essentially a dialectics enables the indigenous critic to question stereotypes and myths of Italian American culture that the mainstream media have created. Viscusi calls this creation of discursive power our "only project," and he perceptively concludes that it is thus a "project of our language" (9). Viscusi's goal is to create a self-critical discourse, a discourse that Italian American culture has traditionally lacked. I share his goal. What follows is my contribution to the creation of a culture-specific criticism that is sensitive to both Italian and American cultures.

The first step in establishing an indigenous criticism is to create what

Gramsci calls the self-inventory. Gramsci's notion of a self-inventory—literally, the listing of what is found during a self-examination—requires us to identify the signs that result from the self-fashioning that is created in and through literature; this list, in the case of Italian American literature, will contain the characteristics that distinguish this literature from other American literatures. We will track these characteristics through both Italian and American cultures, the two national cultures from which the Italian American self is fashioned. I will present a way of reading the Italian signs in texts produced by Italian American writers, and I will compile a self-inventory of Italian signs that will help readers learn more about cultural differences and cultural identity. We will look linguistically at the instances of code switching in the presentation of Italian dialects and ideolects; stylistically at oral and literate models in narrative performance; and formalistically at the forms identified with the dominant and minority cultures. Finally, I will discuss the attitudes expressed by Italian American writers in terms of the ideological culture to which they belong. This examination will follow a paradigm based on the historiographic work of Giambattista Vico.

Trying to place Italian American narratives—from the early immigrant works through contemporary ones—into traditional historical categories such as modernism and postmodernism can create confusion. For example, when critics examined the first novel by Pietro di Donato, who was forging a new stage of Italian American literary activity, they found it to fall short of the ruling aesthetic standards of both the modernist and the proletarian writers of the time. Thus, di Donato was, in spite of his status as a best-selling author, relegated to the freak show corner of the American literary circus. Minority-culture writers have suffered from a lack of sensitivity to and understanding of the relationship of what Werner Sollors calls cultures of "descent" and "consent," and Edward Said calls "filiate" and "affiliate" cultures, a sensitivity that Erich Auerbach so eloquently describes in "Vico and Aesthetic Historicism": "The largeness of our aesthetic horizon is a consequence of our historical perspective; it is based on historism, i.e., on the conviction that every civilization and every period has its own possibilities of aesthetic perfection; that the works of art of the different peoples and periods, as well as their general forms of life, must be understood as products of variable individual conditions, and have to be judged each by its own development, not by absolute rules of beauty and ugliness" (183–4). Such a perspective is often perceived as relativism, which terrifies traditional cultural gatekeepers. It is also a major concern of many contemporary critics, who see much of what enters the mainstream from minority cultures as entering via a type of affirmative action aesthetic based on politics.

In my attempt to create a horizon that would enable readers to view Italian American literature in the context of its relationship to Italian, American, and Italian American cultures, I found that I needed a new way of looking at narratives by minority writers, a way of reading that would enable readers to include such work in ongoing discussions of American literary history and would help all of us achieve that sense of foresight that Vico refers to as "consciousness of the certain." In this way, our criticism might even become predictive rather than simply reactive.

Vico and Italian American Literary History

Philosophy contemplates reason, whence comes knowledge of the
true; philology observes that of which human choice is the author,
whence comes consciousness of the certain. . . . This axiom shows
how the philosophers failed by half in not giving certainty to their
reasonings by appeal to the authority of the philologians, and likewise
how the latter half failed by half in not taking care to give their authority the sanction of truth by appeal to the reasoning of the philosophers.
If they had done this they would have been more useful to
their commonwealths.
Vico, axiom 10, *The New Science*

The Italian American critical project is both a philological (or historical) and a philosophical one. Key components of it are the development of a literary history and the creation of an aesthetic by which to read Italian American texts. In discovering these components we can be helped by the application of Vico's notion of *corso* and *ricorso*, a cultural rise and fall that happens and will happen again as cultures and civilizations age and mature. I grant that applying this notion literally to American history would be quite problematic, for as a nation of nations, America could not easily follow Vico's universal pattern of rise and fall as long as cultural diversity persists. However, *corso* and *ricorso* can illuminate the recent rise in power of minority American literature.

If we consider each of the ethnic groups in the United States as an individual nation within a society of nations, Vico's theory provides a way of mapping the rise and fall of such literatures as Anglo-American, African American, and Jewish American. In brief, I suggest that we are now witnessing the descent of Anglo-American literature into a *ricorso*. Having moved through a *corso*, from the *vero narratio* (telling it like it is) of its earliest writers, evidenced by oral traditions and autobiographies, through the mythic period (or the mimetic), which is historically characterized as the period from the American renaissance through high modernism, and finally into the philosophic, or what has been referred to as postmodernism, American literature, as traditionally defined, has reached its period of decadence. It has become, in John Barth's words, a "literature of exhaustion." According to Vico, the next stage of cultural history will be a descent into barbarism. While such a descent is inevitable, it can be delayed by a return to the culture's fundamental principles, its roots. What is enlivening American culture at this time, and delaying the descent, is the rise of the artists and intellectuals of America's other-cultural components. These writers are like Vico's plebeians (the powerless), who struggle for the laws and the benefit (the power) of the patricians (the ruling class). The contemporary struggle for inclusion by minority cultures into the mainstream of the dominant culture parallels the political struggle that Vico sees in the movement from aristocratic rule to a popular democratic liberty (*New Science*, 55).[11]

The process is described by Paul Lauter in his essay "Caste, Class, Canon," in which he raises and examines an important question: How is the canon a function of critical technique? Lauter sees the canon as "a product . . . of our training in a male, white, bourgeois cultural tradition, including in particular the formal techniques of literary analysis" (59). He tells us that we must look at the full range of cultural traditions if we want to change the body of literature that we consider in our American literature courses. Focusing his discussion on the writing that emerges from the working-class and African American cultures, Lauter observes that "the conception of the functions of art are [*sic*] here very different from those propounded, say, by Aristotle, or Milton, or Coleridge — or formalist criticism" (63). And so, in order to develop appropriate critical tools, we must explore working-class art "in terms of its use" (65). This development requires an understanding of the social and political contexts out of which a particular work emerges. In essence, Lauter advocates a multi-cultural approach that uses elements from Marxism and New Historicism to bring works that have been traditionally marginalized into the center of public consciousness. This task, Lauter reminds us, has traditionally been accomplished not by academic critics but by social activists: "It was not the work of critics that refocused attention to the distinctive concerns of women writers any more than black aestheticians initially established the conditions for recognizing the traditions of African-American composition. On the contrary, it was the movements for social, economic, and political changes of the 1960s and 1970s that challenged long-held assumptions about was significant for *people*" (79). In other words, criticism alone does not expand a canon. Such change requires the mobilization of social and political forces and "our work as political people" (80). But scholars and critics can begin the process by attracting new attention to the texts that mainstream society has kept at the margins.[12] Vico's political allegory of the plebeians and the patricians conceptualizes and historicizes the context for the current situation of American multiculturalism. Thus, I will adapt Vico's stages describing the development and decay of a culture as a framework by which to historicize contributions by American authors of Italian descent to American literature. Those historical stages, in Vico's vocabulary, are the poetic, the mythic, and the philosophic.

Vico's developmental framework can be seen as a variant of one discussed by Werner Sollors in his analysis of the relationship of ethnicity to literary forms:

We are accustomed to think of the development of American literature as "growth," as a process of increasing formal complexity from travelogues and letters . . . , sermons, essays, and biographies to the increasingly successful mastery of poetry, prose fiction and drama. Analogously, we may see the historical unfolding of ethnic writing as a process of growth; and again, the beginning is with immigrant and immigrant letters. . . . The literature then "grows" from nonfictional to fictional forms . . . ; from folk and popular forms to high forms . . . ; from lower to higher degrees of complexity . . . ; and from "parochial" marginality to "universal" significance in the literary mainstream. (*Beyond Ethnicity*, 240–1)

The problem with this "growth" paradigm, as Sollors points out, is that it tends to set up a false opposition between "parochial ethnicity" and "modern movements in art and literature" (241), which in turn leads to the creation of an equally false opposition between ethnicity and Americanness. To avoid this problem we need to develop a way of reading literature according to the "growth" model, a way that is not so much reading such works as products of ethnic writers as reading them for the ethnic signs produced by their American writers. These signs play to two audiences: those familiar with their culture of "descent" (the culture into which one is born and raised), and outsiders (those familiar with the author's culture of "consent"). The critic of multicultural literature needs to know how to read the signs generated by all the cultures that have shaped an author.

Using Vico's notions of a culture's three ages — the Age of Gods, the poetic stage; the Age of Heroes, the mythic stage; and the Age of Man, the philosophic stage — we can create an interesting retrospective approach to reading the history of Italian American narratives. We can read the preimmigrant past as the Age of Gods, the early period of social development in which men create gods in their own image and set up the socioeconomic rules for survival, resulting in what Vico calls divine societies; the immigrant experience can be read as the Age of Heroes, in which aristocratic rule is developed; and the postimmigrant experience as the Age of Man and Woman, in which the rebellion of the servile class creates a democratic society. I apply this notion of national evolution as a metaphor that describes Italian American literature's cultural history.

Vico's three stages give us a way of reading the movement from a culture based on oral tradition to one based on literary tradition. This process reflects Vico's notion of the movement from *vero narratio*, the poetic, during which we find the codes of a culture ruled by the divine imbedded in the stories transmitted through the oral tradition; to the mythic, during which the codes of culture shift to rules based on heroic models; and finally to the philosophic, during which Man and eventually Woman rebel against traditional models and subsequently re-create or reinvent the models of behavior. Thus, I read oral traditions and the narrative autobiographies of immigrants as *vero narratio*, the early auto-biographical fictions as the creation of myth, and later, more sophisticated and self-reflexive postmodern narratives as the philosophic.[13]

As representative of *vero narratio* I have chosen Constantine Panunzio's *The Soul of an Immigrant* (1921), Pascal D'Angelo's *Son of Italy* (1924), and Marie Hall Ets's *Rosa: The Life of an Italian Immigrant* (1970). Narrative development in the poetic mode is characterized by models of behavior based on divine models and a strong sense of destiny as the means determining one's fate. These narrative constructions are rooted heavily in Italian folk culture, reveal a dominance of Italian over American traits, and display a fairly extensive use of Italian language. Within this mode we can observe a shift from folktale to autobiography as evidenced by the shift of subject from other to self. Finally, within narratives in the poetic mode, there is a movement of the Italian alien subject toward conformity with mainstream American society.

As representative of the mythic mode I have selected John Fante's *Wait until Spring, Bandini* (1938), Pietro di Donato's *Christ in Concrete* (1939), Jerre Mangione's *Mount Allegro* (1943), Mario Puzo's *The Godfather* (1969), Gay Talese's *Honor Thy Father* (1971), Helen Barolini's *Umbertina* (1979), Tina DeRosa's *Paper Fish* (1980), and Carole Maso's *Ghost Dance* (1986). Narratives developed in the mythic mode present models of behavior based on heroic figures who inspire a struggle with destiny. While there are elements of folklore present in these narratives, the sense of folklore is not as dominant as it is in the poetic mode. There is an obvious dominance of Italian American traits over both Italian and American traits, yet there is a significant presence of Italian words and phrases. It is in this mode that we can observe the transition from auto-biography to autobiographical fiction. The subjects in these narratives rebel against both Italian and American cultures and thus fashion the hybrid Italian American culture.

The philosophic, or incredible, mode (a mode that challenges and destroys belief in previous models) is represented by Giose Rimanelli's *Benedetta in Guysterland* (1993) and the narratives of Don DeLillo and Gilbert Sorrentino.[14] Narrative development in the philosophic mode features models of behavior based on humans as makers of their own destinies. Folkloric elements, when present, are used to deconstruct the dominant/official culture. This mode evidences a transition from autobiographical fiction to experimental fiction as well as a dominance of American traits over Italian and Italian American traits. Although linguistic signs of Italianness are not obvious, they are visible to the trained reader. The subjects in these narratives are likely to rebel against any tradition.

The movement from mode to mode can be read as movement from an imaginative idealism through social realism to an intellectual idealism that accompanies a decadent postmodernism.[15] These three stages represent periods that mark the evolution of narrative production. By no means are they meant to be categorically applied to "generations," or to a single author's oeuvre, for as we will see, a writer's narrative strategy can develop and shift among these modes throughout his or her career.

Criticism as Ethnography: Reading the Italian American Sign

The semiotic process involves not so much a particular group
of things as it does their being grouped in a certain way. It is, in short,
a position of reading.
William Boelhower, *Through a Glass Darkly*

In an early essay attempting to determine appropriate critical approaches to ethnic literature, John M. Reilly presents the idea that

ethnic literature is not ethnography, nor even politics, though imaginative ethnic writing will help describe culture and may justifiably advocate political positions. Rather ethnic literature can only be fully explained by an approach that studies writing as the expression of the cognitive orientations of the authors. Ethnicity is a constant among these orientations, but it is varied and modified by authorial disposition, assumptions about social and personal relationships, self-image, and assumptions about the way the natural and social world works ("Criticism of Ethnic Literature," 12)

While Reilly does not define or elaborate on how to study an author's "cognitive orientation," the study of the development of an author's thought, and thus expression, can be helped by the science of semiotics and the field of ethnography.

In terms of ethnic semiotics, the work of William Boelhower provides a way of understanding Reilly's idea of the "cognitive orientations" of ethnic writers. Boelhower situates the ethnic sign in an inferencing field created by what he calls the "cognitive gaze." This gaze, the act of seeing/reading, which he illustrates through Henry James's experience of the "staring silence" that occurred when he encountered Italian workmen on the Jersey shore, "generates a cognitive map equivalent to an ethnic world" (*Through a Glass Darkly*, 39). When Henry James looked at these workers, he interpreted that they were inferior to the Italians he knew. Such an interpretation, says Boelhower, depends entirely on the mode of development of one's way of thinking. The same can be said for the writer. The diction that a writer uses can say much about his or her relationship to the subject of his or her writing. In the case of Henry James, we can read his disappointment, if not disdain, that the Italian American laborers did not reflect the Italy of which he knew and wrote. Boelhower's point here is that the reader of a scene — and the same is true of any text — comes to the experience with "a position of reading" (*Through a Glass Darkly*, 39), with certain expectations based on previous and often preformulated expectations. James's observation of the Italian American workers, and his conclusion that they were inferior to the Italians with whom he was familiar, were based on his limited ability to read the Italian signs and his inability to transcend his previous experience with the subject. The notion of the Italian in America as preconstructed by writers such as Henry James is one I plan to challenge by providing a means of reading (or revising) the signs generated through the written expression of Italian Americans. By constructing a dialogical scene between what is Italian and what is American, we can begin to read the consequential sign production and thus understand that there is an Italian American perspective. The signs that will appear will be the key to understanding Reilly's notion of cognitive orientation of the author and as such will enable us to better understand how ethnicity is modified by Reilly's checklist of "authorial disposition, assumptions about social and personal relationships, self-image, and assumptions about the way the natural and social world works" ("Criticism of Ethnic Literature," 12).

In effect, identifying and analyzing the ethnic signs produced by the writers whose works I examine in this book can be seen as the creation of a literary ethnography. A brief survey of recent developments in the field of anthropology and the postmodern criticism of ethnographies that has arisen from a concern with how best to (re)present the "other" will make this clear. As James Clifford writes in his introduction to *Writing Culture*: "It has become clear that every version of an 'other,' wherever found, is also the construction of a 'self,' and the making of ethnographic texts . . . has always involved a process of 'self fashioning.' Cultural *poesis*—and politics—is the constant reconstitution of selves and others through specific exclusions, conventions and discursive practices" (24). Contemporary critics of ethnographies (especially Clifford Geertz, James Clifford, George E. Marcus, Michael Fischer, and Stephen Tyler) have revolutionized anthropology by employing poststructuralist literary theory. They have read ethnographies not as transparent windows into other cultures but as texts built by writers. These and other critics see ethnographies as working more like two-way mirrors: while providing a look at the culture under study, they also reflect the person who is doing the studying. Approaching literature through ethnographically oriented readings is the foundation of the school of criticism called New Historicism, which focuses attention on the cultural contexts in and from which a particular author writes. My discussion will identify elements of ethnography that can provide the basis for a working approach to American literary criticism.[16]

Ethnographic insight into a text's cultural role can eliminate, in Roland Barthes's words, "distinction derived from logic which turns the work itself into a language-object and science into a metalanguage, and thus to forgo that illusory privilege which science attaches to the possession of a captive language" ("Science versus Literature," 413). In other words, the movement in poststructuralist theory has been from a focus on the decontextualized language that appears in any written text, to the relationship that the text describes between the context and the author. By approaching a text ethnographically, we can better understand it as a communicative event determined by the cultural constraints within which the writer performed. A judgment of the author's competence and performance will necessarily be tied to the cultural contexts in which the writer worked. Too often in our examination of cross-cultural texts we read only the American side of the "other" American effort, leaving the other either unexplored or, at best, obscured by the shadows of the dominant Anglo-American cultural standards. The ethnographic critic can shed much light on problems ignored by the critic who is textbound and limited to a mono-cultural — i.e., canonical — sense of competence and performance. If an ethnographic critic is to be successful, he or she must be able to read the culturally specific signs generated in the multicultural text. In the case of Italian American literature, and other American literatures as well, the critic must be aware of the cultural codes that generate those signs.

For the purposes of this study, I will define an Italian sign as one signifying *Italianità*, or the qualities associated with Italian culture. The most obvious signs will be the lexical units that appear in the Italian language or dialectal variants. Beyond language, there are two cultural codes that govern public behavior: *omertà*, the code of silence that governs what is spoken or not spoken about in public, and *bella figura*, the code of proper presence or social behavior that governs an individual's public presence. These codes were carried to America through the oral traditions of southern Italian culture, and so it is important to first consider the folkloric basis of Italian American culture.

Vico believed that a "critical, etymological study of the classic myths of the Greeks and Romans would prove invaluable for reconstructing the prehistory of classical civilization" (Bidney, "Vico's New Science," 261), and he analyzed the language used to create the texts that contribute to the making of a culture. Likewise, each minority culture also has a prehistory that can and must be reconstructed. For Italian Americans, this is a history largely found in the immigrants' words and figures, or tropes, discovered in both the early writing (usually letters and journalism) and the oral traditions that inform this early literature. In "Vico's New Science of Myth," David Bidney reminds us that Vico believed that to study a society completely one must consider both elite and popular culture: "Through the study of the folklore of a people, the ethnologist and folklorist may reconstruct its ethnic history and provide new generations of poets and artists with a genuine source of inspiration for further ethnic creativity" (267). Such study has certainly renewed Native, African, Asian, and Mexican American cultures. Thus, in this book I will consider the elements of folk culture — the stories, proverbs, etc. — that form the basis of Italian

American culture. I will examine representative aspects of Italian American narrative forms, including the novel and the autobiography, that have emerged during the period between 1920 and the present. Developments in literary and cultural theory will lead us to ways of reading a literature that for too long has remained in the shadows of the new light that critical attention to ethnicity has shed on previously marginalized narrative texts. By situating these representative texts within the context of American cultural history and criticism, replacing the concepts and constructs of realism, modernism, and postmodernism with a Vichian paradigm of poetic, mythic, and philosophic, I will provide a model for entering into an Italian American discourse through the reading of the Italian signs it contains. I will also examine how different writers represent Italian American ethnicity. The reconstructive methodology required to continue the re-creation of Italian American culture requires a consideration of the interactions between American and Italian cultures, and thus an intimate familiarity with both cultures is necessary. Reconstruction through etymological study of the appearance and function of the Italian signs in Italian American literature is a good place to begin an analysis of Italian American literature.

In Chapter 1, we will search for Italian signs in representative texts created by immigrants. We will consider writers who, primarily through autobiography, created a storytelling tradition in writing, a tradition I call *vero narratio*. Their texts, while heavily influenced by American models, contain relationships to Italian culture that have rarely been explored. It is here that I begin my historical reading of Italian American writing as it is informed by the oral traditions on which many of the earliest Italian American social realist narratives (primarily autobiographies) written by immigrants are based: Constantine Panunzio's *The Soul of an Immigrant*, Pascal D'Angelo's *Son of Italy*, and Marie Hall Ets's *Rosa*. These narratives represent early attempts to negotiate an American identity.

Chapters 2, 3, and 4 examine works representative of the mythic mode often used by Italian American writers. These texts reveal a shift from the poetic (Age of Gods) into the mythic (Age of Heroes): the dominant heroes are the figures of the immigrant and the godfather, figures prominent in the works of Mario Puzo, Gay Talese, Giose Rimanelli, Helen Barolini, Tina DeRosa, and Carole Maso. Chapter 2 focuses on works of fiction created by children of Italian immigrants. Situated in the mythic period, these texts use such figures as Christ and the Madonna to encode *Italianità*. The primary texts we will consider in this chapter are Pietro di Donato's *Christ in Concrete* (1939), John Fante's *Wait until Spring, Bandini* (1938), and Jerre Mangione's *Mount Allegro* (1943). Chapter 3 examines the impact of the use of the Mafia myth in Mario Puzo's *The Godfather* (1969), Gay Talese's *Honor Thy Father* (1971), and Giose Rimanelli's *Benedetta in Guysterland* (written in the 1970s but published in 1993). I have placed Rimanelli's novel at the end of this chapter not because it represents the mythic mode of narrative development, but rather because it represents the deconstruction of that mode and thus becomes a threshold into the philosophic mode. Chapter 4 analyzes the work of three contemporary writers who advance the mythic period and who invest the figure of the immigrant with heroic qualities. These authors employ what I call the postmodern prerogative by exercising the option of visibly identifying with their Italian American heritage through their use of Italian American subjects. This reconstruction/deconstruction of history is a strong component of contemporary Italian American literature. By returning to the roots of a culture's foundation, it is possible to delay its descent into the inevitable *ricorso*; this recovery is essentially the means by which a culture in decay can be renewed. At a 1983 conference of the Associazione Italiana di Studi Nord-Americani, Daniel Aaron warned that "Italian American writers will never merge into the mainstream of the national culture, complete their 'passage,' until they have come to terms with themselves and their suppressed 'Italian foundations'" ("The Hyphenate American Writer," 25).[17] The immigrant past is re-created in the writing of the grandchildren of immigrants through the self-reflection that is created by an increased distance from the immigrant experience; this most distant historical perspective is gained by inquiry into the ethnic experience, which results in the re-creation of the immigrant experience in America through more distinctively fictional forms. In essence these portrayals rewrite immigrant myths, with the immigrants, usually grandparent figures, as the heroes.

By the third generation, Italian Americans had assimilated into the larger American culture via educational institutions, intermarriage, and exodus from the "little Italy" ghettos. Through this assimilation they gained greater political, social, and economic control over their lives. This sociological assimilation created a shift in the focus of the fiction produced by Italian American writers. Their fiction has become less a means of presenting what it means to be Italian in America and more descriptive of what it means to carry the cultural trappings of *Italianità* into everyday American lives. As Aaron notes, "Today many new ethnic writers and intellectuals recover their identities by locating their ancestral roots, digging them up and displaying them" ("The Hyphenate American Writer," 27). Chapter 4 discusses the use of the Italian American subject as a means of recovering and/or reinventing ethnicity (the visible Italians). This reinvention is demonstrated through an examination of the works of Helen Barolini (*Umbertina*, 1979), Tina DeRosa (*Paper Fish*, 1980), and Carole Maso (*Ghost Dance*, 1986).

Chapter 5 analyzes works produced by American authors of Italian descent who, while abandoning the ethnic self as subject, retain fragile yet definite connections to their Italian American cultural conditioning. Even the most invisibly Italian American writers retain signs of their ethnicity that, when identified and read appropriately, can situate their works in a truly Italian American tradition. This phenomenon is demonstrated through an examination of postmodernist works by Italian American writers, focusing on the early stories and first novel of Don DeLillo and the early novels of Gilbert Sorrentino. This chapter discusses the disappearance of a distinctive Italian American subject in light of the advance of postmodernism and uncovers submerged signs of *Italianità* that are imbedded, consciously or not, by these writers.

The book concludes with a brief consideration of the short fiction of Mary Caponegro as representative of the future possibilities of reading American writers of Italian descent. I present suggestions for applying this cultural specific paradigm to other texts as a way of generating new readings of narratives produced by American writers of Italian descent.

One

Narrative in the Poetic Mode

If the peoples were established by laws, and if among all these
peoples the laws were given in verse, and if the first institutions of these
peoples were likewise preserved in verse, it necessarily follows that all
the first peoples were poets.
Giambattista Vico, book 2, "Poetic Wisdom"

The poetic mode of narrative development, rooted in an oral tradition, represents the beginning of the growth of a distinct literary tradition that follows Vico's depiction of the movement from *vero narratio*, or the poetic stage of cultural development, into the mythic. Vico refers to this period as the Age of Gods, and thus the literature produced during this period reveals strong beliefs in the divine. Vico sees the poets as the "sense" of the human race (110) and the earliest "makers" of human stories or history. I use this meaning of poet-as-maker when I apply the phrase "poetic mode" to *Rosa* (1970), the as-told-to autobiography of Rosa Cavalleri; to *Son of Italy* (1924), by Pascal D'Angelo; and to *The Soul of an Immigrant* (1921), by Constantine Panunzio. These narratives are representative of texts created out of elements of the oral tradition, and they represent some of the earliest Italian American narrative contributions to American culture.

Immigrant Autobiography: From Oral Tradition to Written Word

Immigrant Autobiography, informed by a pre-metropolitan self, witnesses
through its very own shock-ridden plot, the birth of the modern
self and condition, the American condition *par excellence*.
William Boelhower, *Immigrant Autobiography in the United States*

Italian Americans are heirs to a rich oral culture, one that once was passed on from generation to generation not by diaries, lettters, short stories, or novels, but by word of mouth. In the villages and towns of Italy, the *cantastorie*, or "history singers," were (and in many cases still are) the custodians of local tradition. Within the family, children learned by listening, watching, and imitating. Books were not a part of peasant life in southern Italy, nor were they an integral part of Italians' adaptation to American life. In America, Italian oral culture collided with the literary traditions of Anglo-Saxon culture, and for a long time learning how to write (more often than not for the first time) in the language of the adopted country would be synonymous with becoming American. Creating texts through narrative contributed to the re-creation of selves forged out of the elements of Italian and American cultures. Rosa's voice, D'Angelo's text, and Panunzio's *figura* of the model American each represent key stages in the self-refashioning that occurred through the immigrant experience as it was (re)presented in writing.

Narratives in the poetic mode are strongly connected to the oral traditions of Italian preindustrial culture. Familiarity with distinctive characteristics of these narratives will help us to identify these texts as bridges between the primary oral culture and the newly literate culture. In *Orality and Literacy*, Walter Ong identifies a number of elements found in oral and literate cultures. Of these, "the heroic tradition of primary oral culture and of early literate culture with massive oral residue, relates to the agonistic lifestyle. Oral memory works with heavy characters and the bizarre" (49). All three narratives under discussion in this chapter contain rich examples of such characters. From wizards and witches to bosses and "big brothers," these characters represent the powers that influence each narrator's worldview. The sentence structure of oral stories, Ong tells us, is characteristically simple. These simple sentences accumulate information rather than imbedding it in complex sentences filled with dependent clauses. Such a structure facilitates recall, a necessity in cultures that rely on human memory for information storage and transmission. This characteristic is more obvious in the as-told-to narrative of Rosa Cavalleri, but it is also found in a lesser degree in the more literary autobiographies of D'Angelo and Panunzio.

Other identifying characteristics of a primary oral culture recognizable in these texts are the use of repetition and the use of present tense—techniques that live storytellers often employ to create a sense of things happening right before the listeners' eyes. Ong also tells us that "oral cultures tend to use concepts in situational, operational frames of reference that are minimally abstract in the sense that they remain close to the living human lifeworld" (*Orality and Literacy*, 49). This predominance of the concrete over the abstract is more obvious in Rosa's narrative, but again, it also appears to a lesser degree in the narratives of D'Angelo and Panunzio. All three narratives contain a rich sampling of these elements while they also provide the materials out of which we can begin to fashion the origins of an Italian American culture.

The Signifying Donkey: From Voice to Text to *Figura*

Signifyin(g), in other words, is synonymous with figuration.
Henry Louis Gates, Jr., *The Signifying Monkey*

Most of the Italians who immigrated to America between 1880 and 1920 came from a peasant culture based on oral traditions. Books were not among the possessions they carried along in the move to America. In Italy, literacy was a tool used by those in power to exercise and protect their power over others. The Italian institutions of church and state controlled access to this power by controlling access to literacy.[1] It is no wonder, then, that the majority of Italians who immigrated to America were illiterate people who had had no power to control their lives in Italy. In essence, they were considered subhuman by those who held power over them. There are many references to the plight of the Italian peasant being the same as that of the donkey, the typical beast of burden in southern Italy.[2] Ignazio Buttitta's poem from the early 1920s, "Lu sceccu," or "The Ass," is a prime example. In the poem, here translated from the Sicilian into English by Justin Vitiello, Buttitta uses the donkey as a metaphor for the peasant:

The Donkey

The wretch drags the chain
and the dumb donkey bears it,
harnessed from dusk till dawn
to the mill, back and forth —

a thrashing is the rule
as the boss strides the rump.

Bray, the bridle will slash,
paw, the spurs will grind,
tote wheat, but straw
and chaff is what you eat.
Such is the lot of the wretch
under the whip and rein,
his neck, under the yoke,
groomed with a curry comb

and trampled by the procession
of kings, nobles, prelates
drawing blood from the eyes
of the poor, blind and sick.
Ecce "the family of man" —
evil is the wretch's lot.

This is precisely the way of life that many of those who immigrated to the United States were hoping to change. While immigration was the first step in gaining greater control over one's life, the acquisition of literacy in America would become a way of maintaining and increasing that control. Acquiring the ability to signify the immigrant experience would become the key to shifting from the powerlessness of an oral culture ruled by destiny to a written culture in which one could exercise greater control over one's life. This transition, however, did not happen cleanly or completely in the life of every immigrant. The texts created by the three narrators under consideration here fluctuate between the oral and literate styles just as they fluctuate between identification with Italian and American cultures. *Rosa* is consistently much more closely tied to oral traditions than *Son of Italy*, and *The Soul of an Immigrant* is even less connected to the oral than the other two. Together, however, these three narratives represent a foundation on which a distinct Italian American literary tradition can be built.

It has taken three generations and more than one hundred years of Italian presence in America to produce a literature that can be called

Italian American.[3] The number of autobiographies produced in this literature is few in comparison with the number produced by other major ethnic groups. The paucity of self-reflective written works can be attributed to a number of causes: distrust of the written word, (an Italian proverb warns: *Pensa molto, parla poco, e scrivi meno* [Think a lot, speak little, and write even less]); the immigrant's distrust of social and educational institutions, which represent the ruling classes; and parents' failure to encourage children to pursue literary careers because the family needed the money each child could earn as soon as he or she was old enough to be employed.[4] In spite of the low priority given to writing by Italian Americans on the whole, however, a number of authors have emerged to document the Italian American experience and create a literary tradition out of a strong oral tradition.[5] In this respect, Italian American writers have much in common with writers from American Indian, Mexican American, and African American traditions. The strong storytelling traditions in Italian American oral culture are filled with tales that explain the reasons for traditional rituals and provide information about how to live one's life. These tales also enable us to examine the evolution of the Italian American's self-concept and its progression into the public discourse.

"The conscious awareness of the singularity of each individual life is the late product of a specific civilization," writes Georges Gusdorf in his essay "Conditions and Limits of Autobiography." "Throughout most of human history, the individual does not oppose himself to all others; he does not feel himself to exist outside of others, and still less against others, but very much *with* others in an interdependent existence that asserts its rhythms in the community" (29). The body of available literature on Italian oral traditions supports Gusdorf's observations. Telling the story of self in public was not part of any public cultural tradition south of Rome (the region from which more than 80 percent of the Italians who immigrated to America came). This point is supported by a number of studies of the traditions of Italian storytelling.[6]

In *Italian Folktales in America: The Verbal Art of an Immigrant Woman*, Elizabeth Mathias and Richard Raspa present an in-depth look at what happened when a traditional tale teller, Clementina Tedesco, trained by a master storyteller in her native village of Faller in northern Italy, immigrated to America in 1930. Mathias and Raspa note that Tedesco's repertoire expanded from traditional *märchen* and legends representing an Italian communal experience to include personal, factual accounts of her immigration experience: "What emerged with Clementina in the new setting was a different way of communicating with others, still artistic, still startling in its power to evoke life, but no longer a part of a traditional art" (60). In the Italian oral tradition, the self is suppressed; it was not used as a source for storytelling in the communal settings of Italy, where one function of such stories was to create a temporary respite from the harsh realities of everyday peasant life. In his book about Tuscan oral traditions, *Folklore by the Fireside*, Alessandro Falassi cites a proverb that reveals a second function of traditional storytelling: *La novella non è bella se non c'è la giuntarella* (The story isn't good if it doesn't have its moral [37]). Traditional stories served both to entertain and to inform the young, while reminding the old of traditions that had endured over the years. Personal experience was kept to oneself.

Southern Italian culture is replete with aphorisms and proverbs that advise against revealing information that can be used against the self or the family: *A chi dici il tuo secreto, doni la tua liberta* (To whom you tell a secret, you give your freedom); *Di il fatto tuo, e lascia far il fatto tuo* (Tell everyone your business and the devil will do it); *Odi, vedi, e taci se vuoi viver in pace* (Listen, watch, and keep quiet if you wish to live in peace). This tendency to keep to oneself has often been misinterpreted by other American groups, who see this characteristic silence, or *omertà*, as un-American.[7] Mathias and Raspa suggest that this behavior changes through immigration. Once the Italian storyteller is uprooted, a sense of self begins to emerge as the dominant material for storytelling. This idea is echoed in *Italian-American Folklore*, a recent work on Italian American folklore by Frances Malpezzi and William M. Clements: "The storytelling that flowered among Italian Americans involved their own experiences and those of their family members who had gone through adventures which, though not as magical as the events that befell the heroes of the *marchen* and the protagonists of supernatural legends, involved just as much peril and had the advantage of immediacy and obvious relevance to those in the audience" (153). But even as storytellers shift toward recalling more personal stories, they continue to exercise caution concerning what can or cannot be communicated. Rosa, for example, changes the names of the people she talks about for fear that she might harm them or that they might be able to harm her or members of her family. And D'Angelo and Panunzio rarely include surnames of those who either helped or harmed them. In the immigrant experience we can locate the sources of an autobiographical tradition that pits Italian culture against American culture, creating a tension that guides the narrative.[8] This tension emerges in the overriding theme of immigrant narratives, the flight to a better world or a promised land.[9]

In America the immigrant had to learn a new system of codifying cultural signifiers, one that often conflicted with the immigrant's previous way of interpreting life. The resulting conflicts are obvious in the turn-of-the-century language encounters between Italian-speaking immigrants and the English-speaking Americans.[10] Arrival in America also required the immigrant to develop a new sense of self in the context of the larger society. The experience of leaving the old country and arriving in the new is the primary subject of such early narratives as Constantine Panunzio's *Soul of an Immigrant* and Pascal D'Angelo's *Son of Italy*, and autobiographies narrated to those who could write English such as *Rosa, the Life of an Italian Immigrant*. Panunzio's autobiography contains two stories of conversions, both of which relate to his Americanization. The first is his conversion from Roman Catholicism to "American" religion (Protestantism), the second from Italian to American citizenship. His use of selections from English and American poetry to introduce each chapter provides evidence that he has come to understand and accept "the genius of the Anglo-Saxon mind and character of the soul of America" (*Soul of an Immigrant*, vii).

D'Angelo's story of his rise from illiterate, "hunger-artist" immigrant to citizen of literary America (through winning a national poetry contest) can be read as a version of the American success story modeled after Benjamin Franklin's *Autobiography*.[11] D'Angelo's *Son of Italy*, like many African American slave narratives, is introduced by an established American, who functions as both authenticator and model reader. In D'Angelo's case the American is Carl Van Doren, former editor of the *Nation*, the magazine that awarded D'Angelo first prize in its 1922 poetry contest. Both Panunzio's and D'Angelo's autobiographies may have been subjected to editing; both authors apologize to their readers for their inadequacy with the English language.[12] Indeed, we can assume that each experienced a great deal of editorial control in preparing his work. *Soul of an Immigrant* and *Son of Italy* are among the earliest Italian American autobiographies; they also represent the insertion of Italian contents into the more traditional American autobiographical forms of the conversion and success story.

Another dominant subject in immigrant autobiographies is the detailed descriptions of the incredibly difficult work the authors had to perform in order to survive. Like the figure of the donkey in Italian folklore, these peasants were "beasts of burden" until they were transformed into people by achieving the ability to signify their experiences in a language that Americans could understand. And while this signification rarely occurred in writing, the following three examples represent three distinct stages in the evolution of the Italian American narrative from its origins in oral tradition.

Rosa: The Voice of the Emergent Self

One of the strongest Italian American immigrant narratives is the story of Rosa Cavalleri as told to Marie Hall Ets, a social worker who met Rosa at the Chicago Commons, a settlement house for poor immigrants, in 1918.[13] The illegitimate daughter of a famous Italian actress whose name she refuses to reveal,[14] Rosa was abandoned at birth and spent her early years in a Catholic orphanage before being placed into a foster home. *Rosa* documents a young girl's life in an impoverished northern Italian village and her forced immigration to America to join her husband (a marriage arranged by her foster mother, who would not allow Rosa to marry the man to whom Rosa had earlier declared her love). The bulk of Rosa's narrative deals with her life in Italy; only the last ninety pages relate her experiences in the United States.

It is important to keep in mind that Rosa's story comes to us through the filter of an American recorder and editor.[15] In this sense it is, stylistically, a bicultural document. Since Rosa, illiterate in both Italian and English, had no control over the writing, it is no wonder that the use of Italian in the text is limited to a few words and phrases; however, the sound and structure of Rosa's Italian American dialect has been preserved and works as a constant signifier of Rosa's *Italianità*. Obvious Italian signifiers appear in the italicized words in the text and through the syntax of Rosa's sentences, which include phrases such as "Quiet, quiet I ran" (*Rosa*, 12), a translation of the Italian *piano piano* (softly, softly). In terms of content, Ets explains that she chose not to include the many traditional stories that Rosa had told her because they "held little that would interest moderns" (7).[16] Unlike Mathias and Raspa, Ets chose to preserve only "the amazing story of her [Rosa's] life and of the fears and superstitions and beliefs of the people of her village" (7). The written narrative demonstrates Ets's cultural bias toward what it is that constitutes autobiography. For Ets, it is Rosa's story as an individual that is worth writing down. Rosa creates her self, not only through her personal stories but also through the stories she relates about her culture and her people. Through this narrative Rosa passes on stories that her people used to tell in Italy. There is one account of monks praying in a church that gets struck by a lightning bolt which runs along the floor and pulls the nails out of their shoes so that they are barefoot. She says that she doesn't know if the story is true and refers to it as "just a story to laugh" (40). Attached to this story is a comment in which Rosa explains that in Italy, priests were often the butt of jokes and were made fun of in stories. She cannot tell these stories in America because she fears that "the people in America won't understand. They think we are not reverent to our priests if we tell these funny stories" (40). Because it is important for Rosa to maintain *bella figura*, in this case to have people think nicely of her, she will not relate stories that will make her look bad according to American standards.

Rosa's ability to sing, dance, and tell stories, an ability she attributes to being the daughter of a famous actress, enabled her to survive her uprooting from the stables of Bugiarno and transplantation to the kitchens and classrooms of America. During a play produced in the Italian convent where Rosa had been sent to learn from the nuns and to work for a silk manufacturer in exchange for room, board, and an education, Rosa is sent onstage to fill a lull in the performance. What comes to her mind is to sing and perform a village song of "the stupid peasant and his donkey" that she used to sing with a friend. "First I was the stupid peasant walking with bent knees and heavy feet behind my donkey. Then I was angry and swearing and waving my whip. Then I was singing to him. And the people, they went crazy for that song" (103). Rosa's performance is so successful that a rich man in the audience offers to reward the whole convent if she does an encore. Rosa performs the song again, and from then on she is treated better by the nuns.

This ability to tell stories is what first attracted Ets to Rosa (5). Winifred Farrant Bevilacqua has observed that Rosa sought to "transcend her limited and limiting circumstances and to assert her individual self" and achieved this aim through the "cultivation of the art of telling stories, which earns her the attention and pleasure of others, gives her an identity that is related to her community and expressive of her individuality, and is an outlet for the richness of her inner world, so in contrast to her external poverty" ("Rosa," 548).

Rosa's entré into America was through her dual role as worker and storyteller, and her narrative is filled with references to characters of Italian folklore. While Rosa acknowledges the existence of *maliardi*, or "evil ones," she believes that "no one can witch me. I'm too strong in believing in God and the Madonna" (159). Rosa's narrative is fundamentally based on her belief in God as the maker of destiny and is punctuated with references to the Madonna and the miracles she creates to protect the faithful. Vico's theory of the poetic origin of language regards the human need to interpret natural signs such as lightning as the signification by a powerful creator, or God, to human beings (*The New Science*, 118). Rosa, for example, believes that "it was God and the Devil fighting that made the sky crack open like that. God was striking the Devil with the lightning" (38) Early in the narrative, Rosa recounts the experience of nearly being killed by a lightning strike. The event, in which one of her friends is struck while attempting to hide under a tree, is interpreted by the peasants as a miracle: "The Madonna put it in your mind to run back. It was the Madonna who saved you" (37). It is her belief in the Madonna as the intercessor between poor women and children and God that sustains Rosa throughout her life.

Rosa's narrative is strongly rooted in the folk culture of her homeland. Her repertoire of folktales comes from her experience of listening to "men in the barns on cold winter nights" (40). Unfortunately, few of these tales made it into the narrative transcribed by Ets.[17] Nevertheless, Rosa's narrative follows the models of folktales through her anecdotal accounts of the miracles she has witnessed. She relates the story of Gionin, who lost his cows during a storm and after praying received a vision of the Madonna, who told him she had returned his cows to him because of his devotion to the Madonna del Monte (45). She also tells of the pilgrimage she and her stepmother made to the church of Maria Bambina in hopes of healing her stepmother's arm, which no doctor could heal (46). Rosa begins this story in the present tense, "Now I have to tell." This present-tense signifier, trapped in writing by Ets, reveals the connection to oral culture that Rosa's speech signifies in spite of Ets's attempts to turn her stories into literature. This also occurs in chapter 3, which begins, "Now I will tell the story of Mama Lena, they way she all the time told it to me" (20); and at the beginning of chapter 28, "Tonight the Madonna made a miracle to help me. Listen what happened" (241). Phrases such as these appear frequently throughout the text, often as lead-ins to a commentary on the story in progress or to point to a difference between life in Italy and life in America. For example, after Rosa narrates the lightning story, she tells us that "the scare of lightning never passed — I'm afraid yet. The electric storms in the old country — in Lombardy — were terrible. Here in America they are too, but not so bad" (39). And in Italy, "there used to be more miracles than now in America. That's because the American people have not the faith and the strong religion" (44). Rosa takes great pains to separate the cultural differences between Italy and America, as in her criticism of American medical practices: "The American doctors they ruin the people. I say, 'People don't go to the doctors! Let them alone!' Here in America everybody runs to the doctor. And those doctors! When you get a pain down here in your leg, they look in your mouth and say, 'You have to pull out the teeth, that's all.' You get a pain in your stomach, and they say, 'Take off the tonsils.' . . . In Italia we don't take off nothing — we keep everything, and we are not sick" (252).

More often than not, Rosa's criticism of America is indirect; often, it appears in the context of the wrongs that were done to her. Her first husband, Santino, forced her to move and manage a whorehouse he had purchased. Ironically, in relating this story she breaks the code of *omertà* which she believes will protect her and her family: "But I don't ever want my children to know about that bad business my husband bought. I never told them — never! I can't even tell them now. That man, maybe he's alive yet, and rich. He can kill me if I tell about him. He's got the policemen and all those high-up politicians for his friends. He makes them the present of a pile of money, and when someone tries to make him trouble, the politicians help him along" (198). Her husband did threaten to kill her and tried a number of times to slit her throat while she was asleep, but Rosa thwarted his efforts and, with the help of Gionin, who would become her second husband, ran off to Chicago with her children. Rosa's story realistically and graphically depicts the conditions in Italy that forced hundreds of thousands of Italians to migrate at the turn of the twentieth century. A key to understanding the effects of this migration on the Italians can be found by examining the role played by fear in the development of Rosa's self-identity. Rosa's fear in Italy is generated by the Italian class system, which demands that the poor never look into the eyes of the rich; this fear is also present in the traditional male-female relationship, which turns women into the property of fathers, husbands, bosses, and priests. Proper behavior between girls and boys is related in terms of a cultural code. "Girls were not allowed to speak to boys. The boy and the girl, they were like the rich and the poor together, like the man and the woman, like the North Italian and the South Italian — the boy was so much higher than the girl. You didn't dare do anything to a boy" (86).

Rosa's narrative is filled with fear of men and of the Italian authorities who imposed their will upon her. This power of men to control women comes from God, as Rosa's pastor, Don Domenic, tells her: "God gave the man the right to control the woman when He made him stronger. . . . It's a sin for the wife not to obey. Only God and the Madonna come first. Only when the husband wants his wife to sin against God and the Madonna she must not obey him" (82). But Rosa experiences another fear, the fear of God, and this fear is not lost in her move to America. In fact, her immigrant experience strengthens her Italian-created religious convictions. Thus for Rosa, as for many Italian immigrants, there is the experience of two types of fear: the fear that feeds the development of self — the fear of God — and the fear that starves it — the fear of Man — both of which make up her identity. Her last wish indicates the psychological transformation she experienced in the move to America:

Only one wish more I have: I'd love to go to *Italia* again before I die. Now I speak English good like an American I could go anywhere — where millionaires go and high people. I would look the high people in the face and ask them what questions I'd like to know. I wouldn't be afraid now — not of anybody. I'd be proud I come from America and speak English. I would go to Bugiarno and see the people and talk to the bosses in the silk factory.[18] And to Canaletto [the convent where she was educated].[19] Those sisters would not throw me out when I come from America! I could talk to *Superiora* now. I'd tell her, "Why you were so mean — you threw out that poor girl whose heart was so kind toward you? You think you'll go to heaven like that?" I'd scold them like that now. I wouldn't be afraid. They wouldn't dare hurt me now I come from America. Me, that's why I love America. That's what I learned in America: not to be afraid. (254)

For Rosa, and for many immigrants like her, leaving Italy meant leaving a traditional system of life that could be escaped only by death or migration. This dynamic of Old World sense of destiny versus New World sense of freedom from fate, so well portrayed in Rosa's "as-told-to" autobiography, is a dominant theme in Italian American autobiography.

The American ideas of self-reliance and the importance of developing one's self-identity outside one's community created tensions between Italian and American culture as the Italian in America fashioned an Italian American identity. These tensions became evident as the Italian American developed a written tradition out of a predominantly oral tradition. For in the oral tradition of Italian Americans such as Rosa, self became a new and, for the first time, safe subject for public discourse. As the subject of self became the focus of Italian American writing, the contemporary autobiographer who enjoyed greater control of the language of the new country was better able to negotiate the difference between Italian and American ideas and was thus better able to forge an identity that essentially was a synthesis of the two often conflicting worldviews. As a result, the autobiographer, while writing the story of his or her self, also became a spokesperson for his or her community, developing models of self-construction that represented possible ways of moving from an Italian to an Italian American identity.

Essentially, in the writing of Pascal D'Angelo and Constantine Panunzio, control of the American language — something that immigrants such as Rosa who were more rooted in the oral tradition did not have — means greater control of the self as American. With this increased control comes the ability not only to create but also to articulate a truly Italian American identity.

Pascal D'Angelo's Poesis: Text as Bridge between Cultures

As exile/discoverer, as emigrant/immigrant, D'Angelo's
narrator bases the seriousness of his ongoing quest for value and
synthesis on the very form of his autobiography. It is the immigrant
autobiographical fabula, in other words, that ultimately legitimizes his
quest by bridging the metropolis and the happy valley, a world of
mediation, form and transcendence.

William Boelhower, *Immigrant Autobiography*

It was Rosa's voice that found her a place in American culture as a worker-
storyteller, not in the traditional role of *cantastorie* — a teller of timeless
tales — but in the literate tradition of Ets, who recorded only the story of
Rosa's self and its struggle to survive in a new world. Ets transformed
Rosa from a singer of a people's history, the traditional role of the *canta-
storia*, into the singer/sayer of an individual's history. Pascal D'Angelo is a
similar voice struggling for recognition and acceptance in a new world,
but for D'Angelo the struggle takes place in a different medium, one in
which the voice of oral tradition is inscribed and self-transcribed through
literacy into a literary tradition. Like *Rosa, Son of Italy* is introduced by a
"real" American, *Nation* editor Carl Van Doren, who from the position of
someone with cultural power recounts the story of how he came to meet
D'Angelo and how he helped to make the immigrant worker-poet famous.
This five-page introduction serves as an authenticating document, the
likes of which regularly preface the texts of slave narratives and Native
American autobiographies. Van Doren serves as D'Angelo's literary *padrone*. He witnesses D'Angelo's literary signature, as he writes in his introduction to *Son of Italy*: "I accepted some of his poems and sent him to
editors who accepted others. Moreover, I wrote a short article about him
in the department of *The Nation* called 'The Roving Critic.' The result was
another evidence, if anybody needed it, of his authenticity" (*Son of Italy*,
x). Such witnessing was necessary to verify the amazing transformation of
pick-and-shovel laborer into legitimate poet, for to Americans, D'Angelo
says, "I was a poor laborer — a dago, a wop or some such creature" (138).
In the minds of most American readers of the time, such a transformation
was so unlikely that it required a reliable witness to testify to its truth.

In his important and seminal study of D'Angelo's autobiography, William Boelhower points to a number of characteristics of D'Angelo's writing that support my placing of him in the poetic mode of narrative production: "This peasant world runs on magic, its history is natural history. The repeated use of 'we' indicates that human life in this timeless world is far from being individual, separate and inner-directed. Instead, the real protagonist of this Old-World environment is a multiple character, a trans-individual subject which will even endure in the New World under the form of extended familial and extra-familial groupings. D'Angelo, in fact, does not give his people names but presents them as types" (104). As Boelhower suggests, the primitive world from which D'Angelo escaped by joining his father in search of work in America, was one in which "if they cannot communicate with a distant government, they can communicate with the gods of their valley. In knowing their world, they can know themselves" (108). This knowledge, according to Vico's principle of *verum-factum* (i.e., Man can only truly know that which he makes) is the basis for D'Angelo's narrative. Unlike Rosa, who explains her life through miracles of God and the Madonna, D'Angelo explains his life in terms of what he himself has made out of the situations created by himself and others.

The first five chapters of *Son of Italy*, exactly one-third of the narrative, deal with life in Abruzzi, the land of D'Angelo's birth. D'Angelo explains his origins in terms of his people: "We of the uplands of Abruzzi are a different race. The inhabitants of the soft plains of Latium and Apulia where in winter we pasture our sheep consider us a people of seers and poets. We believe in dreams. There are strange beings walking through our towns whose existence, we know, are phantasies. We have men who can tell the future and ageless hags who know the secrets of the mountain and can cure all illness save witchcraft with a few words" (9). One of his earliest memories is of an old man "known as sort of a wizard" (15) being struck by lightning, or, as his mother calls it, "the fires of heaven" (16). Unlike Rosa, D'Angelo's religion is pre-Christian. There are only a few references to God and none to the church. People deal with witches, wizards, and vampires by themselves, without the intercession of supreme beings or members of the clergy. And while D'Angelo alludes to patron saints and mentions God a handful of times throughout his narrative, the Christian foundation that so solidly roots Rosa's narrative is lacking. D'Angelo's spirituality is rooted in the common folk's relationship to their environment.

D'Angelo's birthplace is a "quiet land" where "the old traditions have never entirely died out" (13). Wisdom comes not from the Bible or the mouths of priests, but from the elders and the strangers who wander into his village. Knowledge is transferred through proverbs such as "Humanity is a cyclone that does not come to moisten our fields, but to flood them" (20). Troubles in one's life are attributed to "the will of those whose methods are not for us to understand" (20). Shepherds are holy people who walk with spirits. Essentially, D'Angelo's spirituality is, like that of Native Americans, tied to the land. His homeland sits in the valley of the Monte Majella, "the mother mountain" of which "we are proud to call ourselves the sons" (13). It is the land from which "sprung" the ancient Samnites, who "spread their power all over Italy, making even Rome tremble" (13). It is a land rich in tradition and honored in a number of the poems D'Angelo places at strategic points in his narrative.

Beyond its obvious folkloric roots, D'Angelo's narrative most represents the primitive, poetic mode of *vero narratio* through the poems he includes. The three poems situated in the chapters dealing with D'Angelo's life in Italy relate what Boelhower calls the organic connection between the native and his land (*Immigrant Autobiography*, 103). Nature, in the childhood world of D'Angelo, is in control of everything. To the primitive, it speaks a language human beings must interpret. This is nowhere more obvious than in the first poem, "Midday":

The road is like a little child running ahead of me and
then hiding behind a curve —
Perhaps to surprise me when I reach there.
The sun has built a nest of light under the eaves of noon;
A lark drops down from the cloudless sky
Like a singing arrow, wet with blue, sped from the bow of space.
But my eyes pierce the soft azure, far, far beyond,
To where roam eternal lovers.
Along the broad blue ways
Of silence. (18)

In Italian, the poem's title would be "Mezzogiorno," the name given to the region of southern Italy where D'Angelo was born. It also signifies the time of day in which people stop their work to eat and rest. The road is the way out of this region, and by personifying it as a child, D'Angelo connects travel to the natural curiosity of children. D'Angelo's meditation on the natural setting, which includes the sun, the sky, and a bird, is a way of connecting the human to the world of nature. His world is one in which mountains speak to the sky, nature speaks to man, and man responds through language. This interaction is depicted in the second poem he includes, "Monte Majella":

The mountain in a prayer of questioning heights gazes
upward at the dumb heavens,
And its inner anger is forever bursting forth
In twisting torrents.
Like little drops of dew trickling along the crevices
Of this giant questioner
I and my goats were returning toward the town below.
But my thoughts were of a little glen where wild roses grow
And cool springs bubble up into blue pools.
And the mountain was insisting for an answer from the still heaven. (23)

The pastoral world is one in which the goatherd is witness to the interaction of natural elements: the mountain, its rivers, and the sky. Again, language documents the interaction and becomes the vehicle through which man connects himself to this natural environment. In the third poem, "Fantasio," D'Angelo presents the overriding theme of his narrative: the relationship between darkness and light, between dream and reality. The poem's setting is a pastoral site where a road cuts through the mountains. Night becomes a "black flower" that "shuts the sun within its petals of gloom." The "dim jagged distances are pearl-gray wings / flitting." Onto this scene moonlight is cast as "a hailstorm of splendor / Pattering on the velvet floor of gloom — "; this sight infects the poet with "a fever of youth" that trembles "under the incantation of Beauty" that is "like a turmoil of purple butterfly caught in a web of / light." The darkness flows out of night like "a black foam" and erases the sight of the wings (43).[20]

In D'Angelo's primeval world, night and darkness are reminders that humans do not and cannot control their environment. Man-made roads are reduced to dreams. Movement, and subsequently navigation of this world, is restricted to the elements of nature such as the sun and the moon. These are what control the world in the night. "Fantasio" is the last poem in the section of the autobiography that deals with life in Italy. D'Angelo's observations of America, and the metaphors of his poetry, shift from the world of nature to the world of man. America is a land in which man struggles with nature, a place where man's imprint on the world destroys the natural relationship of his past and creates in its place a tension that often results in confusion.

D'Angelo's early attempt to read American signifiers is a good example of this confusion, for he reads them according to Italian religious signifieds. Of his encounter with street signs he writes, "I began to notice that there were signs at the corners of the streets with 'Ave.! Ave.! Ave.!' How religious a place this must be that expresses its devotion at every crossing, I mused. Still, they did not put the 'Ave.' before the holy word, as in 'Ave Maria,' but rather after. How topsy-turvy" (61). D'Angelo faces similar confusion during his early attempts to speak English. In one situation he is told to go to a store for a dozen eggs. He hears "aches" and in communicating it to the storekeep the word becomes "axes" (70). The result is a hilarious account of the clerk's attempt to sell him a dozen axes. What becomes obvious at this point is the sharp contrast between the colloquial and humorous qualities of his prose and the formal and serious qualities of his poetry. The poems included in his autobiography mark epiphanic occasions and demonstrate his ability to fashion art from his mundane experiences.

The first poem that appears in the American section, "Night Scene," demonstrates the intensity of the struggle in men's lives when they become disconnected from nature.[21] In this poem D'Angelo compares a man walking home from work to an approaching storm. He characterizes the storm as "an unshaped blackness," a "mountain of clouds" that "rises like a Mammoth" (75). The black clouds are illuminated by the fires of a foundry. The man is characterized first as a "form" nearly indistinguishable from the black clouds, but as it nears, the figure on the road becomes a man—a man who, oblivious to the beauty of the world around him, curses something, perhaps his life, his fate as a worker. This experience is like a storm in nature when elements clash to disrupt the peace of the pastoral world. This poem comes at the end of chapter 6, in which D'Angelo recounts his first jobs and the "endless, continuous toil" as a pick-and-shovel man and his realization that such work is getting him, materially and spiritually, nowhere. He needs more than work and the meager life it brings. He needs poetry, which lives longer than manual labor: "Who hears the thuds of the pick and the jingling of the shovel. All my works are lost, lost forever. But if I write a good line of poetry — then when the night comes and I cease writing, my work is not lost. My line is still there. It can be read by you to-day and by another to-morrow. But my pick and shovel works cannot be read either by you to-day or by anyone else to-morrow" (74–5). D'Angelo keeps the beauty of the world of his past alive through his poetry. Through poetry, the ugliness of the present can be transformed into beauty. There were only two ways for D'Angelo to deal with the terrible situation he was in: he could return to Italy as his father did, or he could search for the "light" in America — the poetry that could get him out of the perpetual darkness. "There was a lingering suspicion that somewhere in this vast country an opening existed, that somewhere I would strike the light. I could not remain in darkness perpetually" (115). But such light would be a long time coming. D'Angelo then recounts his life doing railroad work, living in a boxcar, and the terrible work accidents he witnessed. Work, he says, "was a war in which we poor laborers — Poles and Italians — were perpetually engaged" (117). The next poem in the narrative is placed at the end of this chapter, and while D'Angelo maintains the interplay between darkness and light, his subject shifts from nature to man.

In "Accident in the Coal Dump," D'Angelo presents a narrative of a man who has died "in crushed splendor under the weight of awakening" (117).[22] He had been a friend to D'Angelo and a family man, now transformed by death into "an extinguished sun still followed by unseen faithful planets / Dawning on dead worlds in an eclipse across myriad stars" (118). After they have dug out his body they leave. A "youngster who was trying to fool himself and his insistent thoughts" attempts to joke about "the dead man" (118). Snow begins to fall "like a white dream through the rude sleep of winter night," and "a wild eyed woman came running out of the darkness" (118). This juxtaposition of darkness and light is characteristic of D'Angelo's depictions of his American experiences. Most of his imagery is presented in this *chiaroscuro* fashion. But unlike the dark/light portrayals of Italy in which man is connected organically to the natural world, those of America present man in conflict with nature and the ruling divinities.

This shift comes through clearly in "Omnis Sum," a Whitmanesque lyric that opens the chapter in which D'Angelo recounts a work injury that forced him out of his job and brought him the opportunity to begin learning the English language. In this poem D'Angelo juxtaposes the image of himself as Christ in the darkness of thought.[23] Light is created by a Thor-like god who rules the night. Like Christ, D'Angelo suffers a terrible wound to his hand, after following a foreman's order against his own better judgment and other workers' advice. After the accident, which renders him unable to work, D'Angelo meets Michele, a fellow worker who speaks good Italian and talks to him of Dante — whom the illiterate D'Angelo thought "was an ancient king" (132). When D'Angelo shows him his wounded hand, Michele says, "Boy, a stupid world drove nails through other hands — other hands." The literal-minded D'Angelo doesn't understand the allusion to Christ (132), but his interaction with Michele is educational and enables him to realize that in his present state he is "nothing more than a dog. A dog. But a dog is silent and slinks away when whipped, while I am filled with the urge to cry out, to cry out disconnected words, expressions of pain — anything — to cry out" (137). Depressed, he resigns himself to his fate: "the gradual eking out of my life. Word and food" (139).

Through an encounter with Mexican American laborers, who show him a Spanish-language newspaper, D'Angelo's interest in reading is renewed. He decides that English is more to his liking, and he begins to decipher local newspapers. As he learns new words, he writes them "in big letters on the mouldy walls of the box car" (141) and "on a railroad tie" (144). Attending a vaudeville show in New York, he decides that he can do better than the short farce included, and he is motivated to write. He includes this "'prehistoric' attempt" in his autobiography along with all its mistakes (142). American workers berate him for trying to learn the language and engage him in a vocabulary duel during which D'Angelo presents them with twelve words, "none of which they could understand" (147). But in spite of his attempts to master the English language, he still sees himself as a pick-and-shovel man, a lament he voices in the present tense (145) in the middle of the past-tense narration of these events.

A turning point comes when he learns about opera, which "revealed to me beauty, which I had been instinctively following, in spite of my grotesque jokes and farces" (149). D'Angelo attempts to learn music, but he fails to master an instrument and turns to writing poetry instead. The poem that D'Angelo includes in this setion, "Song of Light," announces a reconnection between D'Angelo and the natural world, a reconnection that comes through poetry:

The sun robed with noons stands on the pulpit of heaven
Like an anchorite preaching his faith of light to listening space.
And I am one of the sun's lost words,
A ray that pierces through endless emptiness on emptiness
Seeking in vain to be freed of its burden of splendor. (155–6)

D'Angelo begins immersing himself in reading and attends the opera when he has the chance. These experiences help him through the difficult days of seemingly endless work, and they inspire him to create his own beauty. "The quality of beauty that is in 'Aida' I have found only in the best of Shelley and perhaps Keats. There were parts of such overwhelming loveliness that they tore my soul apart" (150).

Literacy enables D'Angelo to challenge the fate that his fellow immigrant workers try to convince him to accept: "Some maintained that my knowledge of English would help me to advance in this world and others insisted that a man who was born a laborer could never rise" (158). Felice, an old worker, warns him that unless he defies such a fate, he will end up like himself, an "illiterate" who "walks like a duck; with a deformed hunchback" (159). Felice challenges D'Angelo: "And you, who they say can write in English — what good does it do you to know the language of America while working here? You are not getting a cent more than a parrot like me who goes wherever they take him. You live in the same box car. You eat the same food. And if you stay here long enough you will become the same as I. Look at me and you are looking into the mirror of your future!" (159). Motivated by Felice's words, D'Angelo decides to move into New

York City and write poetry. At this point in the narrative he includes part of a poem that he says was later printed in "a leading magazine."[24]

In the dark verdure of summer
The railroad tracks are like the chords of a lyre gleaming across the dreamy
    valley,
And the road crosses them like a flash of lightning.
But the souls of many who speed like music on the melodious heart-strings of
    the valley
Are dim with storms;
And the soul of a farm lad who plods, whistling, on the lightning road
Is a bright blue sky. (160)

This poem shows a marked change in D'Angelo's characterization of himself, from the curious child content to ponder nature to the "farm lad" who takes off down the road to the city with a "blue sky" optimism.

D'Angelo's move to the city does not change his condition. In fact, his life becomes more miserable after he takes a room in Brooklyn. After a few weeks he writes "The City," a poem that again is filled with black, white, and gray images that characterize the duality of the city's power to create darkness and at the same time offer the light through "lifting street-lamps" that illuminate the night.[25]

The factory smoke is unfolding in protesting curves
Like phantoms of black unappeased desires, yearning and struggling and
    pointing upward;
While through its dark streets pass people, tired, uscless
Trampling the vague black illusions
That pave their paths like broad leaves of water-lilies
On twilight streams (163)

This is the first poem D'Angelo sends out for publication, beginning a string of rejections that leads him to realize that he is "alone in my struggle to acquire a new language and a new world" (165). After seeing what he calls "the most blatant and silly trash imaginable" (166) on the editorial page of a "respectable metropolitan newspaper," D'Angelo is motivated to travel door-to-door in search of a publisher. During this quest he survives on a diet of "steel [stale] bread," rotten bananas, and bone soup. His determination to publish leads him to what he calls "the great lesson of America. I had learned to have faith in the future. No matter how bad things were, a turn would inevitably come — as long as I did not give up" (171).

The final chapter of D'Angelo's narrative recounts his horrible living conditions, which become even worse when the pipes in his building burst and all his food and possessions are spoiled by sewer water.[26] His desire to produce beauty and truth is so powerful that when he receives no response from the *Nation*, in whose contest he had entered his poems, he dashes off a long letter to the editor. The letter, which takes up the bulk of his last chapter, pleads for recognition:

I am one who is struggling through the blinding flames of ignorance to bring his message before the public — before you. You are dedicated to defending the immense cause of the oppressed. This letter is the cry of a soul stranded on the shores of darkness looking for light — a light that points out the path toward recognition, where I can work and help myself . . . what I want is an outlet to express what I can say besides work. Yes to express all the sorrows of those who cower under the crushing yoke of an unjust doom. . . . Let me free! Let me free! Free like the thought of love that haunts millions of minds. . . . Lift me, with the strength of the prize, out of this ignoble doom and place me on the pulpit of light where I too can narrate what the Nature-made orator has to say in me. (180–4)

Like most of his poems, this letter, with its references to darkness and light, reveals the astonishing change that comes over the poet as he evolves from farm lad to pick-and-shovel man to poet. By characterizing himself a "Nature-made orator," D'Angelo points to a reversal of fate that poetry has enabled him to accomplish. As a poet, he becomes like the sun, like the gods who create light, who control destiny. He is, in essence, reconnected with the beauty of the land of his birth through the power of creating art. Van Doren, as he says in his introduction, responded positively to D'Angelo's plight, and soon D'Angelo became a celebrity. Though he would die young (at thirty-eight), destitute and dependent on friends for a proper burial, D'Angelo's short-lived triumph was proof that one born in poverty could change one's destiny. D'Angelo's narrative ends with a commentary on what this reversal of fate meant to his parents: "And sweeter yet was the happiness of my parents who realized that after all I had not really gone astray, but had sought and attained a goal from the deep-worn groove of peasant drudgery" (185).

Boelhower fittingly labels D'Angelo "an Italian-American Prometheus," for D'Angelo brings the control of his destiny out of the hands of the gods and into his own. He connects the world of nature with the world of man, the Old World of Italy and the New World of America, through his lyrical texts and the poetic narrative they create. Yet, throughout his narration, D'Angelo speaks only for himself and, as Boelhower points out, "from the periphery, as a marginal figure. It is precisely as such that his poetic word has value. In this way, instead of denying the dominant stereotype of the Italian by simply canceling it . . . , D'Angelo confirms it as a positive imge" (98–99). In the next example of the poetic mode of narrative, Constantine Panunzio obtains a position at the center of the culture of his adopted land by setting himself up as the *figura*, or model, of the Italian immigrant.[27]

The *Figura* of Constantine Panunzio: Writing the Self American

Unlike Rosa Cavalleri and Pascal D'Angelo, Constantine Panunzio's evolution from Italian to immigrant to American brought him into a position of power from which he could speak for other immigrants. The structure of the first half of *Soul of an Immigrant* strongly resembles *Rosa* and *Son of Italy*. But during the second half, Panunzio shifts away from self as subject and begins exploring the plight of the immigrant in America. William Boelhower sees this shift as something that detracts from the narrative as story and turns the autobiography into a rhetorical argument: "In taking on a public *figura*, he sacrifices the existential dimension on the altar of the general view, and one is left with a strategy of sublimation rather than a more convincing praxis of synthesis. In this way, the second half of the autobiography becomes a sort of antinarrative, since the protagonist's movement through space is greatly diminished . . . and it proffers little really new knowledge [about Panunzio's life]" (*Immigrant Autobiography*, 68–9). But through this shift Panunzio moves beyond his personal story and assumes a political pose as an advocate for his people.[28]

The Americanization of Constantine Panunzio follows closely the example set by immigrants of other ethnic backgrounds and by some American Indians.[29] Like many of these early writers, Panunzio was influenced by Benjamin Franklin's *Autobiography*. Like Franklin, Panunzio opens his autobiography by explaining why he is writing it. He then moves into an explanation of his genealogy. After acknowledging his debt to the English and Anglo-American poets (vii) from whom he quotes throughout his work, Panunzio tells of the many times he has told this "round unvarnished tale" (ix) to his American friends. Realizing that it not only "evoked interest" but "awakened sympathy toward the 'foreigner,'" (x) he decided that he "owed it to my adopted country to give the story to the public" (x). In his foreword, he recounts how one night he told it to a Wesleyan College schoolmate, and "since that night I have had to tell the story hundreds of times to audiences varying from one person to hundreds of men and women" (ix) and all around the country.[30] Although for nearly fifteen years he was able to refrain (due to embarrassment) from writing down his story, the aftermath of World War I and the nation's subsequent preoccupation with the assimilation of the immigrant forced him to realize that "if the story were to do any good it need go out at this time" (x). The values of his story, as he sees them, arise out of "the fact that it recounts the struggles of an *average immigrant*"; it "depicts the *inner, the soul struggles* of the immigrant more than his outward success or failure" (xi); it shows that "even a southern Italian can make something of himself under the inspiring influence of America, when he has the proper opportunity and is thrown in the right environment" (xii). Aware that northern Italians were usually better received in America than their darker-skinned southern counterparts, Panunzio stresses his "southern" roots to make a case for the potential of the southern Italian, who, for the most part, had immigrated under quite different conditions. Thus, from the beginning of his autobiography, Panunzio takes on the responsibility of speaking for all Italian immigrants, and he offers his life story both as a *figura* for other Italian immigrants and to educate those Americans who have and will come into contact with immigrants from Italy. By taking on this spokesperson's role, Panunzio does indeed advocate assimilation, but not without weaving into his narrative much criticism (both explicit and implicit) directed at his model reader, the Anglo-American.[31]

Panunzio's autobiography was written at a time when the United States Congress was considering ways to stop the flood of immigrants from southern Europe. He completed it sixteen days before Congress enacted the Emergency Quota Act on May 19, 1921, and three years before passage of the National Origins Act (1924), which limited immigration from southern Europe to a tiny percentage of the immigrants already in the United States. Although Panunzio was not personally affected by such laws, he was quite familiar with the earlier injustices the government had inflicted on immigrants. Before writing his autobiography, he published a study entitled *The Deportation Cases of 1919–1920* (1921), designed to "call public attention to practices that are inconsistent with the American tradition of justice and fair-play" (5).[32] Panunzio uses his autobiography to build an argument that pleads for understanding and acceptance of his people by the Anglo-American culture, without whose assistance the immigrant cannot become a good citizen. After setting himself up as a spokesman for his people, Panunzio recounts his own life story. His recollections follow a four-part structure. He starts with his childhood in Italy and moves into his initiation into American life, which builds toward his conversion to Methodism and is followed by his accounts of ministering to Italians in ghetto communities. The fourth and final section recounts his experiences on the road to becoming an American citizen. Part of this fourth section includes a visit back to Italy during which he realizes that he can no longer live there and so must return to America.

Panunzio begins his autobiography by giving some historical background on his birthplace, Molfetta, Apulia. Like D'Angelo, he notes that his hometown has roots in Roman history, and he recounts some of the ancient legends of Italia Antica (4). He gives examples of the social and religious lives his people led prior to and after their conversion to Roman Catholicism (7). By doing this, Panunzio draws readers' attention to the fact that he comes from a civilized land with a recorded history. But he notes that in his homeland, religion was something the men would "speak disparagingly of . . . , if religion it could be called. They would speak of the corruption of the Church . . . [and] complained of the exorbitant expenditure of money in connection with the numerous feasts" (19). Unlike Rosa and D'Angelo, Panunzio had enough education to enable him to read Italian. However, reading the Bible was something he feared he "would be punished for" (19), and he refers to it as "the 'Bad Book'" (19).

Panunzio takes great pains to describe the intimacy of his family's interactions with each other. By demonstrating the importance of family in his native culture, Panunzio makes his readers aware of the commonalities Italian culture shares with American culture. He devotes a number of pages to the story of his grandfather, after whom he is named, who was "the moving spirit of a small group of patriots" (9) who fought to free their people from the Bourbon "tyrants" during the 1848–49 revolution. He also describes his father's devotion to his country and the role he played as a public servant. Although Panunzio clearly establishes the many similarities between his native Italian culture and American culture, he does not avoid discussing the many differences, such as religious practice. "Religion," he tells us, "was primarily considered a woman's function, unnecessary to me, and a matter about which they [the men] continually joked. Even for the women of our household, religion consisted simply in going to confession perhaps once a month and in going to mass every Sunday" (18). This admission takes on great importance later in his story when Panunzio refers to his conversion to Methodism as *the great awakening.* He remarks that the New Testament was "the first piece of moral and religious teaching which I understood" (145). In essence, his life before conversion to the "American" religion could be viewed by his readers as one in which the potential for Christianity lay dormant, an idea that was a staple of conversion narratives.

In an early chapter entitled "The Call of the Sea," Panunzio establishes his difference from the typical Italian boy. Instead of conforming to the Borghese traditions that he is expected to follow, he rebels and chooses a different path; he becomes a sailor. In essence, he views his call as his destiny to find freedom from Old World ways, ways that expect him to conform to the image of his grandfather, his namesake. Panunzio cushions the impact of his rebellion against his family by inviting a comparison between himself and Columbus, an identification that strengthens his connection to America through the references to a major *figura* in America's founding myth. While he is away at sea, his parents both die during a scarlet fever epidemic, leaving him the ward of an uncle, who permits him to continue his life as a sailor. After sailing throughout European and Mediterranean waters he takes advantage of an opportunity to sail to America, a land for which he had already formed a longing. "Of course, like every Italian boy, I had heard from earliest childhood of America, the continent which 'Colombo,' one of our countrymen, had long ago discovered" (59). In bringing up Columbus, Panunzio establishes a natural connection between Italy and America.

Panunzio's image of America, formed by Italian literature and children's stories that portrayed Indians as cannibals (60), was rather distorted. His only other sources of information about America were American sailors and the Italians who had worked in America and then returned to home with "much money" and "strange habits like not drinking wine or not speaking our dialect any more, wearing white collars and purple neckties when they belonged to the 'gente' [common folk]" (65).

Though he had received an education in Italy, Panunzio arrived in America, at the age of eighteen, unable to read or write English and ignorant of American laws and customs. His immigration, appropriately on July 4, 1902, was unintentional and is recounted in a chapter entitled "In the American Storm." Having landed in Boston aboard the *Francesco*, the Italian merchant ship on which he worked, Panunzio becomes homesick and decides not to remain on the ship for its next voyage to Montevideo. He plans to find work in America that will enable him to purchase return passage to Italy. He immediately befriends a French immigrant sailor, and the two take off in search of work. What follows is an account of Panunzio's initiation into and journey through America. He is victimized by the *padrone* system, in which Italian Americans exploit naive immigrant "greenhorns," essentially enslaving them to employers and extracting a large percentage of their wages for finder's fees, housing, and meals, which they would provide to the immigrant workers. Panunzio begins to learn the English language through his work. His first American words are "peek" and "shuvle," which refer to the type of work he is expected to do. Because he cannot speak the language and because of his ignorance of the American system of justice, he is victimized time after time by people who hire him for jobs and then do not pay him. Panunzio repeatedly interrupts the narrative of his hard times on the road to becoming an American to connect his experiences to those of other immigrants. Many of these interruptions identify and argue against the false assumptions that Americans often make about his people. One such false assumption is that if Italian immigrants come from a farming economy, they should be comfortable working on American farms. As Panunzio explains, however, "the *contadini* were not farmers in that sense at all, but simply farm laborers, more nearly serfs, working on landed estates and seldom owning their own land. Moreover, they are not in any way acquainted with the implements of modern American farming. . . . When they come to America, the work which comes nearest to that which they did in Italy is not farming, or even farm labor, but excavation work" (78). He makes similar references to false assumptions about southern Italian immigrants and the harsher American climate (97), and their difficulties in learning the English language (108) and dealing with the American justice system (111–18, 129–30). Throughout his life Panunzio experienced the shattering effects of racial prejudice, which, he says, "have been dealt by older immigrants, who are known as 'Americans,' as well as by more recent comers. All have been equally heart-rending and head-bending. . . . I have seen prejudice like an evil shadow, everywhere. . . . It passes on its poison like a serpent from generation to generation, and he who would see the fusion of the various elements into a truly American type must ever take into cognizance its presence in the hearts of some human beings" (82). Panunzio refers to false assumptions and prejudice as stumbling blocks to assimilation and then cites his own experiences to demonstrate that in spite of such hurdles the Italian can become a faithful American. Because he has succeeded in overcoming these obstacles, first by being converted and then by becoming a Methodist minister, Panunzio decides to work as a mediator between the Italian immigrant and the dominant American culture: "I began to have a desire to do what I could to interpret America to the immigrant, especially to the Italians, and an equal desire to interpret the life struggles of the immigrant to the American public. . . . I felt it my duty on general humanitarian grounds to participate in the work of mutual interpretation" (203).

His work takes him for the first time into urban ghettos, and his experiences there enable him to understand the reasons Italians were not easily made into enthusiastic Americans (228). Inherent in his reflections on the plight of the immigrant is a strong thread of social criticism that is couched in Panunzio's repeated praise for the ideals of American life: individuality, self-reliance, freedom, democratic justice, and Christian values. These ideals are all possible for immigrants to achieve with assistance from good Christian Americans. Such educated, white Anglo-Americans are the audience (his model readers) to whom Panunzio writes, and he pays tribute to them in his chapter "My American 'Big Brother.'"

After detailing the great and "kind assistance" that an American (who remains anonymous to the reader) provided him when he needed it most (219–22), Panunzio draws yet another generalization designed to elicit sympathy and support for the immigrant from his WASP audience: "Americans are not made by simple formulas. They are born out of the embodiment of ideals; they are molded into shape by the hand of those who have mastered the art of treating men as human beings, whatever their color or nationality. When we realize this and act accordingly, then all the problems of the 'alien' in America will largely vanish and our country will realize in a fuller measure a true assimilation of its varied people and a truer national consciousness and unity" (224). Panunzio adopts an assimilationist stance that argues for giving immigrants opportunities for education and conversion. He has been successful because he has not been restricted to life in a ghetto, where "the real America" cannot be experienced. In a chapter entitled "My American Philosophy of Life," which is written as a letter to his brother Vincent, who remained in Italy, Constantine documents the exact changes he has gone through in becoming an American. He explains that his experience shows "that a transformation in the thought-life of the foreign groups could actually take place, if in some way or other they had access, as I have had, to the real life of America" (276).

Panunzio had the opportunity to return to Italy during World War I when he enlisted for service with the YMCA in France. From France he was sent to Italy, where it was his privilege to "raise the first Stars and Stripes which, to my knowledge, ever flew near the lines of the Italian army" (316); it was a small flag he had carried "folded against my heart" from America. This episode provides the final brick in Panunzio's foundation as an American: he has answered his country's call during a time of war. He ends his autobiography with a short oration paraphrasing "America the Beautiful," which is directed beyond the reader to America itself:

I love Thee, America, with manhood's strong love, born out of the unfolding of the mind, the evolving of the soul, the sufferings and joys, the toil and the larger loves of the years. I love Thy very life. I love Thee as I can love no other land. No other skies are so fair as Thine; no rugged mountains or fruitful plains so majestic and divine. I am of Thee; Thou art mine; upon Thy sacred soil shall I live; there I fain would die, — *an American*. (329)

Panunzio's documentation of his journey from European civilization through the American wilderness and finally into American civilization establishes his authority to speak for the concerns of all immigrants. Writing his autobiography becomes a way of negotiating not only for his own acceptance by the dominant American culture but also for the acceptance of all Italians who immigrate to America. Though his experiences certainly qualify him for such acceptance, it is the public self presented in his autobiography that demonstrates to all his readers that he has made himself over into an American, and that his experience can provide a model for all immigrants, especially if his criticism of the treatment of immigrants is heeded.[33]

While Panunzio's autobiography opens in the poetic mode, its closing represents the beginning of the shift into the mythic mode, obvious in Pietro di Donato's autobiographical novel *Christ in Concrete*. While Panunzio's philosophical basis is fundamentally Christian, he takes great pains to establish the fact that he comes from a culture strongly rooted in folk beliefs, in which organized religion means little. The two halves of his story separate folktale from autobiography and mark a move into the mythic as his protagonist becomes the heroic model immigrant. This shift also marks the movement of Italian alien subject toward conformity with mainstream American society. By prefacing each chapter with poems by such figures of the Anglo-American canon as Matthew Arnold, Henry Van Dyke, Christopher Morley, and William Wordsworth, Panunzio reinforces the notion that education, in the Arnoldian tradition of exposure to the best a culture has to offer, is the way to convert the immigrant into the American.

Two

The Early Mythic Mode: From Autobiography to Autobiographical Fiction

Semiology has taught us that myth has the task of giving an historical intention a natural justification, and making contingency appear eternal.
Roland Barthes, "Myth Today"

The founding myth for the Italians is this memory of how the rich expelled the poor into the world invented for them by the great Amerigo [Vespucci].
Robert Viscusi, "A Literature Considering Itself"

The three texts I have chosen to represent the early period of the mythic mode of narrative development were written by children of Italian immigrants, the protagonists in what Robert Viscusi calls the "founding myth" of Italian America. Those immigrants were guided by the myth that American streets were paved with gold and believed they could *fare l'america* or "make America." The goal for many was to dig for the gold and then bring it back to Italy. These "birds of passage," who did just that, returned to Italy with stories that exaggerated their successes, fueling the desires of peasants who longed for a better life. The stories of those who remained in America, their voyages, their troubles, their failures and successes, became the building materials for early Italian American fiction. John Fante, Pietro di Donato, and Jerre Mangione were among the earliest Americans of Italian descent to use these materials to create histories of mythic proportions.

In *The New Science*, Vico identifies the mythic stage of history as developing after families and social institutions were established. During this stage an aristocracy would develop against which the common people would revolt as they attempted to gain greater control of their lives. Out of this struggle would rise heroic figures who, as culture heroes, replaced the divinities of the poetic age as models for human behavior during the mythic age. This shift would be accompanied by a new symbolic or figurative language that would be used to narrate the acts of these heroes. Vico notes that this shift occurred along with the shift away from agrarian culture and into an urban culture, away from a theology based on fear of the gods to one in which men and women began to struggle with the gods. He also sees the advent of myth as a means by which humans rewrote the stories of gods as divine creatures, giving them human qualities that would then enable man and woman to "sin with authority." While Vico attributes these aspects to the Greeks and Romans, the same qualities are shared by the early developers of Italian American myths. The key to understanding the mythic mode lies in Vico's suggestion that "poets do not make ethnic myths; they simply record in allegorical poetic form, the histories of their people" (Bidney, "Vico's New Science," 274). That is what Pietro di Donato and John Fante do. Through autobiographically based fiction they record the histories of their people. Jerre Mangione's autobiographical narrative, in spite of its presentation as nonfiction, shares a similar function.

By 1930 various stereotypes of the Italian immigrant in American culture had been well established as the myths through which the Italian American presence would be read.[1] If the Italian was not seen as a gangster or a knife-wielding, mustachioed foreigner who had taken away American jobs from the earlier immigrants, then he was depicted as "a restless, roving creature, who dislikes the confinement and restraint of mill and factory," "very slow to take to American ways," "volatile, and incapable of effective team work" (Orth, *Our Foreigners*, 182–3). In spite of the quotas established on Italian immigration in the mid-1920s, restrictionists in Congress pointed to the Italians as a major reason for unemployment and crime. Nativists argued for total exclusion and even wholesale deportation of Italians.[2] If these views were not enough to marginalize Italians, the rise of fascism in Italy during this same period renewed suspicion of and hostility toward the Italian in America. Before the 1930s much of what the Italian had to say about his or her situation in America appeared only in Italian-language newspapers, and therefore had little, if any, effect on an English-reading American public. But during the 1930s, a new American-born generation would come of age to write the stories their parents could barely recount in English, to document the injustices faced by the immigrants, and to describe their own experiences as new Americans. Through their writing, they would create new myths; by recording reality, they would explain the differences between Italians and Americans and bridge Italian and American cultures, creating a synthesis that can be called Italian Americana.[3]

Unlike the few earlier Italian immigrant writers, whose works essentially argued for acceptance as human beings and pleas for recognition as Americans, the children of Italian immigrants used their writing both to document and to escape the conditions under which they were born and raised. Recovery and consideration of their works will help us to re-create a literary history that is sensitive to the process by which the children of immigrants forged Italian American identities out of the materials of Italian and American cultures. A common thread in the works of Fante, di Donato, and Mangione is the different lives led by the parents and their children. The parents' generation, characterized by hard work and the acceptance of injustice as destiny, gave way to the child's ability to fight injustice through writing. While these three writers are mostly concerned with the experiences and exploitation of the working class, none of them follows any of the prescribed formulas for the creation of proletarian literature.[4]

These authors share with their contemporaries working in modernism the propensity to prop their narratives on prevailing cultural myths. As Viscusi notes, "The allegorical destiny of Italian American heroes [is] to endure ritual death and processional reidentification in the process of becoming divinities" ("A Literature Considering Itself," 272). Viscusi defines *processional* as "a habit that produces a visible event in which the contradictions of the communal life become the materials of a public ritual" (271). The example Viscusi uses to illustrate this point is the Italian American religious festival, or *festa*, a distinctive event through which *Italianità* is publicly signified. This processionalism originates in the cultural code of *bella figura*, the maintenance of a proper public presence. A similar signification occurs in many other nonformal presentations in the narratives of Fante, di Donato, and Mangione. For John Fante, the processional comes not through large public gatherings but through the smaller, more personal interactions between his Italian and American characters.

John Fante's American *Fantasia*

John Fante was born in Denver, Colorado, on April 8, 1909, to a father who had immigrated from Abruzzi, Italy, and a mother born in Chicago to immigrant parents from Potenza, Italy. He was one of four children raised in Boulder, where his father, a stonemason and bricklayer, found work in the building trades. At an early age he was encouraged by Catholic nuns to write. He attended Regis College and the University of Colorado at Denver, but he left college to hitchhike to California, where he took jobs in fish canneries and shipping docks to help support his mother and siblings after his father left the family. From these experiences came his earliest writings, which he sent to H. L. Mencken, then editor of the *American Mercury*.

Fante dreamed of becoming a great writer. His early debut as a story writer, at the age of twenty-one, was aided by Mencken's desire to combat the Anglocentric hegemony of the New England literary establishment. By 1940, Fante had already published half of his lifetime production of short stories in national magazines such as *American Mercury*, *Atlantic Monthly*, *Harper's Bazaar* and *Scribner's*. He had also published two novels and a collection of his stories (*Dago Red*, 1940). James Farrell praised Fante's 1938 bildungsroman, *Wait until Spring, Bandini*, as one of the "few [1930s novels] of genuine merit and value" ("End of a Literary Decade," 208). In spite of receiving such support and praise by two of the period's leading literary figures, however, Fante's writing has received little critical consideration.[5]

Most of Fante's works concern the development of the social and aesthetic consciousness of a child of Italian immigrants and the contribution of that consciousness to the child's fantasy of assimilation into mainstream American culture. The subject of much of his writing is the relationship between the individual and his family and community, and the subsequent development of a single protagonist's American identity that requires both an understanding and a rejection of the immigrant past that the parents represent. Fante's early writings focus on the development of an American identity through attempts to distance his characters from their Italian and working-class roots. Because of this Fante focuses more on the personal, and thus ethnic, than on the political and class-based dimensions of his characters' lives.[6] Not having been born or raised in a little Italy, Fante, as most of his writings bear out, became hyperaware of the ethnic differences between his family and the other members of his community.

His four-book saga of Arturo Bandini, of which *Wait until Spring* is the first, follows a young Italian Catholic who lights out for California with the intent of escaping his family and its ethnicity by becoming a writer. *Wait until Spring* deals primarily with the young man's parents and their struggles to establish themselves in a strange world, but more importantly it sets up the theme of assimilation into the American Dream. In *Ask the Dust* (1939), Fante's second novel, Bandini abandons his Italian American home and makes his way to California. In the process he denies the ethnicity that he questions in the first novel, by calling attention to the ethnicity of others, such as Camilla, the Mexican waitress with whom he falls in love and whom he continually calls a "greaser." In essence, Bandini believes the way to become American is by identifying others as non-Americans.[7]

But I am poor, and my name ends with a soft vowel, and they hate me and my father, and my father's father, and they would have my blood and put me down, but they are old now, dying in the sun and in the hot dust of the road, and I am young and full of hope and love for my country and my times, and when I say Greaser to you it is not my heart that speaks, but the quivering of an old wound, and I am ashamed of the terrible thing I have done. (47)

Fante's works provide an insight into the process by which an American-born child of Italian immigrants fashions an American identity through the process of denying other immigrants and their children the same possibilities. The development of this offensive behavior is a necessary defense for Arturo Bandini, the son of Italian immigrants coming of age in America during the rise of Italian fascism.

During this period Fante was at work on *The Road to Los Angeles*, which had been contracted by Alfred Knopf but was published posthumously in 1985. The protagonist of this novel, Arturo Bandini, sees himself as a hero, and he uses his exposure to the works of European bourgeois intellectuals to set himself apart from the masses: "I said to Mona [his sister], 'Bring me books by Nietzsche. Bring me the mighty Spengler. Bring me Auguste Comte and Immanuel Kant. Bring me books the rabble can't read'" (85). Throughout the novel, Bandini comically regurgitates his readings in rebellion against his home environment. He uses his identity as a writer to separate himself from the working class, which reminds him of the past he is trying to escape. In this novel Fante sets up the myth of the artist as hero in a society that has no need for what the writer produces. In *1933 Was a Bad Year* (1985) Fante shifts into the sports-figure-as-hero myth as he depicts a young boy's desperate struggle to assimilate into American culture. The protagonist, Dominick Molise, attempts to separate himself from his poverty and ethnicity and rise above the masses through baseball. Fante juxtaposes the experiences of Molise's dream of "making America" through sports with the reality of the life of leisure led by the protagonist's wealthy best friend. In all these works, the protagonist is never successful in his attempts to transcend his social position.[8]

Although nearly all of Fante's novels and stories are presented through an Italian American perspective, they also use elements linked to the literature of the period in which he wrote. Fante's novels are strongly connected to the West Coast road books of John Steinbeck. In *Ask the Dust* (1939), for example, Fante creates a protagonist typical of the "picaro" Philip H. Melling identifies as dominant in the writing of this period: "The novel of the 1930s is dominated by the figure of the itinerant traveller who lives on the periphery of society and is forever seeking new adventures. This character is seldom cerebral or self-involved and he wanders aimlessly through a land devoid of cultural tradition" ("Samples of Horizon," 118). Fante invests his protagonist with a more cerebral perspective and a greater self-involvement than most other picaresque heroes exhibit. At the same time, he shares the modernist movement idea of America as a cultural wasteland: "I call my book *Ask the Dust* because the dust of the east and the middle west is in these streets, and it is a dust where nothing will grow, supporting a culture without roots and the empty fury of a lost hopeless people, frenzied to reach a peace that cannot ever belong to them" (Prologue to *Ask the Dust*, 12). While Fante shares some of the concerns of those traditionally identified with the modernist movement, his ethnic and Marianist Catholic orientation combine to create philosophical obstacles that prevent critics and historians from including him in the Marxist and New Critical studies that have shaped the definition, and thus our awareness, of the modernist American literary tradition.

Fante's contribution to the Italian American tradition is his depiction of the myth of assimilation as a way of achieving the American Dream. The dream, achieved by "making America," guided many children of Italian immigrants away from their Italian heritage, through materialism, and toward full membership in American culture. Fante creates this myth through his depiction of the Italian American family in *Wait until Spring, Bandini* and their attempts to achieve the American Dream with dignity. The father and mother are depicted as heroic figures who seem unconnected to any historical period. An early reviewer notes their "timeless quality," a quality he has seen before "in Giovanni Verga and in Ignazio Silone" (Chamberlain, Review, 70). Fante represents *Italianità* through three figures: the father, Svevo Bandini; the mother, Maria Toscana Bandini; and the grandmother, Dona Toscana. In contrast to these figures are the American bankers, clerks, and the widow Hildegarde. Caught somewhere between these extremes of Italian and American identities are the three Bandini children — Arturo, Federico, and August — who achieve a synthesis of Italian and American identity.

The novel opens as Svevo Bandini is angrily walking home, frustrated at having failed to find work as a bricklayer due to the Colorado winter. Svevo is heroically pitted against both natural elements and a man-made economy that he had run to in the hope of finding a life better than the one he had lived in Italy. Without work he must live on the credit extended begrudgingly by local merchants. The Colorado winter presents him with a situation he rarely faced in the old country. Svevo curses his situation, calling out, "*Dio cane*" (God is a dog). His defiance of God is countered by his wife's piety and her belief that everything comes from God. When Svevo swallows garlic bulbs to cure a bad case of the flu, his wife attributes his recovery to her prayers and to God, from whom the garlic comes.

Among Svevo's enemies is his house, a constant reminder of his inability to "make America": "It was his enemy, that house. It had a voice, and it was always talking to him, parrot-like, forever chattering the same thing. Whenever his feet made the porch floor creak, the house said insolently: you do not own me, Svevo Bandini, and I will never belong to you. . . . Once it had been a challenge, that house so like a woman, taunting him to possess her. But in thirteen years he had wearied and weakened, and the house had gained in its arrogance" (*Wait until Spring*, 16–17). Another enemy is Helmer, the banker with "eyes that looked like oysters" (17). It is before this American that Svevo has to stand and "say that he had not enough money to feed his family" (17), admitting that he cannot pay the mortgage. These problems combine to make Svevo Bandini a bitter man who takes out his anger on his wife and children. In spite of his behavior, his wife sees him as "pure as bread," a simile that comes from the Italian *buone come pane* (good as bread) — a reference to the most important element in the southern Italian's diet. Svevo's language is peppered with Italian curses such as *"Dio Maledetto!"* (accursed God) and *"povera America!"* (poor America), which reveal his frustration with life as an immigrant in a land that was "the rear end of God's creation, always frozen, no place for an Italian bricklayer; ah he was cursed with this life" (25). Svevo's curses, more than verbal vents for his frustration, are also spoken to affect his wife. "To use the name of Christ carelessly was like slapping Maria across the mouth. . . . The first English words he learned were God damn it. He was very proud of his swear words" (37–38).

Besides his foul language, Svevo has a propensity for violence. His past is full of fights with his father, whose arm he broke after pushing him down the stairs (20). His belief in disciplining his children through physical punishment forces similar confrontations between him and his children. Especially affected is his oldest son, Arturo, who becomes a parallel protagonist in this novel. Svevo's behavior and Italianness become the qualities against which Arturo rebels. "His name was Arturo, but he hated it and wanted to be called John. His last name was Bandini, and he wanted it to be Jones. His mother and father were Italians, but he wanted to be an American. His father was a bricklayer, but he wanted to be a pitcher for the Chicago Cubs" (33). Fante goes on with a litany of the differences between Arturo and the father he worshipped even as "he lived in dread of the day when he would grow up and be able to lick his father" (34), who "wasn't satisfied with being an Italian, he had to be a noisy Italian" (35). Arturo is torn between love and hate of the people he calls "these Wops" (37).

Whenever Svevo tells his kids about life in the old country, where he "made four cents a day carrying stone on his back" (41), he shows his son that if there is no dignity in his present condition, there is at least a type of heroism in his immigration story. "The progression of years, the crossing of an ocean, the accumulation of mouths to feed, the heaping of trouble upon trouble, year upon year, was something to boast about too, like the gathering of great wealth" (41). Ironically, Arturo comes to understand his father through his attempts to separate himself from his Italian heritage. Like Svevo, Arturo hates winter, because it keeps him from playing baseball (51). He too must wait for spring, to regain his position as a star baseball player in his community. In spite of his wish to be as unlike his father as possible, Arturo identifies with his father's plight to the point of tears:

Everywhere it was the same, always his mother — the poor things, always poor and poor, always that, that word, always in him and around him, and suddenly he let go in that half darkened room and wept, sobbing the poor out of him, crying and choking, not for that, not for her, for his mother, but for Svevo Bandini, for his father, that look of his father's, those gnarled hands of his father's, for his father's mason tools, for the walls his father had built, the steps, the cornices, the ashpits and the cathedrals, and they were all so beautiful, for that feeling in him when his father sang of Italy, of an Italian sky, of a Neapolitan bay. (55–6)

The force that maintains Svevo's connection to Italy and to the past is his friendship with Rocco, a boyhood friend from the old country with whom Svevo occasionally takes off on weekend drinking and card-playing binges. Together, they represent a way of life that is insular in that it separates Italian men from Italian women and is antithetical to the "American way."

Arturo understood his mother's hatred for Rocco. Maria was so afraid of him, so revolted when he came near. Her hatred of his life-long friendship with Bandini was tireless. They had been boys together in Abruzzi. In the early days before her marriage they had known women together, and when Rocco came to the house, he and Svevo had a way of drinking and laughing together without speaking, of muttering provincial Italian dialect and then laughing uproariously, a violent language of grunts and memories, teeming with implication, yet meaningless and always of a world in which she had never belonged and could never belong. (71)

The world created by Svevo through his interactions with his *paesano* Rocco is one evidence of the family's "un-Americanness." Another is Fante's juxtaposition of Maria with American women, which emphasizes the impossibility of assimilation for Arturo's mother.

Sometimes when she opened the pages of a woman's magazine whenever one came her way; those sleek bright magazines that shrieked of an American paradise for women: beautiful furniture, beautiful gowns: of fair women who found romance in years: of smart women discussing toilet paper. These magazines, these pictures represented that vague category: "American women." Always she spoke in awe of what "the American women" were doing. . . . She came away drugged with the conviction of her separation from the world of "American women." (73)

Religion is Maria's only escape from her husband's verbal torture and her own failure to become an American woman. She incessantly recites the rosary: "That string of white beads, the tiny links worn in a dozen places and held together by strands of white thread which in turn broke regularly, was, bead for bead, her quiet flight out of the world" (75).

Svevo shares a similar need to escape, which he achieves through the religion of work and the employment of his skills as a bricklayer. "He was a bricklayer, and to him there was not a more sacred calling upon the face of the earth. You could be a king; you could be a conqueror, but no matter what you were you had to have a house; and if you had any sense at all it would be a brickhouse; and, of course, built by a union man, on the union scale. That was important" (74). A rupture occurs in the family fabric when Svevo leaves home on hearing that his mother-in-law is coming to visit. Dona Toscana makes his list of enemies by constantly reminding him of his inability to provide better for her daughter and grandchildren and by accusing him of infidelity. When she arrives Dona Toscana yells out, "The man you married is a brutal animal. But he married a stupid woman, and so I suppose he will never be exposed. Ah, America! Only in this corrupt land could such things happen" (93). "Strange times" follow Dona Toscana's departure. Maria becomes listless and stops cooking and cleaning. All day long she would "lay like one dead, the rosary in her hand" (132). Arturo finds her one day "in the darkness of the coal shed with his father's trowel" (135). Arturo can no longer stand to watch his mother suffer and decides to look for his father.

During Dona Toscana's visit Svevo lives with Rocco and takes out an ad in the local paper with the hope of finding some way to use his skills to make money. The widow Hildegarde responds to the ad and is titillated by his *Italianità*.

So he was Italian? Splendid. Only last year she had traveled in Italy. Beautiful. He must be so proud of his heritage. Did he know that the cradle of western civilization was Italy? Had he ever seen the Campo Santo, the Cathedral of St. Peter's, the paintings of Michelangelo, the blue Mediterranean? The Italian Riviera. No, he had seen none of these. In simple words he told her that he was from Abruzzi, that he had never been that far north, never to Rome. He had worked hard as a boy. There had been no time for anything else. (176)

His sexual encounter with the rich American widow becomes Svevo's way of making America. "He laughed the triumph of his poverty and peasantry. This Widow! She with her wealth and deep plump warmth, slave and victim of her own challenge, sobbing in the joyful abandonment of her defeat, each gasp his victory. . . . And when he left her sobbing in fulfillment, he walked down the road with deep content that came from the conviction he was master of the earth" (199). After a few days of living with the widow, Svevo returns home "with new shoes on his feet, defiance in his jaw, guilt in his heart" (158), and Christmas gifts for everyone. Sensing his infidelity, his wife scratches his face bloody and throws the money he offers into the stove. Svevo returns to the widow's house.

While all this is happening to his parents, Arturo is in the process of struggling with his Catholicism and professing his adolescent love for a classmate, Rosa Pinelli, for whom he steals a family heirloom to present as a Christmas gift. Rosa's mother suspects the theft and returns the jewelry. One of Rosa's friends, the blonde Gertie, hands Arturo a letter during class. The letter confirms his fears of not being accepted as an American:

Dear Arturo Bandini:
Some people are too smart for their own good, and some people are just plain foreigners, who can't help it. You may think you are very clever, but a lot of people in this school hate you, Arturo Bandini. But the person who hates you most is Rosa Pinelli. She hates you more than I do, because I know you are a poor Italian boy and if you look dirty all the time I do not care. I happen to know that some people who haven't got anything will steal, so I was not surprised when someone (guess who?) told me you stole jewelry and gave it to her daughter. (241)

Arturo's reaction to this note becomes the subject of a "whispered hubbub" throughout the classroom, but the attention shifts away from him when the teacher announces that Rosa has died that day of pneumonia. As a means of consoling her son, Arturo's mother sends him off to the movies. Later in the story, Arturo comes upon his father at the widow's house. His dog runs onto her property and she responds by screaming out, "You peasants! . . . You foreigners. You're all alike, you and your dogs and all of you." Svevo's response reconnects father and son: "That's my boy. You can't talk to him like that. That boy's an American. He is no foreigner" (265).

In his preface to the 1983 reprint of *Wait until Spring*, Fante points to the novel as the source of "all the people of my writing life, all my characters are to be found in this early work" (9). *Wait until Spring, Bandini* is also the source of the myth of assimilation that is constantly retold throughout Fante's later works.⁹ Whether he approaches assimilation through the sports hero or the artist-as-hero, Fante's autobiographical fiction sets up an important myth through which Italian American culture can be read.

Pietro di Donato's Revolutionary Revision of Christ

Born in Hoboken, New Jersey, in 1911 of Abruzzese parents, Pietro di Donato became a bricklayer, like his father, after his father's tragic death on Good Friday 1923. "Christ in Concrete," his first short story, recounts his father's death. It was first published in the March 1937 issue of *Esquire*, then reprinted in Edward O'Brien's *Best Short Stories of 1938* and expanded into a best-selling novel that was chosen over John Steinbeck's *Grapes of Wrath* as a main selection of the 1939 Book-of-the-Month Club. Unlike Fante, di Donato never dreamed of becoming a writer, but *Christ in Concrete*'s success placed him in a national spotlight that many critics believe forever blinded his artistic vision. In an early review, E. B. Garside calls him "a shining figure to add to the proletarian gallery of artists" (292) and then goes on to predict that di Donato "would never create a prose equal of Leopardi's *A Silvia*, nor will his latter-day rebellion rise to the supple power of *Pensieri*. But it must be understood that the Italian soul is essentially 'thin.' The Italian peasant and work man live themselves out fully as part of a family, or of an aggregate of some sort all committed to the same style" (Review, 292). Louis Adamic, more sensitive, perhaps, to di Donato's immigrant characters, saw that *Christ in Concrete* was unlike the staple fare of the laboring class, "reflections of the economic treadmill on the tenuous cheesecloth fabric of an ideology" (5). Yet, in spite of this sensitivity, his review betrays a stereotypical notion of immigrant *Italianità* when he characterizes the writing as "robust and full-blooded and passionate, now and then almost to the point of craziness; and also like Fante he has imagination and a healthy sense of the source of poetry in the Italian. . . . Sometimes one feels as though bricks and stones and trowelfuls of mortar have been thrown on the pages and from them have risen words" ("Muscular Novel," 5). Warren French's *The Social Novel at the End of an Era* (1966) is the only book-length study of the literature of the 1930s to even mention di Donato. Yet, while French acknowledges the "fresh and vigorous viewpoint" that *Christ in Concrete* "brought to the American social scene," he portrays di Donato as an example of "the very irresponsibility that destroyed the age" (17). French includes di Donato, along with Richard Wright, in an epilogue subtitled "Beginners' Luck."

Only recently have critics begun to realize what a truly revolutionary figure di Donato was. In his resurrection of di Donato's contribution to the Third American Writers' Congress, Art Casciato helps us to understand why writers like di Donato were ignored by the established critics and scholars of the period. As Casciato points out, di Donato, in his brief speech at the 1939 American Writers' Congress convention in New York (which Malcolm Cowley asked to be rewritten so that it would conform to Cowley's expectations), refused to adopt "the prescribed literary posture of the day in which the writer would efface his or her own class or ethnic identity in order to speak in the sonorous voice of 'the people'" ("Bricklayer," 70). Di Donato's style resisted the modern, and "thus supposedly proper ways of building his various structures," making him "less the bricklayer, than a bricoleur who works not according to plans but with materials at hand" ("Bricklayer," 75–7). Di Donato was the only one of the three writers I discuss here to join the Communist Party, which he did at the age of sixteen on the night that Nicola Sacco and Bartolomeo Vanzetti were executed. The following excerpt from di Donato's contribution to the Third American Writers' Congress is an example of what Cowley found so troublesome about his attitude. "I am not interested in writing for class-conscious people. I consider that a class-conscious person is something of a genius — I would say that he is sane, whereas the person who is not class conscious is insane. . . . In writing *Christ in Concrete* I was trying to use this idea of Christianity, to get an 'in' there, using the idea of Christ" (Casciato, "Bricklayer," 69). Needless to say, di Donato's paradoxical use of "comrade-worker Christ" (*Christ in Concrete*, 173) as a metaphor for the working-class man would prove to be quite problematic when viewed from a Marxist perspective. Yet, in spite of his absence from serious critical studies of American writers, di Donato is perhaps the best known of the early Italian American writers because of the impact *Christ in Concrete* had and continues to have on its readers. He has often been referred to as the "grandfather" of Italian American literature.

In the eyes of many critics, di Donato's first novel is the prototypical Italian American novel, in spite of the fact that many others were published long before his. One of the reasons for this comes from the fact that the signs of *Italianità* are foregrounded in this novel as in no other writing yet produced by an Italian American. Di Donato's *Italianità* is most obvious through the novel's diction. His word choice and word order recreate the rhythms and sonority of the Italian language.[10] In his essay "Rehabilitating di Donato, a Phonocentric Novelist," Daniel Orsini notes that "throughout *Christ in Concrete* di Donato strives to disclose what Husserl calls 'a pre-expressive and pre-linguistic stratum of sense' that separates fact from essence, language from being, worldliness from transcendentality" (192). Orsini points to a key element in understanding the revolutionary effect of di Donato's linguistic representation of *Italianità*: "In short, di Donato discovers, for himself, and for his readers, that the way to a representative Italian identity is through speech acts construed as phonocentric — that is, through words conceived as elemental, self-present, and hence pure sounds which he employs not to write about, but rather to speak of, the vividly worldly consciousness of his characters" (199). According to Orsini, di Donato captures the *Italianità* of these immigrants to America "by fracturing conventional grammar, punctuation and syntax, and also by using — and exploiting — dialectical clichés" (199). As a result, di Donato's diction reminds us of what Vico was referring to when he labeled primitive human speech poetic. This language picture of the immigrants, as Robert Viscusi points out, helps to enhance the mythic mode of the novelist's narrative voice.[11]

In "*De Vulgari Eloquentia*: An Approach to the Language of Italian American Fiction," Viscusi points us toward an understanding of di Donato's diction and its relation to his mythical portrayal of life in Italian America: "The Italian American writers fills his English with Italian that serves the ritual purpose of invoking and celebrating the power of a mythical Italy. By *mythical* I mean that this Italy has exchanged physical for psychological presence. Though the actual place be absent, the mythical Italy is a universal presence that Italian American writers devote themselves to, sometimes unconsciously" (24).

In Viscusi's view, di Donato effects this mythical state through two linguistic registers: "the English equivalent of the Italian the characters are actually speaking" and "broken English" (35). These two registers "exert a pressure upon the idiomatic English of the narrator" (36) and create a truly Italian American English (37). Viscusi concludes, "Here is the language of neither Italy, nor America. This tongue — liturgical, patriarchal, heroic, diplomatic — belongs to a people whose expression arises in two countries, employing the mythical dignity of a mythical Italy as a consolation for, as an incantation over, a real America" (37). Yet, while critics have acknowledged and applauded the inventiveness of di Donato's linguistic experiment, none has yet explored the twist di Donato gives to the Christ story.[12]

While Fante was busy portraying characters who struggled to fit into American life, Pietro di Donato was rejecting the American dream through a rewriting of the story of Christ by documenting the disintegration of the Italian family caused by American capitalism. Before his death in January 1992, he had completed a novel entitled *The American Gospels*, in which Christ, in the form of a black woman, comes to Earth at the end of the world to cast judgment on key historical figures of contemporary America. The theme of Christ as a woman can be found in much of what di Donato has written. It is a theme that is usually left in the shadow of the more obvious interpretation of the great Italian American myth created in his first novel. Di Donato's Catholicism had its roots in pre-Christian matriarchal worship.[13] He admitted to being "a sensualist, and I respond to the sensuality of the Holy Roman Catholic Church, its art, its music, its fragrances, its colors, its architecture, and so forth — which is truly Italian. We Italians are really essentially pagans and realists" (von Huene–Greenberg, Interview, 36). Annunziata, the mother in *Christ in Concrete*, is the key figure in di Donato's rewriting of the Christian myth. She controls her son's reaction to the work site "murders" of his father, Geremio, and his godfather by calling on him to put his trust in Jesus, the son of Mary. This same trust has led immigrants to accept poverty as their fate and passivity as their means of survival in a world bent on using and then disposing them. Trust is a myth that di Donato, through his protagonist, Paul, refuses to accept.

Christ in Concrete (the most mythical text of Italian American literature) is an important bridge between the poetic and mythic modes of Italian American narrative. As a myth it presents a heroic figure, Paul, who searches for God, in the form of Christ, whom he believes, as he was trained to believe, can save his family from the terrible injustices brought upon them by a heartless society. The novel is divided into five parts: "Geremio," "Job," "Tenement," "Fiesta," and "Annunziata," each focusing on the key figures in the myth. In "Geremio" and "Job," di Donato presents Job (i.e., one's work) as the antagonist that controls the Italian workers through the human forces of Mr. Murdin, the heartless foreman; the state bureaucracy, which sides with the construction company during a hearing into Geremio's death; and the Catholic church, through an Irish priest who refuses to do more than offer the family a few table scraps from his rich dinner. Job, which never appears with the expected article "the," is depicted as a living thing that "loomed up damp, shivery gray. Its giant members waiting" (*Christ in Concrete*, 9). Job serves as the means by which "America beautiful will eat you and spit your bones into the earth's hole" (3), as one worker predicts. In "Tenement," young Paul comes to learn about the forces of good and evil in the world and that good comes only from the workers' community, which is portrayed in "Fiesta." Paul's mother, Annunziata, pregnant at the opening of the novel, is the Madonna figure and also represents the immigrants' faith in God, whom she invokes through prayers such as "God of my fathers, God of my girlhood, God of my mating, God of my innocent children, upon your bosom I lay my voice: To this widow alone black-enshrouded, lend of your strength that she may live only to raise her children" (63). In the chapter devoted to her "widowhood," Annunziata attempts to raise her children according to the Christian myth, but in the process her son Paul loses the faith she hopes to pass on to him through recollections of her husband's show of faith.

A heroic struggle occurs between man and God through the figures of

Geremio and Job. Geremio believes he can gain the means to live and eventually to achieve the American Dream — a haven from Job where "no boss in the world can then rob me of the joy of my home" (11). But the money saved for the house must be used to bury Geremio, who along with the other workers becomes a sacrificial victim to Job through the greed and insensitivity of the company. As Paul begins to take up the struggle where his father left off, he begins to see through the masked mechanism of this myth and realizes that the only way to beat Job is by not becoming a part of the system and by fighting against it. This realization is vividly depicted by di Donato through one of Paul's dreams.

Toward the end of the novel, Paul dreams that he is about to die just as his father did. His godfather attempts to save him and is tossed off a scaffold by the foreman who was threatening Paul. Paul fails to save his godfather but remembers who can save him: "It is our Lord Christ who will do it; he made us, he loves us and will not deny us; he is our friend and will help us in need! Bear, oh godfather, bear until I find Him" (285). Paul then takes off in search of Christ and runs into his father, who is on his way to work. The work site becomes a shrine for the workers, who have now become saints; Mr. Murdin, the foreman, appears as a magician who "each time he revolves and shouts at Geremio and Paul he has on a suit and mask of a general, a mayor, a principal, a policeman" (288). Job falls apart, and Paul is the only one who tries to save himself. Paul sees himself in his father's crucified form. He is then carried off to the Cripple, the hag who earlier in the story had conducted a séance for Paul and his mother. Paul sees his father hovering over the Cripple, and as they embrace, Geremio sighs, "Ahhh, not even the Death can free us, for we are . . . Christ in concrete" (290). Paul's dream quest ends here with the failure of Christ to save him and his family. Eventually he realizes that only he can save himself, a realization that is dramatized in the last scene of the novel.

By the novel's end, Paul's faith is nearly destroyed, as evidenced by his crushing of a crucifix offered to him by his mother (296–7). However, the final image of the novel suggests that the matriarchal powers still reign. The image we are left with is an inversion of the pietà; the son is holding a mother who is crooning a deathsong/lullaby that hails her son as a new Christ, one that her children should follow (303). But this haunting image can also suggest that the mother has become the new Christ, who in witnessing what America has done to her son, dies and through her death frees her son from the burden of his Catholic past. This death is quite different from the death of his father, which led Paul in search of Christ. His rejection of Christ as the means to survive in this world contributes to his mother's collapse. She then becomes the basis for a new faith in himself toward which his mother urges her children as she cries out "love . . . love . . . love . . . ever our Paul" (303). This figure of the dying *mater dolorosa* replaces Christ as the figure through which man can redeem himself.[14] There is no redemption through the father; if Paul stays in the system, if he continues to interact with Job, he will share the destiny of his father, Geremio.

For di Donato, the immigrant laborer may become a hero through martyrdom, but his life becomes not a model to emulate but something to avoid. In the eyes of Geremio, America remains an immigrant's dream anchored in God and the belief that God will provide the means by which the immigrant will prevail. Geremio's hope that all his children will be boys is tied into his perception of the American dream: "I tell you all my kids must be boys so that they someday will be big American builders. And then I'll help them to put the gold away in the basements!" (5). And so, the dream of an immigrant Italian becomes a nightmare for the child Paul, who, as witness to the tragedies that have befallen his immigrant family, must become not a new Christ but more a Saint John the Baptist figure who wanders through life preparing humanity for the revolution, seeking redemption through the women he encounters.

By directing his characters' rage at the employers who exploit immigrant laborers, Pietro di Donato argues for solidarity among American workers and requires that they look to each other to solve their problems. Just as the Italian community keeps Geremio's family together, the extended family of the workers must help its members. Di Donato's revision of Christ points to the failure of American Catholicism to support the immigrants' struggle. He reveals Catholicism as a force that controls and subdues the immigrants' reactions to the injustices of the capitalist system that exploits the Italian immigrant as it maims and kills him. Di Donato's deconstruction and remaking of the Christian myth force us to reread *Christ in Concrete* as more revolutionary than it has been portrayed to be by past critics.

Di Donato's rewriting of the Christ myth led him away from organized Roman Catholicism and toward paganism, a return that is explicit in nearly all his subsequent work. His ability to see through the repression created by a Christianity that aligned itself with a capitalist power structure led him toward socialism. Cultural critic Louis Fraina foretold di Donato's dilemma in his 1911 essay "Socialism and the Catholic Church": "The economic suffering of the peoples makes them turn to religion, and the dominant church being allied with the exploiting-properties elements, the toiling masses, too ignorant as yet to embrace Socialism, turn for 'relief' to a religion in opposition to the established church. The desire for happiness is the *conditio sine qua non* of religious faith" (5). For di Donato, this "religion" came not in the form of an organized church but rather through a spiritual quest for truth that would lead him back to a pre-Christian pagan (quasi-Sadistic) sensualism that he would record in his next novel.

This Woman (1958), di Donato's long-awaited sequel to *Christ in Concrete*, was greeted with a flood of negative reviews.[15] As a work of art, this second novel does not achieve the status of the first; however, for di Donato interpreters it is an incredibly important work. In it, di Donato describes the path taken by the young protagonist, Paolo di Alba, after his rejection of both the American Dream and the traditional myth of Christ. Paul becomes "the boy who later felt the terrible exultation of pagan freedom when his mother died in his arms" (*This Woman*, 14). This freedom from the strictures of Italian and American traditions enables the protagonist to re-create himself through a new moral order built on a triad of masonry, sex, and soul: "The three-act drama of his mental theatre would revert first to the factual solidity of building construction, evolve to the mercury of sex, and then culminate with the spiritual judgement" (8).

The central story of the novel concerns Paolo's innumerable and incredible sexual encounters with women in a manner reminiscent of the Marquis de Sade and his faithful Italian disciple, Gabriele D'Annunzio.[16] His main conquest, Isa (short for Isis), is the widow of a German American hotel manager. Eventually Paolo's obsession with possessing this woman collides with his obsession with her husband's ghost. The novel dramatizes the classic madonna/whore complex through the figures of Paolo's dead sister, Ann, and his lover, Isa.

Why wasn't his Madonna-sister alive instead of Isa, and he returned to free clear days! Why did he have to be crucified with the identity and need of this woman! With his Catholicism there was the cleansing, and this woman would not be cleansed. She had to pay, she had to pay! "Purification!" intoned his Soul! "Have the young living husband confront her with the older husband!" chanted the chorus of the Soul. "Purification through desecration! Purification through pain! Purification through the profane! Purification through exhumation! Purification through revelation and witness! Purification! Now! Now!" demanded his Soul. (186)

In a particularly gruesome scene, Paolo rapes Isa, now his wife, on top of her former husband's grave. Later, Paolo returns to the site and digs up the corpse so that he can see the dead man who haunts him through the photos and personal effects Isa refuses to destroy. Paolo does this believing he can exorcise the dead man's memory from his and his new wife's minds: "The unseen cannot die. The dead, viewed, remain truly dead without interruption" (193). He forces Isa back to the grave to see the mutilated corpse, and the experience drives her to a nervous breakdown. Later, and incredibly, the story ends happily with Isa and their son prancing about the beach in a scene that becomes, for Paolo, "a vaulting apocalypse" in which "his immediate pagan satyr mortal, and Catholic Soul eternal dashed into close secret embrace" (220).

Much of di Donato's later work continues to portray this conflict of the sacred and the profane.[17] In *The Penitent* (1962) he recounts the story of Alessandro Serenelli, the man who killed the virgin Maria Goretti, who was later sainted by the Catholic church. Di Donato attempts to understand the murder as a crime of passion committed by a man who as a fisherman lived the pagan life of the sea (*The Penitent*, 205): "Was purity more important than the denial of nature, the agony and loss of one life, the ruin of another and the sorrow of two families?" (203).

After destroying the traditional myth of a Christianity corrupted by temporal powers, di Donato builds a new myth for his readers. This new myth portrays man as surviving best within the naturally spiritual institution of family, which is constantly threatened by a world corrupted by the artificial institutions a material-hungry capitalism creates. Di Donato's final novel is an attempt to resolve the sacred/profane dilemma presented in much of his earlier work. The redemption of the victims of capitalism through the final judgment of a female Christ is the subject of *The American Gospels*, which at this point remains unpublished. Through this novel, which should be read as his primal scream out of the world just as *Christ in Concrete* was his cry into the world, di Donato takes his "revenge on society" by revealing "all the nonsense of authority and of Church" through what he calls a "conscious evaluation of myself" (von Huene–Greenberg, Interview, 33–4). To di Donato, salvation for the world lies in man's ability to become his own god, to take responsibility and control of the world he has created and to act for the good of all.

Jerre Mangione: The Writer as Diplomat

The kingdom of the home
The republic of the street
Felix Stefanile, "Stone"[18]

Jerre Mangione chose a much more orthodox approach in achieving his goal of becoming a writer. During the 1930s, Mangione, born in 1909, had numerous articles and book reviews to his credit and served as the national coordinating editor of the Federal Writers' Project. In 1943 Mangione completed a book that Malcolm Cowley lauded as having "more lives than any other book of our time."[19] In *Mount Allegro* Jerre Mangione neither rejects the American Dream, as di Donato does, nor does he accept it, as Fante does. Through this autobiographical narrative, which describes his long trek from the ethnic ghetto into mainstream American life, Mangione debunks the melting pot myth and replaces it with the myth that the two cultures can be synthesized into a new culture, Italian America. Mangione's narrative argues that one can remain rooted in one's culture of descent, to use Werner Sollors's term (*Beyond Ethnicity*), while consenting to the identity changes demanded of the dominant culture. In this respect, Mangione functions very much as the *figura* presented by Constantine Panunzio. He serves as a diplomat of the new world of Italian America that he fashions in his writing. Mangione realized the existence of these two different worlds, the Italian and the American, at an early age, and the knowledge posed a problem he would attempt to resolve through his many works on the subject:

My mother's insistence that we speak only Italian at home drew a sharp line between our existence there and our life in the world outside. We gradually acquired the notion that we were Italian at home and American (whatever that was) elsewhere. Instinctively, we all sensed the necessity of adapting ourselves to two different worlds. We began to notice that there were several marked differences between those worlds, differences that made Americans and my relatives each think of the other as foreigners. (50)

Jerre Mangione had to escape from the world of his relatives in order to establish a career as a writer. Unlike di Donato, Mangione had wanted to be a writer since his college days, during the late 1920s: "My true ambition, which I tried to keep secret from my parents as long as possible, was to be a writer. It seemed to me that I had no talent for anything else; that, moreover, it offered the fastest avenue of escape to the world outside that of my relatives" (*An Ethnic at Large*, 19). Mangione left the ethnocentric world of his family when he entered Syracuse University. During the 1930s he wrote extensively about the effects of fascism on Italy and about those who fought fascism in Europe. In fact, nearly all his fiction and much of his literary criticism is devoted to antifascist themes. One of his earliest book reviews is of Ignazio Silone's *Fontamara*. Entitled "Happy Days in Fascist Italy," it represents Mangione's earliest attempt to explain fascism to an American audience. "Fascism," Mangione says, "contrary to the impression it tries to give to the world has made his [the peasant's] lot considerably worse. It has borne down on him in many instances the naive faith the ignorant peasant had in 'his government' and depriving him of his means of livelihood" (37). Mangione uses this review as an opportunity to present an alternative view of fascism; he shows that the illiterate Italian peasant was "tricked" into accepting the veiled offer of hope and progress extended by Mussolini's Blackshirt movement: "Silone's canvas takes in the whole of Fontamara, the money-mad, tyrannical officials; the politician who calls himself 'friend of the people' and then betrays them at every turn; those peasants who, before they realized the true implications of Fascism and implicit faith in God and 'their' government. . . . Fascism has wiped Fontamara off the map, but Silone has put it on again in such a way that no Fascist bullets can destroy its significance" (38). Unlike di Donato and Fante, Mangione, at this early stage of his career, began the task of interpreting Italian culture and life under Mussolini. He reviewed translations of Pirandello's books *Better Think Twice about It* and *The Outcast* in the August 28, 1935, issue of the *New Republic*. Entitled "Acrobat to Il Duce," the review points out Pirandello's influence on fascist literature:

Long inclined to emphasize the cerebral and anti-realistic aspects of writing, Fascist literature needed only an impetus like Pirandello's to give it direction; that he has succeeded in giving it, is shown by the sheerly psychological and fantastic themes used and abused by modern Italian writers in every branch of literature. . . . it is hard to read very far in his two latest books without seeing Pirandello, the acrobatic metaphysician, jostling aside the characters and stealing the stage for his own pet somersaults. (82–3)

During the same year, Mangione reviewed *Mr. Aristotle*, a translation of Ignazio Silone's collected short stories. The review's title, "Pirandello Didn't Know Him," refers to the fact that when Mangione interviewed Pirandello during the playwright's visit to the United States, Pirandello said he had never heard of the author of *Fontamara*. This ignorance, Mangione says, "indicates that Italy has been more subtle than Germany in her suppression of intelligent books. Instead of making a bonfire of them, she has simply buried them, leaving no obituaries. . . . [Silone] is an intellectual who can see clearly the plight and frustration of the peasant living under fascism" (23–4).

The predominance of Italy as a subject in Mangione's writing stems from his travels there during Mussolini's regime. Mangione first visited Italy in 1936 and was an eyewitness to the fascists' methods of control. He first documented this trip in articles he published during 1937 and 1938 in the *New Masses*, the *New Republic*, *Travel*, and *Globe* magazine, and *Broun's Nutmeg*, and later it would become a significant portion of his first book, *Mount Allegro* (1943). His left-wing publications and his friendship with Carlo Tresca haunted his first trip to Italy, during which his mail was censored and his movements monitored by the fascist authorities. In 1936 Mangione traveled through Italy and Sicily fearing that at any time he might be arrested and forced into military service.[20] This trip is recounted in his classic memoir, *Mount Allegro*. In it, he describes the effects of fascism on Italy and Sicily as observed through his encounters with Italians and his Sicilian relatives. He prefaces the section covering this trip as follows:

In my years of becoming an American I had come to understand the evil of Fascism and hate it with all my soul. One or two of my relatives argued with me on the subject because they had a great love for their native land and, like some men in love, they could see nothing wrong. Fascism was only a word to them; Mussolini a patriotic Italian putting his country on its feet. Why did I insist on finding fault with Fascism, they asked, when all the American newspapers were admitting Mussolini was a great man who made the trains run on time? (239–40)

In 1937 Mangione left a New York publishing job to work for the New Deal.[21] In the course of this period of his politicization he came to understand the terrible threat that European fascism presented to the world. As he worked to understand it better he befriended Carlo Tresca, an Italian antifascist and anarchist who had come to America in the early 1900s to aid the exploited Italian immigrant laborers. Out of his interactions with Tresca came the material on which he built his second novel, *Night Search* (1965). Based on the assassination of Tresca, *Night Search* dramatizes the experiences of Michael Mallory, the illegitimate son of an antifascist labor organizer and newspaper publisher named Paolo Polizzi (a character based on Tresca), as he searches for the murderer of his father. Through his investigation of his father's murder, Mallory, an apolitical public relations writer inclined toward liberalism, learns to take action, and in doing so comes to understand where he stands in relation to contemporary politics. Mallory very much resembles Stiano Argento, the protagonist of Mangione's earlier and more strongly antifascist novel *The Ship and the Flame* (1948).

Mangione's antifascism is informed by his reading of Sicilian writers. During the late 1930s he interviewed Luigi Pirandello and convinced the publishing firm that employed him to accept a translation of Ignazio Silone's now classic antifascist novel *Bread and Wine*. He explores the effects of fascism in "Fontamara Revisited," in which he describes a visit to Realmonte, his ancestors' homeland in southern Italy. In *The Ship and the Flame* he creates an allegory for the sorry state of political affairs in Europe prior to America's entry into the Second World War. Aware of the dilemma of the liberal and the fate of the revolutionary in the world, Mangione invents a microcosm of the larger world of his time, suggesting that the struggle against fascism can be won through heroic action that would not compromise a Catholic's beliefs and that would require breaking away from the traditional mindset formed over many generations. What makes Mangione's first work mythic is his depiction of the immigrant enclave and the heroic struggle of one man to escape the life he was born into.

Immigrants from southern Italy brought to America a belief in a destiny that humans were powerless to change, a belief indoctrinated by centuries of domination by outside forces. Parents could not expect that their children's lives would ever be better than their own. Such proverbs as *Fesso chi fa il figlio meglio di lui* (Only a fool makes his son better than himself) pointed to the futility of expecting progress through subsequent generations. The tension between the Sicilian adherence to destiny and the American sense of freedom and opportunity is best observed in the body of work created by Jerre Mangione, one of the most celebrated of Italian American writers.[22] His *Mount Allegro* has remained in print most of the time since it first appeared in 1943, a feat that has required six publishers to date.

The American-born son of Sicilian immigrants, Mangione grew up in a multiethnic neighborhood in Rochester, New York.[23] Though originally contracted to be a memoir about life in the Rochester neighborhood, *Mount Allegro* was first published as a work of fiction, over Mangione's protests.[24] Despite this initial confusion, *Mount Allegro* survived to acquire the appropriate subtitle: *A Memoir of Italian American Life*. *Mount Allegro* is the first of four nonfiction books written by Mangione that can be read as an autobiographical procession from Italian identity into Italian American. Each book represents a progressive stage of identity development — from Sicilian to American and eventually to Sicilian American. Our reading of the development of an Italian American autobiographical tradition in general and Mangione's writings in particular can be greatly illuminated through a metaphorical paradigm that Robert Viscusi set up in his reading of Italian American literature.

In his essay "*Il caso della casa*: Stories of Houses in Italian America" Viscusi employs four prototypes of Italian American houses as metaphors for possible readings of Italian American writings: the house as shrine, villa, *palazzo*, and embassy. Viscusi explains that these are not stages of development so much as characteristics found in the writings of Italian Americans: "Any house may be all four of these at the same time, for these nouns merely name purposes, and a house, as we know, can do many things at once" (1). Mangione's first book, *Mount Allegro*, is essentially a "shrine to the old country."[25] The first prototype Viscusi identifies is the house as "shrine. *Lares* and *penates* are what make an American house Italian American, and we have innumerable examples to choose from because anything that bears the mark of Italy can become a household god in Italian America. This extends from such obvious artifacts as the statue of Santa Rosalia or the panorama of the Golfo di Napoli to the subtle but all-enveloping atmosphere of cookery" (2). Applying this notion to *Mount Allegro* enables us to identify specific elements of this Italian American autobiography that work to enshrine and eventually mythicize the old country inside the Italian American home, inside Italian American writing. Such elements are easily distinguished in references to home decor, meals prepared, and subjects of conversation. The autobiographer in this type of work submerges the self in deference to a historical and at times mythical ancestral past communicated through others; he becomes a memoirist who in defining his past, dignifies his present.

As in the stories told by Rosa (discussed in Chapter 1), the fear remaining from life in the old country overshadows life in the new country, despite Mangione's American birth. The source of this shadow for Mangione is the Old World notion of *destino* (destiny), which was instilled in the daily life of his Sicilian American family by their experience of Sicily's political realities and religious practices. Though Mangione's life and writing in many respects attempt to escape *destino*, they are nevertheless greatly affected by it. His relatives' lives are governed by traditions and myths, a way of life that Georges Gusdorf says does not foster autobiography because of a characteristic "unconsciousness of personality" that is found in even "advanced civilizations that subscribe to mythic structures . . . governed by the principle of repetition" ("Conditions and Limits of Autobiography," 30). Such civilizations, Gusdorf concludes, fix their attention and energies on "that which remains, not on that which passes" (30). The Italian notion of *destino* is an example of what Gusdorf calls a theory of "eternal recurrence." Mangione writes that *destino*, a barrier that kept his relatives from becoming Americans, contained "strong elements of fatalism" that were "ingrained in the Sicilian soul by centuries of poverty and oppression. . . . In their minds, *Destino*, the willingness to resign oneself to misfortune, was the key to survival; to refuse to believe that an almighty force predetermined the fate of all people was to court disaster" (*An Ethnic at Large*, 32). Mangione can overcome this barrier only by leaving his relatives. Throughout *Mount Allegro* we get the sense that the narrator is documenting the decline of a people and the end of an era, an era that becomes history the moment the narrator separates himself from his immigrant relatives. In fact, Mangione can write this book only after he has left home. By leaving home, then, he begins the process of Americanization. Even the book's structure reveals the duality its writer experienced.

William Boelhower sees *Mount Allegro* as composed of three movements (*Immigrant Autobiography*, 187). In the first movement (chapter 1) we find the narrator focusing on Gerlando (Jerre), a child protagonist questioning his identity as he begins to develop an individual personality separate from the group of grown-ups. This movement opens with his sister's comment, "When I grow up I want to be an American" (*Mount Allegro*, 1). What follows is an argument among the siblings, during which Gerlando replies, "We're Americans right now. . . . Miss Zimmerman says if you're born here you're an American." His brother argues that they are Italians; soon the argument is resolved by their father's pronouncement, "Your children will be *Americani*. But you my son are half-and-half" (1). This duality is one that Mangione experienced throughout his life. The second movement (chapters 2 through 10) presents life in Mount Allegro through a series of anecdotes and vignettes reported by a detached narrator who forgoes references to himself in favor of letting the relatives relate their own lives in their own words. This movement is presented primarily through dialogue among family members as they interact and through monologues in which key personalities relate their experiences along with traditional folktales, all of it filtered through the narrator, who has mastered the use of English. This movement is, in essence, a synthesis of Rosa and Ets. The final movement (chapters 10 through 14) returns to what Boelhower calls a "sharp focus . . . on the now mature protagonist" (*Immigrant Autobiography*, 187) as he makes his way out of Mount Allegro by going off to college, then traveling to Sicily, and finally moving into the American mainstream.

First by leaving the family house in Mount Allegro, and then by re-creating, or rebuilding, it in his writing, Mangione confronts his divided self and attempts to make a whole of the two halves.[26] The residents of Mount Allegro are not part of the outside community; their interactions with the larger community are more often than not portrayed as confrontations which become the tales told at family gatherings. When Mangione announces his plan to leave Mount Allegro to attend college, his family expects that he will do so only to return in a position of power, as a doctor or a lawyer. When they realize he has the talent and temperament for neither career, a wise uncle suggests a compromise: he should become a pharmacist. Mangione chooses instead to become a writer, a choice that signals a total break from the Old World, for there is no real need in the Sicilian American oral-based community for writers; to become a writer is to elect to become an outsider. Mangione tells us in *Contemporary Novelists* that "the experiences that became the substance of *Mount Allegro* accentuated for me the sharp contrast between the philosophical values of the old world and those of the new. It also succeeded in casting me in the role of outsider who, belonging to neither world, tries to create his own world by writing" (571).

The building of Mangione's American identity was accelerated by a 1936 trip to Italy, recounted at the end of *Mount Allegro*. Mangione leaves for Italy with the caution that he not travel far from American consulates, for his relatives fear that, as the son of immigrants, he might be kidnapped and forced to serve in Mussolini's army. In Sicily, Mangione is identified as the "Americano." He speaks an older dialect of Sicilian and uses words that are part of a creole invented out of necessity as Sicilians imposed their native language on American experiences that had no Sicilian equivalent. He immediately recognizes his Sicilian relatives as versions of those back in America. These similarities enable him to realize that it is futile "for anyone to believe that Sicilians could become conventional Americans in the course of a single lifetime" (265). However, he also becomes aware of a great difference between Sicilians and Sicilian Americans, especially in this time of fascism: the former still have a fear of "speaking out of turn. It lay on their hearts and minds like a heavy poison. But Sicilians had to talk, for it was in their nature. Some talked to me because I was an American relative and would not give them away" (266). Mangione can see this fear; he recognizes the limitations it forces the Sicilian to live with only because he has come to understand and exercise a more Americanized notion of freedom and self-reliance. His experiences outside Mount Allegro, as well as the books he has read about life in America, have enabled him to transcend the immigrant world, to free himself from *destino.*

And so, *Mount Allegro* can be read as a shrine that Mangione has built of and to his Sicilian American past. The recorded memories of his many uncles and aunts and their immigrant experiences preserve a time that is forever gone. As a shrine, *Mount Allegro* can also be read, as Boelhower has pointed out, as a group biography. However, Mangione's work is not so revolutionary or untraditional as Boelhower and other critics would have us believe. Boelhower believes that *Mount Allegro* "signals the very death of the genre, of the autobiographical paradigm as it is traditionally understood, for here the protagonist's time dissolves into the time of the community. Out of the ashes of the typology of the single solitary self will arise the transindividual self, the group-biography" (*Immigrant Autobiography*, 192). Critic John M. Reilly also does not read *Mount Allegro* as an autobiography in the traditional sense. In his essay "Literary Versions of Ethnic History from Upstate New York," Reilly describes *Mount Allegro* as a memoir in which "the self serves as an armature . . . but the subject is less the unfolding of personality than it is passage through events and relationships that may be known also from other, perhaps more objective, writings" (190–1).

Both of these critics correctly point out that *Mount Allegro* is not a traditional American autobiography through which one observes the progression of an individual's development of self over time. However, a more accurate explanation of its difference can be given by noting the Italian tradition out of which Mangione wrote. Mangione's style of submerging the self and inserting the narrator as an invisible protagonist/observer, according to Ben Morreale, is a typical characteristic of control practiced by many Sicilian writers: "Coming from an island that had been the crossroads of armies bent on world domination for centuries, having insecurities that some have translated into a psychological *paura storica*, or history of fear, the Silician has learned not to reveal himself. This reticence might be the core of Sicilian style in literature" ("Mangione and the Yearning for Home," 41). Morreale's observation is crucial to reading Mangione's memoirs, fiction, and social histories. Morreale finds a similar style at work in the writers associated with the Sicilian school of Italian literature: Giovanni Verga, Luigi Pirandello, Giuseppe di Lampedusa, Elio Vittorini, and Leonardo Sciascia. In the works of all these writers the narrative self is subservient to the voices of others; the self is rarely placed in a consistently dominating position. This narrative mask enables the true self to remain flexible and thus untraceable. It is also a politically safe position for a narrator who must negotiate his way through a repressive political system. This was an important stance for Mangione to take, especially when he had to deal with two very different political systems: democracy in America and fascism in Italy.

The guiding principle of Mangione's style and a dominant theme in his work is that one can challenge destiny, one can make one's own destiny. He writes out of a need to explain the people who have affected his notions of self; he also writes in order to bridge the gap between the Italian immigrant and the American. He knows the sophistication and wit these illiterate immigrants are capable of communicating to each other but not to outsiders, who mistakenly equate the immigrant's struggle for self-expression in a foreign language with ignorance. The fact that Italian immigrants had much to offer America in the process of becoming Americans led Mangione to question the viability of the melting pot theory: "Was it in the chemistry of human life for my relatives to become Anglo-Saxonized — the apparent goal of the melting pot theorists? So long as they believed in freedom and democracy — and their long history showed those ideals to be as ingrained in them as their religion — was it necessary that they try to change themselves? Didn't America need their wisdom and their warmth, just as they and their children needed America's youth and vigor?" (*Mount Allegro*, 239). In his attempt to find answers to these questions, Mangione journeys into the past, first through reading and then through travel to his ancestral homeland. Mangione pursues the solution to the Sicilian versus American identity conflict dramatized in *Mount Allegro* in his later writings, until, in *An Ethnic at Large*, he finally settles comfortably into an identity as Italian American. Like Mount Olympus, the source of many of the founding myths of Western civilization, *Mount Allegro* would become the source for many of the myths on which much of Italian American culture would be built and through which Italian American culture would be interpreted.[27]

Beyond the insights into Italian American ethnicity to be gained from the works of these three writers, a closer reading of their writing reveals aspects of the mainstream writing of the 1930s that have more often than not been overshadowed by their ethnic differences. The radicalism of di Donato, the liberal pragmatism of Mangione, and the political apathy of Fante represent three different political positions taken by American writers during the 1930s. Each has an interesting mainstream counterpart: for Fante, John Steinbeck; for di Donato, James T. Farrell; and for Mangione, Edmund Wilson. In spite of their different political beliefs, their works are united by the social criticism of the larger American scene that comes from their positions on the banks of America's cultural mainstream.

Like Mangione, Fante and di Donato juxtapose depictions of the injustices faced by their parents with the hopes that their own lives will be different—by avoiding the blind devotion to the Catholic church of their mothers, and by identifying with American institutions; Fante through magazine writing; Mangione through the university, the publishing industry, and government service; and di Donato through identification with the worker. In contrast with the myths that appear in the writing of Italian Americans during the late 1930s and early 1940s, the myths employed by later writers would capture the imagination of Americans in ways these early writers could only dream of. The myths posited and explored by Mario Puzo and Gay Talese and parodied by Giose Rimanelli would permanently affect, some might say even grotesquely distort, others' image of Italian Americans.

Three

The Middle Mythic Mode: Godfathers as Heroes, Variations on a Figure

Three narratives will represent the middle mythic period of Italian American narrative: Mario Puzo's *The Godfather* (1969), Gay Talese's *Honor Thy Father* (1971), and Giose Rimanelli's *Benedetta in Guysterland* (1993). Within these three works the figure of the godfather surfaces as a direct response to the attempts of Italian immigrants to "make America." Puzo's romanticized version, Talese's historical version, and Rimanelli's parodic version all represent variations on the heroic theme this figure has come to embody. Besides containing the characteristics of the mythic mode that I outlined earlier, these three texts also reveal an intertextual relationship that until recently was a rare phenomenon in Italian American literature.[1]

Interpretations of the Italian American family take on new dimensions in these three books. The image of the honest, hardworking Italian immigrant family portrayed by Fante, di Donato, and Mangione as a community united against an alien and often hostile outside world is abandoned for the portrayal of the family able to gain the power through any means — legal or illegal — necessary to control their environment. This control is represented through the figure of the godfather. Richard Gambino says that the godparent belongs to the second most important category in the hierarchy of Italian family order:

From top to bottom: 1. family members, "blood of my blood," 2. *compari* and *padrini* and their female equivalents, *commare* and *madrine* ("godparents," a relationship that was by no means limited to those who were godparents in the Catholic religious rites . . . and which would better translate as "intimate friends" and "venerated elders"), 3. *amici* or *amici di cappello* (friends to whom one tipped one's hat or said "hello"), meaning those whose family status demanded respect, and 4. *stranieri* (strangers), a designation for all others. (*Blood of My Blood*, 20–21)

These levels are circles or buffers designed to protect the family. With the nuclear family in the center, surrounded by the extended family, then by the *compari* and *commari*, and then the *amici*, the order of the family works like the walls around a castle. *Compareggio* (godparenthood) ranks next to the family because it signifies a trust stronger than any other relationship that unrelated Italians can share. Traditionally, godparents were chosen from the circle outside the "blood" family for the purposes of cementing a familylike bond between those involved. Godparents were selected on the basis of their ability to contribute to the protection and well-being of the family, and selection was often a strategic, political decision.

In America, especially during the Great Depression, those who held power in the Italian American communities (even gangsters) were besieged with requests to be godfathers or godmothers to the children of those who lacked access to power. It was not uncommon for a single individual to be a godparent in a number of families. As an honor to the godparent for accepting the responsibility of *compareggio*, the godfather or godmother's first name often became the second name of the child at Baptism or the third name of the child at Confirmation. The godparent was expected to assist the godchild throughout life and to act as a counselor and a mediator, especially during intrafamily disputes. If a parent should die while the child was still a minor, the godparent would take over the child's upbringing.[2] This, then, is the background of the serious and sacred relationship that would become distorted through the literary and media representations that captured America's attention during the 1970s.

The next three sections of this chapter analyze three representations of the godfather figure created by Italian American writers in order to reveal how they create mythic figures out of historical materials. Mario Puzo's novel, Gay Talese's nonfiction narrative, and Giose Rimanelli's parody represent three very different approaches to representing this very important cultural figure in writing. What is more interesting, however, is how these three representations speak to each other in the construction and the deconstruction of the myth that I call the myth of reverse assimilation.

Mario Puzo's Great Italian American Dream

The book got much better reviews than I expected. I wished like hell
I'd written it better. I like the book. It has energy and I lucked out by
creating a central character that was popularly accepted as genuinely
mythic. But I wrote below my gifts in that book.
Mario Puzo, "The Making of *The Godfather*"

This work of fiction is not really about organized crime or about
gangsterism. The true theme has to do with family pride and personal
honor. That's what made *The Godfather* so popular. It portrayed people
with a strong sense of kinship to survive in a cruel world.
Joseph Bonanno, *A Man of Honor*

The Godfather is Mario Puzo's third novel. His earlier novels represent
his attempts to fulfill a dream of becoming an artist and escaping the
ghetto world in which he was born. Like Fante, di Donato, and Mangione,
Puzo's early encounter with such writers as Dostoevsky in his local library
strengthened his belief in art and enabled him to "understand what was
really happening to me and the people around me" (*The Godfather Papers*,
24). It was not art, however, but war that finally enabled Puzo to escape his
environment "without guilt" (26). Out of his experiences in Europe during and after the Second World War he crafted his first novel, *The Dark
Arena* (1955); ten years later he returned to his life experiences growing
up in New York's Little Italy to create *The Fortunate Pilgrim* (1965). In
The Dark Arena, the protagonist, Walter Mosca (in Italian, *mosca* means
"fly"), returns home from serving with the American occupation army in
Germany. Unable to take up where he left off before the war, Mosca
returns to Germany as a civilian employee of the occupation government
and resumes his life as a black marketeer. While the novel received some
good reviews, Puzo was disappointed that it did not make much money
(*The Godfather Papers*, 33). *The Fortunate Pilgrim* received similar notices
and brought Puzo even less financial reward. Because of the poor sales of
his earlier works, no publisher would advance him the money he needed to
write a third novel. Twenty thousand dollars in debt, he began to look for a
way out. "I was forty-five years old," he writes, "and tired of being an
artist" (*The Godfather Papers*, 34).[3]

    With the publication of *The Godfather* in 1969, Mario Puzo was imme-
diately promoted to celebrity status. Not since the publication of Pietro di
Donato's *Christ in Concrete* had an American author of Italian descent
been thrust into the national spotlight on such a grand scale. The timing
of *The Godfather*'s publication had much to do with its rapid climb to
number one and its sixty-seven-week stay on the *New York Times* best-seller
list. The novel came off the press in the middle of the ethnic revival period

of the 1960s. It also followed nationally televised congressional hearings on organized crime and the publication of Peter Maas's nonfiction best-seller *The Valachi Papers*, in which mobster-turned-informer Joe Valachi describes his activities inside organized crime.

The Godfather has done more to create a national consciousness of the Italian American experience than any work of fiction or nonfiction published before or since. It certainly was the first novel that Italian Americans as a group reacted to, either positively or negatively, perhaps because it appeared at a time when Italian Americans were just beginning to emerge as an identifiable cultural and political entity. Even though this book is much more a work of fiction than any of the earlier, more autobiographical novels written by Italian Americans, it created an identity crisis for Italian Americans throughout the nation. Antidefamation groups denounced Puzo for creating a bad image of Italians in America; young Italian American boys formed "Godfather" clubs; and real mafiosi claimed that Puzo knew what he was writing about. For a while, Puzo wrote a number of essays on the subject of Italian America which appeared in major national magazines. These essays, while often undermining the image of Italians that he created in *The Godfather* and his later novel *The Sicilian*, are also quite critical of the Italian American's behavior in American society.[4]

The effect of this one novel was tremendous. Since its publication, and especially since its film adaptations in the early 1970s, Italian American novelists have been writing in *The Godfather*'s shadow, and Puzo has become a recluse. Though sociologists and literary scholars may forever debate the value of Puzo's work, most would agree that he has left a permanent imprint on the American cultural scene through his representation of *Italianità* and his creation of a mythic filter through which Italian American culture would henceforth be read.[5]

In "The Authority of the Signifier: Barthes and Puzo's *The Godfather*," Christian Messenger reads *The Godfather* through Roland Barthes's essay "Myth Today" for the purpose of determining the role that myth plays in the production of popular culture. Messenger points out that while the Corleone family "appeared to be a proto-family for our collapsing time" (2), it also set up a false dichotomy between good murderers and bad murderers. Messenger reads Puzo's symbolizing as signifiers of a mythic language that result from artificially naturalizing history, a process that Barthes says is the function of myth. Messenger's reading of key scenes in the novel makes clear "the dialectal flow between naturalizing and historicizing" (21) that Puzo's narrative obscures. *The Godfather* portrays the Mafia as a natural force in the Sicilian world from which Vito Corleone comes, a world he attempts to re-create in his new home in America. In this world the Don and his family are portrayed as the "good guys," and the American establishment with which they struggle — the institutions of law and business — are set up as the "bad guys." Messenger suggests that the key question asked by the novel is raised by Jack Woltz and Kay Adams: "What if everyone acted that way?" (3). This question can guide us through a reading of the novel as an exercise in the portrayal of reverse assimilation. In other words, in this novel Puzo presents the question that in effect is the real Italian American dream: What if America assimilated to our ways? Before setting up this approach to reading *The Godfather*, let me first point to some of the aspects of the novel that can be connected to more traditional Western myths.[6]

The Don's system of belief is based on the idea that each man has but one destiny. The Don's own destiny was determined when he killed Fanucci, the thug who extorted money from local merchants and demanded tribute from any criminal activity that took place in his neighborhood. When Fanucci demands a percentage of Vito's and his partners' crime, Vito decides to kill him. "It was from this experience came his oft repeated belief that every man has but one destiny. On that night he could have paid Fanucci the tribute and have become again a grocery clerk. . . . But destiny had decided that he was to become a Don and had brought Fanucci to him to set him on his destined path" (*The Godfather*, 201). Similarly, each of the Don's sons is seen as having his destiny determined by a single incident. Santino (Sonny), the oldest son, is destined to follow his father's ways, not only because of birth but, according to the Don, because he witnessed his father's shooting of Fanucci (221). Michael Corleone's destiny is revealed the night he shoots Sollozzo and the police captain. Fredo's position outside the inner workings of the family business is determined by his inability to defend his father during the assassination attempt.

Puzo borrows a figure from ancient mythology to describe the Don's children. Daughter Connie has a "Cupid-bow mouth" (19). Sonny is described as having the face "of a gross Cupid" (15). His large penis signifies his Dionysian behavior, which interferes with his ability to concentrate on the family business (75). Ruled by his emotions, Sonny is unable to become a good don. Fredo has "the same Cupid head of the family" and lacks "that animal force, so necessary for a leader of men" (16). Predictably, Michael is the only child not described in terms of Cupid.

Throughout the novel the Don is characterized as a god or demigod who can negotiate affairs between humans and the supernatural. This is underscored by the hospital scene in which Genco Abbandando lies on his deathbed crying out, "Godfather, Godfather . . . save me from death. . . . Godfather, cure me, you have the power" (47). The Don replies that he does not have such powers, but if he did, he should "be more merciful than God" (47). Genco then appeals to the Don to stay with him as he faces death: "Perhaps if He sees you near me He will be frightened and leave me in peace. Or perhaps you can say a word, pull a few strings, eh" (47)? When he is not being a god, Don Corleone is portrayed as a heroic figure who is able to struggle with the gods. Puzo characterizes Don Corleone as a rarity, a man of will, a man among "men who refused the dominion of other men. There was no force, no mortal man who could bend them to their will unless they wished it. They were men who guarded their free will with wiles and murder" (287).

In the Don's speech to the heads of the other crime families after the murder of Sonny, he attempts to make peace through an appeal to the American Dream, but the whole speech is an example of *bella figura*, a public posturing designed to shield his true plans and to present the illusion that he is willing to assimilate to the American ways of doing illegal business:

Let me say that we must always look to our interests. We are all men who have refused to be fools, who have refused to be puppets dancing on a string pulled by the men on high. We have been fortunate here in this country. Already most of our children have found a better life. Some of you have sons who are professors, scientists, musicians, and you are fortunate. Perhaps your grandchildren will become the new *pezzonovanti*. None of us here want to see our children follow in our footsteps, it's too hard a life. (292)

The Don uses his power to make friends who will strengthen his position. His competitor, Sollozzo, is driven by the opportunity to make money through the high profits of drug manufacturing and distribution; however, he lacks a key ingredient for insuring the venture's success — the Don's friends in high places. This is the clash between the Old World sense of power bringing wealth and the New World's sense of wealth bringing power. Thus, when the Don pledges not to seek revenge for Santino's murder and to support drug trafficking, he does so because he sees that the only way to keep his family intact is to ensure Michael's safe return from Sicily. After this speech, the Don returns home and announces his semi-retirement and his plans to stay home and work in his garden. But he can do this only because he knows that Michael will take over the business and enact the Corleone family's revenge.

Ironically, Michael, the son destined to take over the Don's power, is the one closest to total assimilation into American life. At the outset of the novel, Michael breaks the code of *omertà* by letting Kay Adams in on the history of his father's business. During his sister's wedding reception Michael tells stories about the "more colorful wedding guests," like Luca Brasi. He explains to Kay what is going on at the meetings held inside his father's study and interprets the ambiguities she, an outsider, is unable to read. Later, on the night that his father is shot, Michael leaves Kay and returns to the family house, and "for the first time since it had all started he felt a furious anger rising in him, a cold hatred for his father's enemies" (123). This fury drives Michael back into the family fold and leads him to avenge his father's shooting.

Up to this point, Michael has been as innocent as the women in the Corleone clan. He has been kept out of the family business and has had a hero's upbringing, the American equivalent of an aristocrat's education, with knightly training in the marines through which he achieves heroism during the war. His military service is part of his attempt to Americanize himself. It represents loyalty to a power that is not Sicilian and rebellion against his father's wishes, as the Don realizes: "He performs those miracles for strangers" (17). Michael's murder of Sollozzo and the police captain takes place under the fated circumstances of an Orestes. His ancestral culture's code demands vengeance for his father's blood, and Michael acts accordingly.

After the murder, Michael flees to Sicily, that otherworldly ground of his being and his subconscious — a locus for so much of Western mythology. There he meets the characters who embody the new condition of his soul, which is physically manifest in his disfigured face. He learns the history of Sicilian culture and the role the Mafia has played in it through Dr. Taza: "He came to understand his father's character and his destiny . . . to understand men like Luca Brasi, the ruthless *caporegime* Clemenza, his mother's resignation and acceptance of her role. For in Sicily he saw what they would have been if they had chosen *not* to struggle against their fate" (324). His bodyguards, like mythological dogs, defend him against the wolves (strangers outside the circles of family and friends) through their use of *lupara*, or "wolf guns." He meets Apollonia, his anima — the pure, good, noble, and beautiful, full of pietàs and innocence. This all takes place in the pastoral setting so thickly described by Puzo during the couple's first meeting (332) and throughout their brief marriage. When Apollonia dies, the victim of a car bomb intended for Michael, it is because he is set on the course that kills the innocence and dirties the moral cleanliness inside himself. She dies in his place as the part of himself that his own actions kill. Her very name and physical appearance signify the *chiaroscuro* contrast, the Apollonian / Dionysian dichotomy that the new Michael has become. Their relationship is typical of the male / female social dichotomy in Sicilian culture in which the woman holds the good, the man shoulders the evil. As Don Corleone earlier reminded his godson Johnny Fontane, women "are not competent in this world, though certainly they will be saints in heaven while we men burn in hell" (38).

While the typical successful hero in traditional myth returns from the otherworld strengthened and complete, Michael returns to America with nothing but a memory of the values represented by Apollonia. Instead of becoming a savior of American society as a fully realized human being, he returns and grows stronger as a monster; a hero in his family's society, he becomes a villain in American society. Unlike Orestes, he never receives the deus ex machina–like compassion of an intervening Athena to save him according to traditional myths. The education Michael receives during his exile in Sicily enables him to take command of his father's kingdom and ruthlessly rule it in the Old World manner.

While there is much in this novel that lends itself to intepretation through traditional myth analysis, Puzo also develops something that transcends the archetype approach. What Puzo has contributed to Italian

American culture is a myth of the assimilation of America into Italian culture. Vito Corleone's goal is to render powerless the forces that attempt to control him. And he does this by re-creating the Old World in the midst of the New.

Many people read *The Godfather* as an allegory of a decadent America in the postwar period.[7] But the novel can just as well be read as the struggle to protect a family and preserve it, no matter the cost, in a hostile environment. If the family is to be preserved, assimilation into American culture must be avoided, and this can be done only if the exact opposite happens; that is, if America assimilates into the culture of the Don and his family. Thus, the novel can be read as proposing the following question: What would happen if an Italian had the power to make America conform to his or her way of seeing/being in the world? In order for this to occur, the Italian would need to create an alternative world within the world, a world that competes with the American world, one that offers a viable alternative. It is inevitable that when these two worlds come into conflict with each other, the subsequent tension often erupts into violence.

The world that Don Vito Corleone replicates in America is built on the solid foundations of a centuries-old social order in which fate or destiny, more often than not through birth, determined the life an individual would lead. In the feudalistic system of Sicily and southern Italy, the peasant could not hope to aspire to a better life by challenging the forces that controlled his life. As a result, attention was focused on what could be controlled, the family unit. This is the reason so many Italians immigrated to America. The world into which they came had been built on the myth that through freedom, people can become whatever they want if only they work hard enough. This puritanical work ethic and the built-in reward system did not require the family to stick together, and often it led to the breakup of the nuclear family.

The Don's Old World notion of a work ethic requires that the family stick together, and any attempt by an individual to leave threatens the livelihood of the entire family. In fact, if a family is to survive with its Old World values intact, it must work against assimilation and strive to have its surrounding environment conform to the family's way of life. Thus, the central conflict of this novel is how to keep the family together for its own good in a land where people no longer depend on the family unit for survival. This conflict is introduced through the opening vignettes in the Don's office. Amerigo Bonasera's family was harmed through the American youth who beat up his daughter, Johnny Fontane lives a mockery of a marriage to a Hollywood star, and to protect his family's honor the baker Nazorine must find a way for his helper, Enzo, a prisoner of war about to be deported, to marry his daughter. All three men have found success by adapting to the American way of life, but when the New World system fails them, when the nuclear family has been threatened or attacked, they return to the Old World through Don Corleone, just as villagers returned to the castle for protection from invasion during feudal times. In return for his assistance, Don Vito requires "that you, *you yourself* proclaim your friendship" (14); in other words, that you conform to his way of life. In this way Corleone not only perpetuates the Old World system but also further insulates and protects his own family. In many ways, Don Corleone is like the king of feudal times who offers protection to those whose problems he has helped to create. His consigliore, Tom Hagen, realizes this: "It was a pattern he was to see often, the Don helping those in misfortune whose misfortune he had partly created. Not perhaps out of cunning or planning but because of his variety of interests or perhaps because of the nature of the universe, the interlinking of good and evil, natural of itself" (391–2). The Don, because he is the center of the world he has re-created in America, is like God who makes all things, good and evil, and is the force that is cursed as it is praised by those who live under his dominion. And so, Bonasera, Nazorine, Fontane, and most of the novel's other characters are monologic, all pieces in the puzzle Puzo produces, which reveals the power of Old World culture to maintain itself in a New World environment. Don Corleone is more concerned with maintaining *l'ordine della famiglia* and expanding its power than with increasing his profits; that is what he transfers to his son Michael, who has become Old World through his exile in Sicily. Michael achieves what Sonny and Fredo cannot because they lack the experience of life in the land of Mafia origins, an experience that would have balanced their beings. The Don does what he believes is necessary for men's families to thrive. He leads his godson, Johnny Fontane, back to taking care of his family and his friends through Nino. He will ensure through an act of Congress that Nazorine finds a good husband for his daughter. And his men will enact the vengeance that Amerigo Bonasera needs in order to return honor to himself and his family.

There are numerous examples of the Don's ability to make America and Americans assimilate to his ways. Tom Hagen, a German American orphan brought into the Don's home, is raised as one of his own, educated in the American system all the way through law school. Given this opportunity to become a successful American, Hagen opts instead to complete his assimilation into the Don's world. "'I would work for you like your sons,' Hagen said, meaning with complete loyalty, with complete acceptance of the Don's parental divinity" (53). Later on, the Don remarks, "Even though you're not a Sicilian, I made you one" (298). Yet, in spite of Hagen's near-native knowledge of Sicilian ways — he is the one able to read the Sicilian sign of the fish wrapped in Luca Brasi's bloodstained vest (118) and is appointed acting consigliore on Genco's death — and because he is not of Sicilian blood, not "born to the ways of *omerta*" (50), he is relegated to marginal status when Michael takes over. Tom breaks the code of *omertà* at the end of the novel when he explains to Kay why Michael had to kill Connie's husband, Carlo (445). It is as though Vito Corleone is a Midas whose very touch turns people into Sicilians. In spite of the power that the movie producer Jack Woltz has gained in the American system, he too must assimilate to the Don's world, he must give in to the Don's wish that his godson Johnny Fontane get the role that revives his film career and his loyalty to the family. It is Don Vito whose subtle machinations remind Johnny of how he neglected his responsibilities to help his boyhood friend and *paesano* Nino. The Don provides Johnny with the means to succeed, and ironically it also becomes the means by which Nino is destroyed.

The character who best illustrates this reverse assimilation hypothesis is Kay Adams. Kay, who can trace her ancestral lineage to the *Mayflower*, embodies all that is American, and her assimilation into the Corleone family is the strongest evidence of reverse assimilation. When Michael brings her to his sister's wedding, he does so to "show his own future wife to them, the washed-out rag of an American girl" (17). He sits with her "at a table in the extreme corner of the garden to proclaim his chosen alienation from father and family" (17). When the Corleones meet her they are unimpressed: "She was too thin, too fair, her face was too sharply intelligent for a woman, her manner too free for a maiden. Her name, too, was outlandish to their ears. . . . If she had told them that her family had settled in America two hundred years ago and her name was a common one, they would have shrugged" (17). No matter how much he loves and trusts Kay, Michael realizes that she is an outsider when he sees her after his father has been gunned down (120). Michael does tell her enough about his father to give her the opportunity to back out of the relationship (121), but she does not. Even when she finds out from Michael's mother that what she had heard about Michael is true, she still holds on to the hope that she will see Michael again. Two years go by and Kay finds work teaching grade school, and she decides one day to call Mrs. Corleone. While talking to her, Kay finds out that Michael has been back in the country for six months. She becomes angry with Michael, his mother, and "all foreigners — Italians who didn't have the common courtesy to keep up a decent show of friendship even if a love affair was over" (357), yet still accepts Mama Corleone's invitation to visit her at the Corleone home. During their reconciliation, Kay tells Michael he could have trusted her, that she would have "practiced the New England *omerta*. Yankees are pretty closemouthed too, you know" (360). Kay accepts Michael's proposal for a Sicilian marriage, one in which she would be his wife but not "a partner in life" (362), after he confides to her that the family will be legitimate within five years and after he provides her with a "final explanation" (365) of his father's business philosophy.

The next we hear of Kay is when Michael is returning home from Las Vegas. We learn that they had been married in a quiet New England ceremony and that Michael was "surprised at how well Kay got along with his parents and the other people living on the mall" (392). She is described as "a good, old-style Italian wife" who gets pregnant "right away" (392). At the birth of her second child, Kay comes to understand that she is "on her way to becoming a Sicilian" after she realizes that the story Connie tells her about Carlo's fuss over the right baptismal gift must be transmitted to Michael (405). Kay leaves Michael when she realizes that he did have his own brother-in-law murdered. Then, against her own better judgment, she accepts Tom Hagen's explanation and returns to Michael and converts to Catholicism, something that does not please Michael, who wants "the children to be Protestant, it was more American" (441). Nevertheless, she is converted to his world and accepts the role of the woman subservient to man. Ironically, the conversion takes place because of her interaction with Tom Hagen, who both breaks the code of *omertà* and treats her as an equal. The final scene of the novel finds Kay at Mass, praying, like Mama Corleone, for the "soul of Michael Corleone" (446). And so, Don Corleone's bid to control his world has had its greatest impact. He has been able, through his son, to convert an American *Mayflower* Protestant princess into a proper Sicilian mother.[8]

Through the marriage of Michael to Kay, Puzo represents the ideal, albeit mythical, synthesis of Italian and American cultures. No matter how much Michael expresses his desires to be legitimate and American on the surface, under his skin he is true to the Sicilian world of his father, and he re-creates that world for the next generation. Thus, Puzo forges in fiction what is impossible to create in reality. The key to this novel's success lies in Puzo's ability to make readers envy and even fear the mystery and the power inside the *Italianità* that he represents through the Corleone family. This is the very myth that Gay Talese's nonfiction narrative attempts to destroy.

Gay Talese's Great Italian American Reality

In the past few years the mafioso rivals the cowboy as the chief figure in American folklore, and the Mafia rivals the old American frontier as a resource for popular entertainment. The problems presented by the image of a monolithic, criminal Italian subculture called the Mafia, among the most severe and persistent difficulties which Italian-Americans have had to face, now overshadow all other obstacles to Italian-Americans in overcoming their predicament in the United States.
Richard Gambino, *Blood of My Blood*[9]

Gay Talese is often identified, along with Tom Wolfe and Truman Capote, as one of the earliest practitioners of New Journalism, "a type of expository writing that blends reporting with such fictional techniques as extended dialogue, shifting points of view, and detailed scene setting" ("Gay Talese, 1932–," 390). He says in a 1993 article that he always wanted to write fiction but felt that his early fiction was betraying his family, so he took cover behind the necessary objectivity of the journalist to investigate contemporary issues in American culture.[10]

Honor Thy Father, Gay Talese's nonfiction narrative of the Bonanno family, stems from Talese's curiosity of "what it must be like to be a young man in the Mafia" (*Honor Thy Father*, 499) and his relentless and thorough research into the subject through the life of Salvatore "Bill" Bonanno. Talese started his work during the same period that Puzo was working on *The Godfather* and began to flesh out the reality of something that Puzo never really confronted. While Puzo wrote *The Godfather* "entirely from research," never having "met a real honest-to-god gangster" (*The Godfather Papers*, 36), Talese based his narrative on actual interviews and encounters with the characters he represents in his book. The two books, especially when read together, echo each other in very interesting ways.

On the surface, *Honor Thy Father* can be read as the historical antidote to Puzo's mythic and romantic representation of the Mafia phenomenon. Talese, one reviewer says, demythologizes "as fast as Puzo mythologizes" (Sheed, "Everybody's Mafia," 25). In *The Art of Fact: Contemporary Artists of Nonfiction*, a study of New Journalism, Barbara Lounsberry writes that of all nonfiction artists, it is Talese who "comes the closest to being a *histor.* By making his histories read like novels, he makes them more accessible and memorable than traditional histories" (3). Yet, as we know from recent developments in criticism, histories are no longer the privileged, objectively scientific documents they once were considered to be. Close scrutiny of Talese's narrative reveals the construction of an *Italianità* that is both victim and victimizer of American culture. Puzo's and Talese's narratives achieve the same goal of expanding "the specific dilemma of how to honor one's father in a changing age to the larger question of how to honor the national spirit, the American dream of our *forefathers*, in a similarly changing and diminished era" (Lounsberry, *The Art of Fact*, 3). Thus, like Puzo's novel, *Honor Thy Father* is more about the effects of immigration on a family's attempt to gain power, and thus contol, over its life and livelihood in America than about the criminal activities employed to achieve that power. Unlike Puzo, however, who portrays the Corleone family as successful in maintaining Old World values and traditions, Talese documents the disintegration of a Sicilian family as it suffers from the sins of the father. Talese's narrative is unified not by the story of crime in America but by its "compelling theme of tradition and change in America" (Sheppard, "Second Banana," 83).[11]

In *Honor Thy Father*, Talese employs a fictional style that brings out the inner thoughts of his subjects. He re-creates dialogue and scenes, using material gathered from interviews and research, to heroically portray a son's unquestioned loyalty to his father no matter the cost to his own life and the lives of his family. Bill Bonanno, very much like the fictional Michael Corleone, faces the dilemma of either assimilating into the world of mainstream America through the educational opportunities provided to him as the son of a don or returning to the feudal and patriarchal Old World system of his father.[12] Talese sees this dilemma as a natural phenomenon established at Bill's birth: "To be born of such foreign fathers and to remain loyal to them throughout one's lifetime, was to bear the burden of being an outsider and being alienated from much of America" (*Honor Thy Father*, 68). Lounsberry perceptively sees that men like Joseph Bonanno "brought to the New World their old feuds and customs, their traditional friendships and fears and suspicions, and they not only consumed themselves with these things but they also influenced many of their children" (*The Art of Fact*, 22). Talese sets up Bill Bonanno as the victim of a destiny determined by his birth. The real question that Talese raises in his compassionate account of Bill's life is: Could this son of a Sicilian underworld figure have been anything but a gangster? Thus, the narrative Talese creates reads more like a work out of the tradition of naturalism practiced by Theodore Dreiser, Richard Wright, and James T. Farrell than anything resembling a modernist text.[13]

The narrative is divided into four parts. Part 1, "The Disappearance," opens with the kidnapping of Joseph Bonanno, the family patriarch. This part presents a portrait of Joseph's son Bill that reads very much like Puzo's account of Michael Corleone: "[Bill was] considered something of an eccentric in the underworld, a privileged product of prep schools and universities whose manners and methods, while not lacking in courage, conveyed some of the reckless spirit of a campus activist. He seemed impatient with the system, unimpressed with the roundabout ways and Old World finesse that are part of Mafia tradition" (19). In spite of his

Americanized treatment of Old World values, Bill Bonanno treats his father as though he were God: "It was obvious that he [Bill] was awed by his father, and while he no doubt had feared him . . . he also worshipped him" (19). This aspect of the narrative enables us to read *Honor Thy Father* in the mythic mode of narrative. Joseph Bonanno is characterized as a godlike hero struggling with the powers that attempt to control his and his family's lives. Lounsberry perceptively reads an "ironic Christian typology" in the narrative that helps to connect this work to the mythic mode. She points to Joseph's Christlike propensity to "speak in oracles" and his ability to heal ailments with ancient remedies (*The Art of Fact*, 16). Joseph is also able to read the heavens and predict the weather. Like Christ, Joseph is persecuted for his political activities — his antifascist activities force him to flee Sicily for America (60). Lounsberry's reading of Joseph as a lost or departed God (16), through his disappearance, sets up a scene out of the Old Testament in which Bill, like Moses, also seems lost. Interestingly, the testing of Bill's family loyalty often takes place in the desert lands of Tucson, Arizona, where his father has a second home.[14] Lounsberry employs Christian typology when she reads Bill's wife, Rosalie, as "the Mary figure, first the Virgin Mary 'remain[ing] awake pondering the . . . unexplained origin of her first son,' the son who will be 'her salvation for a while' (115, 121)" (18).[15]

With his father gone, Bill must assume the position of family leader, relying on the training his father gave him earlier in his life in the codes of *bella figura* and *omertà*, which Joseph proferred through the advice, "*Never let anyone know how you feel*" (53) — which, Talese notes, Bill very carefully passes on to his own children (37–8). Talese lets us know that this is a tradition Bill has experienced not only through his father but also through his grandfather, whom Bill recollects "as a heavy white-haired man sitting in the sun in front of the house reciting Sicilian proverbs — ancient truths from a stoical society" (70). Yet, while Bill attempts to reproduce this patriarchal system in his generation, he, like Puzo's Sonny Corleone, lacks the straitlaced values and discipline bred into the men of the Old World. And he too rebels against this system through a love affair, "his first blatantly rebellious act against the Sicilian family strictures that had shaped him and sometimes sickened him. When Rosalie proposed that they separate, he said firmly that he would not let her go" (89).[16] Talese, delving deep into Bill's ancestral heritage, points out that in Sicilian culture there is no social stigma attached to serving in prison (27). This explains why Bill quite willingly goes to jail for his father, who, ironically, never spent any time in prison. Through the experience, Bill becomes a Christlike figure by sacrificing his own freedom/life for his father.

In Part 2, "The War," Talese presents the historical background that led up to the Bonanno family's involvement in organized crime. In a section that reads like Puzo's book 3 flashback to the rise of Don Vito, Talese provides an "*Apologia per mafia mia.*" He tells of the Bonanno family's role in the unofficial governing of the people of Castellammare del Golfo: "They believed that there was no equality under law; the law was written by conquerors. In the tumultuous history of Sicily, going back more than two thousand years . . . the official government was often the enemy, the outlaw often a hero; and family clans such as the Bonannos . . . were held in awe by their townsmen. . . . They were more ambitious, shrewder, bolder, perhaps more cynical about life than their resigned *paesani*, who relied largely upon God" (182–3). Talese characterizes Joseph Bonanno as having achieved "a certain status at birth" (183) due to this history. Orphaned at age fifteen, Joseph inherited the great wealth and power of his father, which he left to his uncles when he moved with his friend Peter Magaddino to Palermo to attend nautical college (192). As a student, Joseph joined an antifascist youth organization and managed to flee in 1924 before he could be arrested by the fascist authorities.

Talese portrays Joseph's rise in the American system of organized crime as a natural outgrowth of his Sicilian heritage. Bonanno turned down his uncle's offer to train as a barber because

he did not sail thousands of miles across the sea, and slip through the dragnet of American security, to devote himself to the trimming of other men's hair. . . . While he was quite certain that he could not attain the respect he sought within the legal confines of an American society that was dominated by Anglo-Saxons, that was governed by men whose grandfathers had muscled their way to the top and had rigged the rules to their own advantage and had learned all the loopholes, he did believe that the ruling classes in America as in Sicily had great respect for two things—power and money—and he was determined to get both in one way or another. (197)

At twenty-six, Bonanno became the youngest don in the New York Mafia as part of the reorganization that followed the famous Castellammarese War of the late 1920s (203).

Thus, Joseph Bonanno successfully carries on the tradition into which he was born, a tradition that Talese portrays as though it is a force of nature rather than the artificial force that it really is. Just as Puzo does with Don Vito, Talese presents Bonanno's career choice as the only viable option for the immigrant unprocessed by American institutions designed to create a melting pot society. Talese does point out that men like Bonanno, unlike the hundreds of thousands of immigrants who attempted to live within the rules of the system, thrived within the American system and never, in spite of their increased persecution throughout the 1950s and 1960s, were interested in overthrowing the system through revolution. Talese's insights into the workings of these gangsters leads him quite often into philosophizing for them: "These men did not want the system to collapse, for if it would collapse they would topple with it. While they recognized the government as flawed, hypocritical, and undemocratic, with most politicians and the police corrupt to a degree, corruption was at least something that could be understood and dealt with. What they were most wary of and what centuries of Sicilian history had taught them to mistrust were reformers and crusaders" (309). After establishing this historical background, Talese returns to the story of Bill's inability to continue the tradition through to his generation, due in large part to the effects of the Banana War, which took place between 1964 and 1969 and was "the last great war in which a leading mafia crime family sought to take over a kingsized portion of organized crime" (Sifakis, *Mafia Encyclopedia*, 24).[17]

Part 3, "The Family," describes Bill's futile attempts to keep the family and its illegal businesses together during a time of intense federal scrutiny and rivalry with other crime families. Bill Bonanno moves his family to San Jose, California, signifying the family's attempt at Americanization. In California, Rosalie finally arrived in an America that seemed right out of the television commercials, "a rather odd place . . . to be awaiting the husband's return from the feudal world of his father" (296). Joseph Bonanno's feudal world, like its environment, is in decay, a decadence represented by Bill's no longer being asked by friends or relatives to serve as godfather to their children. "This meant nothing and everything to him, for it symbolized a loss of his esteem in which he had once been held by other people" (299). This decay is also reflected in Bill's inability to re-create in his own children the awe that his father had instilled in him.

Bill had been magnetized by his father, would have followed him through hell, and when he finally had perceived the full range of his father's power he had been even more impressed and proud. But Bill did not expect to be that persuasive with his own children — he would never be the towering figure to them that his father had been to him; times had changed, the dynasty was disintegrating, the insularity of Italian family life would most likely not survive the third generation, which was probably a good thing for his children. (301)

Although readers are drawn to the book for its descriptions of the Mafia's criminal activities, Talese uses the Bonanno family to make a larger state-ment about the plight of all Italian Americans, especially regarding the increasing and incessant media portrayals of the Mafia that shadow the public image of this ethnic group. In this way Talese confronts what Puzo fails to acknowledge.[18]

Talese presents Bill as a reader of *The Godfather* and remarks that "he became nostalgic for a period he had never known": "The Sicilians de-scribed in *The Godfather* — not only Don Vito Corleone and his college-educated son Michael (with whom Bill identified) but other characters as well — were endowed with impressive amounts of courage and honor, traits that Bill was convinced were fast deteriorating in the brotherhood" (312). While Bill believes that this deterioration is inevitable, he is never-theless saddened by it. Bill's admiration of Puzo's insight into "the secret society" (312) and ability to create believable representations of mafiosi underscore his reaction to an aunt's having seen *The Brotherhood* at Radio City saying it was, in his opinion, "one of the most stupid films ever made," and "real Hollywood crap" (315).

When the average American citizen thought about the Mafia, he usually con-templated scenes of action and violence, of dramatic intrigue and million-dollar schemes, of big black limousines screeching around corners with machine gun bullets spraying the sidewalk — this was the Hollywood version and while much of it was based on reality it also wildly exaggerated that reality, totally ignoring the dominant mood of Mafia existence; a routine of endless waiting, tedium, hiding, excessive smoking, overeating, lack of physical exercise, reclining in rooms behind drawn shades, being bored to death while trying to stay alive.[19] (353)

Talese suggests that the reality of Mafia life changes a member's "perspective of the larger world beyond and his very small place in that world," leading people like Bill to "exploit the fact and fantasy of Mafia mythology as effectively as the FBI director did at budget time, and the politicians before election day, and the press whenever organized crime was topical, and the movie makers whenever they could merchandise the myth for a public that invariably wanted its characters larger than life — tough-talking, big-spending Little Caesars" (354). This is the myth that Talese so carefully destroys through his meticulous portrayal of the reality of Bill Bonanno's choice "to live the lie" (354). Bill perceptively realizes that the Mafia has become "a national symbol of sin" (358) and that "members of the brotherhood were doing their best to live up to their roles" (358). In essence, then, Talese is saying that through the Mafia, the Italian American has become "everybody's other," replacing the Indian as the symbol of evil in American society.

If compared with the publicized atrocities by allied troops on civilians in Asia or with the intrigues of the CIA . . . , the exploits of the Mafia hardly seem to justify the public attention that it receives. And it would not be receiving were it not for the mythology factor, the George Raft reality, the fact that the Mafia today, like Communism in the fifties, has become part of a national illusory complex shaped by curved mirrors that give an enlarged and distorted view that is widely believed because it fills some strange need among average American citizens for grotesque portraits of murderous villains who bear absolutely no resemblance to themselves.[20] (356)

In the final section, Part 4, "The Judgment," Talese uses Bill's trial for credit card fraud and his sentencing as a way of speaking about the plight of contemporary Italian Americans. After sentencing Bill to four years in prison, the judge explains his reasoning:

You have had a relatively good education. . . . You have had comforts provided you in your youth, and there is hardly any excuse for the type of conduct of which you were found guilty here. This was a case where you didn't just yield to a passing temptation but over a period of time engaged in pretty extensive fraudulent use of this card. . . . You arc not the product of a ghetto. I don't see that because of the family relationships to which Mr. Krieger referred you were under any great handicap that required you to use these cards. You could have gotten a job. There was no need to do what you did. (471)

Later, Talese presents Bill's thoughts: "Yes, Bill thought, I could have gotten a job — but doing what? After all the publicity that had been attached to the Bonanno name since the Kefauver hearings twenty years ago — a time in which Bill himself had been called out of a high school classroom to be questioned by the FBI" (477). Talese suggests that Bill's only real option would have been to leave his family and change his name, but had he done that, "he would not have been Bill Bonanno, a son who deeply loved his father" (478). Like most Americans, Talese explains, the judge had no idea what being born into an Old World family meant for second-generation Americans like Bill. Such people were born to carry on the family tradition, something Bill "would not have tried had his father not been so successful and awesome, offering to Bill what appeared to be great opportunities and advantages, a status at birth that had seemed almost regal" (478).

With this book Talese satisfies his own curiosity of what it would be like to be a member of the Mafia.[21] He also counters the myth presented by Puzo's novel by showing that the Bonanno family is not stable, like the Corleone family. Unlike Michael, Bill is constantly moving. Talese, by presenting the reality of everyday life — the kids in school, Rosalie shopping, the constant vigilance of the FBI, subpoenas, court appearances, and jail sentences — pulls the mask off the glamorized Hollywood version of the Mafia. He does this especially well through his presentation of Rosalie's point of view (125) and through his descriptions of her attempts to break away from her husband's world (239).[22] Salvatore Bonanno, the real-life counterpart to Michael Corleone, lacks the mythic powers of the fictional character and is destined to suffer in his attempts to make Old World ways work in the American system. In the end, the reality is that reverse assimilation is impossible: Bill is constantly hounded by authorities, his life is hell, he must run and hide, and eventually he must assimilate to the American ways.

Talese, as the recorder of this family's story, saw himself as the "source of communication within a family that had long been repressed by a tradition of silence" (504). Through Talese the family is able to say things to each other and to the public that they believed they could never otherwise say. What is most interesting about this book, which sold more than 300,000 copies in the first few months, is that in spite of Talese's efforts to change public perceptions about the Mafia and its relationship to Italian America, the Mafia remained and continues to remain a strong filter through which Italian American culture is perceived. Talese, through his portrayal of Bill Bonanno, ironically presents the reality of the lives of many Americans of Italian descent living in an America in which they were unorganized, "voiceless, powerless, frustrated" (484). At the end of the narrative, Talese presents the situation of Italian Americans during the late 1960s (there was "only one senator of Italian origin; in the House of Representatives only eleven of 435 members" [484]) and reports on their brief attempts to become a united political force during an age when public demonstrations fostered changes in the system. This is a subject he takes up later in *Unto the Sons* (1992), the autobiographical study of his own family which in retrospect we can now read as a book for which *Honor Thy Father* is a rehearsal.

Talese's use of fictional techniques to contextualize the material gathered through his investigative reporting created a text with a literary aura and turned the Bonanno family's story into an immigrant epic. The sincerity with which Talese approached the subject of the Mafia after his years of research and his personal contact with members of the Bonanno family, combined with the incredible popularity of the book, contribute to its use as a model for Mafia documentaries and to its vulnerability as a target for parody.

Giose "The Trickster" Rimanelli's Great Italian American Parody

Postmodern parody is both deconstructively critical and constructively creative, paradoxically making us aware of both the limits and the powers of representation.
Linda Hutcheon, *The Politics of Postmodernism*

The trickster summons agonistic imagination in a narrative, a language game, and livens chaos more than bureaucracies, social

science models or tragic terminal creeds; the comic holotrope is a
consonance of narrative voices in discourse.
Gerald Vizenor, "Trickster Discourse"

In 1935, a ten-year-old native of Molise, Italy, entered a Catholic seminary
in Puglia with the intention of becoming a missionary. There he learned
classical Greek and Latin, studied Provençal and French, and encountered
and translated the French symbolists Rimbaud, Verlaine, and Apollinaire.
Five years later he left, realizing that he had lost his vocation. Though he
may have lost his reasons for being a missionary of God, Giose Rimanelli
has in many ways become a missionary of literature. His first novel, *Tiro al
piccione* (1950), is a fictionalized autobiographical account of his early
years in Molise and his experiences during the Second World War. The
novel was translated into English by Ben Johnson as *The Day of the Lion*
and published by Random House in 1954. It received critical praise and
became a best-seller in America. Six years and a number of novels later,
Rimanelli came to America to give a lecture at the Library of Congress,
after which he was invited to teach and travel throughout North and
South America. He decided to remain in the United States, where he
continued to write poetry and fiction, publishing all his writing, except for
some academic work, in Italian. Rimanelli claims to have learned English
by reading *Esquire* magazine and even dedicated his first novel written
in English to the same periodical that launched the career of Pietro di
Donato.

Rimanelli had keen insights into the plight of the Italian American long
before he ever became one. The Italian living in North America served as a
regular subject for his writing in Italy. In *Una posizione sociale* (1959) he
recounts the lives of Italians living in New Orleans in the early 1900s and
examines the lynching of thirteen Italians. In 1966 he collected, edited,
and introduced *Modern Canadian Stories*. *Tragica America* (1968) contains
his reflections of his first years in the United States. In 1975 he gave us a
greater insight into the literature of Italy through *Italian Literature: Roots
and Branches*. Now a professor emeritus at the State University of New
York at Albany, Rimanelli continues writing his fiction in Italian and
publishing it primarily in Italy. Over the years that he has lived in the
United States, however, Rimanelli has been writing poetry and novels in

English and has accumulated a number of unpublished manuscrpts. In 1970 he wrote his first novel in English, *Benedetta in Guysterland*, which was published for the first time in 1993 by Guernica Editions in Montreal and received the 1993 American Book Award of the Before Columbus Foundation.

The first question that comes to the reader of *Benedetta* is why this novel was not published until 1993. After all, by 1970 Rimanelli was a well-known journalist and cultural critic, and an internationally acclaimed writer who had published seven very successful books in Italy that had been translated into eight languages.[23] Since 1961 he had been a tenured professor at American universities such as Yale, promoted on the merits of his writing, not by virtue of his academic credentials. So why didn't he publish this novel right after it was written?

The answer to this question lies in the fact that Rimanelli did not write it for publication; he did not write it for money; he wrote it for love, for love of literature and for his American friends. Though Rimanelli made no attempt to publish it, perhaps because he lacked confidence in his experimental exercises, he did send the manuscript to an impressive list of readers. The readers' responses are catalogued in an appendix attached to the novel. One of the respondents was the noted literary critic Leslie Fiedler, who wrote: "I'm sending back your manuscript with this. It gave me much pleasure, and I think it would be a great loss to all of us if you did not become an American novelist at this point" (*Benedetta*, 191). That was back in 1972, and Fiedler was responding to Rimanelli's sophisticated literary experimentation, an experimentation that few American immigrant authors were capable of producing in the English language. The novel, to Rimanelli, was simply an experiment in English, his first response to the demands of starting over, from scratch, as a writer in a new language, a man of the world with a new toy.

Yet while the language was new, his knowledge of world literature and America was not. North America had entered his imagination long before his arrival in the 1950s. His grandfather was born in New Orleans, and his mother in Canada. We can see images of America forming in his earliest novels.[24] *Benedetta*, the record of his divorce from the native culture that he chose to leave, is the result of his first two decades of immersion into American culture. As writer Anthony Burgess notes in an introduction to

"Alien," Rimaelli's unpublished book of poems written in English between 1964 and 1970, "Rimanelli is one of those remarkable writers who, like Joseph Conrad . . . have turned from their first language to English, and have set out to rejuvenate it in a way few writers could do who were blessed and burdened with English as their first language" ("Alien. Poems," 244). Burgess knew Rimanelli's Italian work well and referred to him as "the *enfant terrible* . . . who, in Italian has done remarkable and shocking things" (224). "The nature of the business," Burgess says, "is to see Western civilization in decline, from the viewpoint of a sort of American who has brought, like Nabokov, all his European luggage with him and regards his primary devotion as belonging to the world, not to a mere segment of it" (244). What Burgess said about Rimanelli's earliest poems in English applies as well to his first English-language narrative.

In the following discussion, my first task is to situate this novel, published more than two decades after it was written, into the body of Italian American literature. My second is to comment on the parodic elements of the text and their relationship to Puzo's and Talese's Mafia narratives, and to discuss how, through parody, Rimanelli elevates the figure of the godfather mafioso beyond the levels achieved by Puzo and Talese and in the process uses this figure to create a sophisticated and complex literary text.

Benedetta in Guysterland occupies a pivotal position in the history of Italian American narrative as the bridge over the border between modernism and postmodernism, between the mythic and philosophic narrative modes. Rimanelli was writing *Benedetta* at the same time that younger Italian American writers such as Don DeLillo and Gilbert Sorrentino were beginning their writing careers. Until this novel was published, it was not possible to talk about a distinctive and visible Italian American presence in postmodernism; a modernist project was needed to serve as a bridge. The completion of such a project, in the eyes of Fredric Jameson, might be marked by parody, a form that, until *Benedetta*, had not yet emerged in Italian American literature. Rimanelli's novel is the missing link between the Italian American modernists and the postmodernists. Because *Benedetta* remained unpublished, and thus outside the range of influence on Italian American writers, we can only speculate as to how it might have stimulated a quicker movement from a modernist to a postmodernist Italian American narrative.

Benedetta in Guysterland is the first Italian American novel to meet one of Jameson's observations of the effects of parody, which is that it "cast[s] ridicule on the private nature of these [modernist texts'] stylistic manner-isms and their excessiveness and eccentricity with respect to the way peo-ple normally speak or write" ("Postmodernism and Consumer Society," 113). Rimanelli embarks on this ridicule at the very outset by appropriat-ing sentences, phrases, and words from such diverse sources as Shake-speare, Theodore Roethke, James Joyce, Curzio Malaparte, Pablo Ne-ruda, American television shows, and Graham Greene. As he explains in his "For-a-word": "This ballad *Benedetta* has been made up by the careful use of famous and infamous quotations, scraps of personal *co co rico* lyrics, confessions of country girls with kitsch and poetry pap, advertisements, newspaper and magazine lines, TV commercials, FBI or MGM releases, interviews, new books, old books read and digested, cartoon-blurbs, etc." (27). Rimanelli boldly acknowledges the sources of his literary thievery in his appendix 3. In appendix 4 he provides a detailed documentation of the appropriations in the novel's first chapter. The appropriations most rele-vant to my reading here are those that come from Gay Talese, one of the three persons to whom the novel is dedicated (1). Talese's *Honor Thy Father* serves as both subject and object of the parody. Rimanelli was far ahead of his time in parodying Italian American culture, for only recently have we begun to see the buds of parody in Italian America.[25] More and more Italian American authors are becoming cognizant of the cultural products of the Italian, American, and Italian American cultures; past parodies of Italian American culture were generally created by non–Italian Americans.[26]

A critic whose work on parody will serve us well in our reading of this novel is Linda Hutcheon, who sees parody as a vital form of expression for marginalized writers:

Parody has perhaps come to be a privileged mode of postmodern formal self-reflexivity because its paradoxical incorporation of the past into its very structures often points to these ideological contexts somewhat more obviously, more didac-tically, than other forms. Parody seems to offer a perspective on the present and the past which allows an artist to speak *to* a discourse from *within* it, but without being totally recuperated by it. Parody appears to have become, for this reason, the mode of what I have called the "ex-centric," of those who are marginalized by a dominant ideology. (*Poetics*, 35).

Rimanelli knows life in the margin, not only the margin between Italian and American culture, but also the margin between Italian and Italian American culture. It is this experience that has given him the perspective that makes parody possible.

Benedetta in Guysterland fills a deep void in Italian American literary history: the cavity caused by the decay of the literary realism characteristic of the standard fare produced by Italian American writers. For too long those imaginations have been held prisoners by the psychosocial borders of the Italian American ghetto. While the emphasis of most Italian American fiction has been the Italian American experience, most authors have been unable to gain the distance from the subject that would enable them to gain the new perspectives necessary to renew the story of Italian life in America. What Mario Puzo romanticized in *The Godfather* (1969), and Gay Talese historicized in *Honor Thy Father* (1971), Giose Rimanelli parodies in *Benedetta*. Through parody he has transcended the Italian American subject, above all, by writing a book about literature using the same subject — the Mafia — used by Puzo and Talese. Like James Joyce, Rimanelli unites high culture with popular culture in this labyrinth of a text that reads like a map of Western civilization.

Rimanelli balances his life on the border of tradition and the avant-garde by making literary forays into both worlds.[27] *Benedetta* demonstrates that one culture could not satisfy Rimanelli. More than an Italian, an American, or an Italian American writer, Rimanelli is a border writer in the tradition of Franz Kafka, Vladimir Nabokov, Jorge Borges, and Gabriel García Márquez. Such border writers, in the view of Emily Hicks, demonstrate a "multi-dimensional perception" (*Border Writing*, xxvi), the possibilities of inscribing a text with an awareness of the referential codes of both cultures that share the same border. While Italy does not share a physical border with the United States, there is a cultural border between the two over which Rimanelli crosses. Hicks points us to an explanation of the difficulties we face when we encounter a text such as *Benedetta*: "The reader of border writing will not always be able to perceive the 'logic' of the text at first. Nor will she be able to hear the multiplicity of discourses within a single language" (*Border Writing*, xxvi). Like much postmodernist writing, *Benedetta* avoids a logical and sequential progression of events through the frame of a traditional plot. By appropriating materials from American, English, French, Italian, Spanish, and Latin American cultures, Rimanelli creates a polyphonic discourse through the English language. While Hicks concentrates her application of border theory on Latin American writers, her work serves well for our reading of Rimanelli. "Border writing," she tells us, "offers a new form of knowledge: information about and understanding of the present to the past in terms of the possibilities of the future" (*Border Writing*, xxxi). This is a notion similar to Hutcheon's perception of the way parody politicizes narrative: "Through a double process of installing and ironizing, parody signals how present representations come from past ones and what ideological consequences derive from both continuity and difference . . . parody works to foreground the *politics* of representation" (*Politics*, 93–4). The politics Rimanelli foregrounds is Americans' obsession with "the other," in this case other as represented by the Mafia. By representing mafiosi as boys who never grow up, Rimanelli pierces through the mystique romantically created by Puzo and realistically documented by Talese to reveal that the Mafia and its mafiosi are social and historical constructions, and anything but natural. Rimanelli's work, again in Hutcheon's words, is "a form of ironic representation . . . doubly coded in political terms; it both legitimizes and subverts that which it parodies" (*Politics*, 101). Rimanelli achieves this representation by turning gangsters into philosophers, giving them a language they could never, in reality, possess; at the same time, Rimanelli turns philosophers into accomplices, hit men of ideas.

One of the guiding philosophers in this work is the poet Theodore Roethke, to whom Rimanelli attributes the novel's epigraph:

Theodore Roethke
to Benedetta Ashfield

The wasp waits.
The ends cannot eat the center.
The grape glistens.
The path tells little to the serpent.
An eye comes out of the wave.

The journey from flesh is longest.
A rose sways least.
The redeemer comes a dark way. (*Benedetta*, 7)

This epigraph is the story of *Benedetta* in brief. Rimanelli creates a tragic self-parody, typical of Roethke, through the protagonist-narrator Benedetta Ashfield, a WASP turned Madonna figure through her encounter with Italian American mafiosi. Benedetta, who was born Clarence Ashfield, is named Benie by Willie Sinclair, a mob lawyer who gives her the nickname because of his familiarity with the Italian American gangsters he hangs out with, who frequently use the word *bene*, which means "good." Through her relationship with Willie, Benedetta is dragged into the underworld, where she becomes the leading "sexophone" player for "Zip the Thunder's" band.[28] The Italians who meet her assume that Benie is short for Benedetta, or "blessed," a word used to identify the Madonna, as in the Hail Mary, which contains the phrase "blessed are thou among women." Benedetta thus comes to embody the paradox of the madonna/whore syndrome. In contrast with Lewis Carroll's Alice — a child who tells the tale of her strange trip into an adult world — Benedetta is an adult who recounts the story of her life in a ferocious world of children, of immature, sexually obsessed adults who play gangsters, or "guysters," as Rimanelli calls them.

Sandwiched between the "For-a-Word" and the "Post-word," Benedetta's narrative incorporates America's obsessive fascination with the Mafia, sex, and violence. *Benedetta* tells the story of America's flirtatious relationship with Italy and debunks the traditional stereotype of the Italian American gangster through Joe Adonis, who, rather tellingly, runs the Mamma Mia Importing Company. The result is a vital sociopolitical parody that shows that sex and violence are in fact displacements of each other. At the same time, the story told here is about the change and the breaking away from roots that happens to all cultural border crossers. Characters who break away from roots include Benedetta, who leaves her home in Appalachia to attend Anabasis College in New England, where she first encounters the Mafia. Santo "Zip the Thunder" Tristano and Joe Adonis also leave their homes in Sicily, as recounted in chapter 3 in a section that parodies Talese's explanation of how Joseph Bonanno came to America.[29]

Through intricate pastische, wordplay, the onomasticon understatement, and the tabula rasa in expressing experimentation, *Benedetta* shows a way of making a truly postmodern Italian American novel. Rimanelli advances the Italian American novel by adding new dimensions to *Italianità* through his defiance of traditional storytelling techniques and his manipulation of previously created Italian American stereotypes. The result is a satire rich in social and political implications presented from an ironic perspective lacking in Puzo and Talese, who take the subjects of Mafia, family, and *Italianità* seriously. Had this novel been published when it was first written, it might have liberated the Italian American artistic imagination from the spell of the gangster that has enchanted it for too long. This parody at long last enables the Italian American narrative to find its way out of the realist and modernist labyrinths and into the wall-less maze of postmodernism.

Benedetta slithers through sense and nonsense along paths paved by James Joyce's *Ulysses*, Lewis Carroll's *Alice in Wonderland*, and Vladimir Nabokov's *Pale Fire*. At the same time, its parodic aim is locked in on details of *Honor Thy Father* that first appeared in *Esquire* magazine, Rimanelli's "teacher" of the English language. Talese appears in the novel as Guy Maltese, the biographer of Santo "Zip" the Thunder, a fictionalized version of Joseph Bonanno. Through Maltese, Benedetta learns the story of Zip's escape to America from Gela (read "Castellammare"), Italy, to avoid persecution by Muscolini (*Benedetta*, 43). Zip becomes the leader of a band of musicians called the Lavanda, or the "washers" (read "Mafia"). The musicians fight amongst each other in the great Gelatari (read "Castellammarese") War (47). Instead of knocking off their enemies and those who break the code of *omertà*, however, they kiss them. The battle here also parallels the 1960s and 1970s activism for women's and gay rights. Santo Tristano leads the Gaia Società guysters from his headquarters, La Gaia Scienza. Joe Adonis forms his guysters into a group of physicians called Normale Società, the Normal Society.[30]

Another interesting parallel arises between Benedetta and Kay Adams from *The Godfather*. Benedetta, like Kay, conforms to the world of the Italian immigrants, rather than vice versa. She is attracted to the world of these "others" and is guided along by Joe Adonis. Her assimilation into their culture eventually drives her insane, and she ends up in an asylum of sorts. Kay Adams finds her asylum in the Catholic church, where she can be "washed clean of sin" and empty "her mind of all thought" (*Godfather*, 445).

Benedetta was born in the town of New Wye, Appalachia, U.S.A., in Nabokov County, and, like Kay Adams, can trace her family back to the *Mayflower* (*Benedetta*, 68), the mythic symbol of Anglo-Americana. Through Joe Adonis she learns to live life with a passion unknown in her hometown: "I am a child of Appalachia but I have slowly broken from the land where there is no laughter except the occasional hoarse cackle of a hen or an old woman defying death. I am learning to speak, to push the earth from my mouth and welcome the day" (109). Her first hometown love is a fellow by the name of Jargon (69). Her second love is Willie "Holiday Inn" Sinclair, who is married to Hester Prynne. Sinclair is a lawyer who associates with guyster (read "gangster") types. Through Willie she learns to "regret (almost) my maverick and hated background" (72). Willie is "kissed" by Zip's band. Her third love is a boy from Yale whom she meets at Anabasis College (73). And after these affairs, she takes a trip to Jersey, where she meets Joe Adonis, who shows her around and introduces her to life in the Lavanda underworld. Benedetta remakes herself into a moll of sorts. As she says near the novel's opening, "I may be a whore, Joe. But I love you. You sang for me, and I am what I am because of you" (67).

Joe tells her that she must "avenge herself of Grendel, the sea monster who tried to destroy" her (81). In essence, he convinces her to destroy the great Anglo-Saxon myth and replace it with a new myth of her origins based on her encounter with his kind. Through a dreamlike sequence she battles the monster, who turns into a priestess, who then turns into Zip the Thunder, who tells her: "Benedetta my child, you must leave behind your fisher-lover Adonis, because you are now your own girl. Go forth into the Wastband and bring forth fruit" (82). Benedetta takes up with Zip's band when Joe is exiled to Italy. It is her association with Zip that eventually drives her mad.

Written during the same time period as Talese's and Puzo's Mafia stories, *Benedetta* takes chances and yet retains a connection to the origins of Italian American oral and literary traditions. It is a source of cultural renewal that at the same time depicts a culture in decay. In essence, it is a document of the border between, in Vichian terms, a *corso* and a *ricorso*, something that happens and will happen again as cultures and civilizations age and mature. This novel, written at a point when American literature was moving into its decadent and self-reflexive stage, demonstrates the possibilities of enlivening a culture through a return to Vico's poetic stage, the move necessary to delay the inevitable descent into cultural decay and resurrection.

Highly philosophic, *Benedetta*'s poetic language also employs formulas of the oral tradition through the use of a number of proverbs such as *"Chi nasce tondo non muore quadro"* (Who is born round will not die square [58]). At the same time the novel appropriates its being from the long experienced literary tradition of the West, as evidenced by the use of lines from Homer, Dante, Shakespeare, Goethe, and other canonical writers. This is the mark of the trickster, the double-talker, whose violation of tradition reminds us how arbitrary solid traditions can be. And this double-talk can be done only by the writer who defies boundaries and crosses borders. The process results not only in the coining of new words but in the true making of new worlds.

Rimanelli's border talk is also evidenced by his inventive use of the Italian and American languages. The wild names Crepadio (May God Die), Failaspesa (He Who Goes Shopping), Santo Tristano (Sad Saint), Scorpione (Scorpion) for Al Capone, Corbello (Blockhead) for Frank Costello, Profeta (The Prophet) for Joe Profaci, LuCane (The Dog) for "Lucky" Luciano, and Venerea Saltimbocca (Venus Veal à la Rome) all function as signs of this hilarious double-talk. His use of such polyvalent terms represents the signifying on American culture so familiar to readers of the texts produced by other marginalized cultures. On another level, Giose Rimanelli is signifying on the hundreds of names dropped by Talese in *Honor Thy Father.* All this is evidence of the literary trickster who transforms culture (hence sense, meaning, import, and significance) through words.

The linguistic mosaic created in *Benedetta* is a metamorphic map of the Americanization process. The result is that Italian American literature is rejuvenated, reborn. As in Native American myths, this is a task accomplished by the stranger who wanders into a tribe at the point of decay and impregnates a maiden who gives birth to a child who will save the culture. This is very much the story of Benedetta. At the novel's end she is pregnant

with the child of Joe Adonis, the man who taught her how to live passion-
ately and in whose image she remakes her self. In a larger sense, Benedetta
is pregnant with Italian American literature, the bastard child of an Ap-
palachian princess and an immigrant mafioso, a child who resides unborn
in the ripe belly of a woman locked away in an asylum. Its birth is the
publication of Benedetta's bildungsroman. As in Native American culture,
this is the story of cultural renewal in which the crossbreed becomes
culture hero. *Benedetta in Guysterland*, written in Albany, New York, in
1970 and published twenty-three years later in Montreal, the birthplace of
the author's mother, is a narrative that reaches beyond its own time,
regardless of its subject, and gives to Italian American culture a needed
and long-awaited presence in American literature.

The interaction between *The Godfather*, *Honor Thy Father*, and *Benedetta
in Guysterland* points to the real development of a literary tradition among
Italian American writers. While we may never know who read whom first,
there can be no doubt that the figure of the godfather gangster in Italian
American literature presents a key to analyzing the representation of *Italianità* in Italian American literature. This key figure also provides a long-
awaited access to the intertextuality at work and play in this tradition.
There are many other works that future readings and writings should
include in this middle mythic period of Italian American narrative. Louis
Forgione's *Men of Silence* (1928), Ben Morreale's *A Few Virtuous Men*
(1973) and *Monday, Tuesday Never Come Sunday* (1977), Mari Tomasi's
Deep Grow the Roots (1940) and *Like Lesser Gods* (1949), Diana Cavallo's *A
Bridge of Leaves* (1961), Raymond De Capite's *The Coming of Fabrizze*
(1960) and *A Lost King* (161), and dozens of other novels written by the
children of Italian immigrants all use the heroic figures of godfathers and
godmothers to represent an *Italianità* that bridged Italian and American
cultures to create the hybrid Italian American culture that laid the foundation for the novels of the later mythic period.

Four

The Later Mythic Mode: Reinventing Ethnicity through the Grandmother Figure

The construction of mythologies and the idealisation of a female
principle serves as a strategy through which an oppositional and
marginalised group can articulate a coherent and fixed identity as the
basis for a critique of the problematic features of modernity.
Rita Felski, "The Novel of Self-Discovery"

Italian American women writers have explored the vital connection
between being a woman and being ethnic in a world (America) which
traditionally has valued neither.
Mary Jo Bona, "Broken Images, Broken Lives"

Beyond Symbolic Ethnicity

W hile many Italian American writers participate in what Ernest Jones
and Karl Abraham have identified as the "grandfather complex"—
which allows the "fantasy" of being "the parents of their own parents . . .
to be acted out symbolically" (Sollors, *Beyond Ethnicity*, 230–1)—this
"complex" is most successfully represented in the narratives constructed by
Italian American women writers. Through the figure of the grandmother,
Helen Barolini, Tina DeRosa, and Carole Maso create models that enable
their protagonists to gain a sense of identity as both ethnic Americans and
women. In "Symbolic Ethnicity: The Future of Ethnic Groups and Cultures in America," Herbert J. Gans suggests that the proliferation of ethnic
signifying in contemporary American culture might be explained by his
hypothesis that "ethnicity may be turning into symbolic ethnicity" (193).
Gans believes that the symbols used by third-generation ethnics to express
identity are more obvious than those used by earlier generations and thus
only seem to be more pervasive. "For the third generation," Gans argues,
"the secular ethnic cultures that the immigrants brought with them are
now only an ancestral memory, or an exotic tradition to be savored once in
a while in a museum or at an ethnic festival" (201). Expressions of this

symbolic ethnicity, according to Gans, come in the forms of rituals, rites of passage, holidays, consumer goods, and ethnic characters in media. Often the symbols take shape in the re-creation of the old country, for the old country is distant enough not to "make arduous demands on American ethnics" (206). This re-creation, Gans explains, is possible because there is less emotional risk for the third generation than for "first- and second-generation people who are still trying to escape it, but even so, an interest in ethnic history is a return only chronologically" (207). Gans's construction of symbolic ethnicity seems to suggest a superficial expression that lacks sincerity and authenticity, yet the Italian American writers of the third generation are anything but superficial in their constructions of *Italianità*. The process of creating these constructions serves as an important and necessary stage that is vital in forming self-identity. While Gans's notion of symbolic ethnicity cannot explain all of the third generation's attitudes toward ethnicity, it can help us read the symbols generated by writers who are the grandchildren of immigrants. The major symbol of this writing is the immigrant figure who serves as an embodiment of an *Italianità* that is being reinvented through the authors' creations of narrative in the mythic mode.[1]

The phenomenon of the third generation's connection to the past was theorized more than thirty-five years ago by M. L. Hansen: "After the second generation comes the third and with the third appears a new force and a new opportunity which, if recognized in time, can not only do a good job of salvaging, but probably can accomplish more than either the first or the second could ever have achieved" ("The Third Generation," 496). The key to reading the literature produced by third-generation Italian American writers is observing the role that the grandparent plays in connecting the writer to his or her ancestral past. A significant difference between second- and third-generation writers, then, is this presence of a grandparent figure who serves to reconnect the protagonist to a past out of which the protagonist fashions an ethnic identity.

Immigrant figures in third-generation writing are central to the construction of narrative myths of origin, and their portrayals in literature take on a mythic function both in documenting the immigrant past and in creating explanations of the cultural differences that were attributed to Americans of Italian descent. Just as the godfather figure represented the attempt to gain the power necessary to negotiate success in America, the immigrant figure—in this case the grandparent—serves as the mythic *figura* who is the source of the ethnic stories created by the third generation. Immigrant *figurae* represent historical mysteries that require explanation. The narratives presented in this chapter all unfold as real or metaphorical journeys into the past with the goal of understanding the impact that both Italian and American cultures have had on the creation of Italian American identities. The result is a combination of memory and imagination that work together to explain the ethnic anxiety faced by those third-generation writers, who are just as alienated from the reality of the immigrant experience as they often feel they are from the very culture into which they were born. The effect of this ethnic anxiety is the sense of what Jerre Mangione calls "a double life." In his essay by that title, Mangione suggests that a quest for identity is a way of resolving problems of duality ("Double Life," 171). This identity quest is the key to reading the narratives of third-generation Italian American writers, for as their grandparents were economic and political immigrants, and their parents social immigrants, they themselves are cultural immigrants.[2]

The immigrant becomes a hero in these quest narratives, a hero who battles forces larger than she or he. The re-creation of these battles and the representation of the sacrifices made by these figures serve more than a symbolic function integral in the formation of a self-identity of the third generation. Unlike what Gans suggests, they become models of what Michael Fischer terms "reinventions of ethnicity." Such reinventions employ "retrospection to gain a vision for the future" ("Ethnicity and the Post-Modern Arts of Memory," 198) and in so doing serve as "powerful critiques of several contemporary rhetorics of domination" (198). Fischer's idea enables a reading beyond the nostalgia suggested by Gans and into the function that a reinvented *Italianità* serves for the third and post-immigrant generations of Italian Americans as they fashion a usable past in which they can locate the cultural elements needed to create integral selves. Understanding this reinvention is accomplished by reading what Fischer calls a narrative's "inter-references between two or more cultural traditions" which "create reservoirs for renewing humane values" (201). Thus we will be able to see that, as Fischer concludes, "ethnic memory is . . . or ought to be future, not past oriented" (201).

One of the earliest third-generation novels to reinvent ethnicity through representing the immigrant experience was Helen Barolini's *Umbertina*

(1979), which came along after the American ethnic revival of the late 1960s and early 1970s during which the generational saga emerged.[3] *Umbertina* tells the story of four generations of Italian American women, focusing on the immigrant matriarchal grandmother, her granddaughter, and her great-granddaughter. Unlike many writers from other ethnic groups, Barolini does not spend much time recounting the story of the second-generation woman. *Umbertina* presents in fiction what most previous Italian American writers offered only through autobiographical and episodic reportage. To do this the author needed to experience what Robert Crichton calls "a sense of removal" (Cammett, *The Italian American Novel*, 28). Barolini explains that she, a grandchild of immigrants, came upon this distanced perspective by traveling to Italy "to see where and what I came from, to gain an ultimate understanding and acceptance of being American with particular shadings of *Italianità*" ("Becoming," 269).

Italian American writers with experiences similar to Barolini's are beginning to surface in numbers just as the term *ethnic fiction* seems to be disappearing.[4] The writers coming from the third generation have produced more effective literature by coming at these "ethnic tensions" — what Fischer calls "ethnic anxiety" — from a more distant perspective, with less of a need to defend themselves, and with the need to negotiate the present in terms of the past.[5] Their writing has also benefited by competing in a critical arena that has been expanded by the work of advocates of culture-specific criticism. They have come along at a crucial junction in what Sollors calls the evolution of ethnic literature. Quite simply, today's Italian American writers represent later stages of the growth of ethnic literature, a process Sollors explains in *Beyond Ethnicity: Consent and Descent in American Culture*:

We may see the historical unfolding of ethnic writing as a process of growth; and again, the beginning is with immigrant and immigrant letters. . . . The literature then "grows" from nonfictional to fictional forms . . . ; or from an autobiography to an autobiographical novel . . . ; from folk and popular forms to high forms . . . ; from lower to higher degrees of complexity . . . ; and from "parochial" marginality to "universal" significance in the literary mainstream (and the American mainstream now includes more and more writers with identifiable "ethnic" backgrounds). (241)

Though contemporary Italian American writers live in what most would call postmodern times, most of them are creating what could formalistically be called modernist projects. In another sense, however, these works are more closely connected to postmodern culture than they might seem, especially if they are examined in the light of what Michael Fischer has termed the "postmodern art of memory." According to Fischer, "Ethnicity is something reinvented and reinterpreted in each generation by each individual and that is often something quite puzzling to the individual, something over which he or she lacks control. Ethnicity is not something that is simply passed on from generation to generation, taught and learned; it is something dynamic, often unsuccessfully repressed or avoided" ("Ethnicity and the Post-Modern Arts of Memory," 195). Fischer suggests that readers pay attention to "the juxtaposition of two or more cultural traditions" found in contemporary ethnic American writing. Thus, in the case of Italian American writers, we need to observe the ways in which American and Italian traditions function in their narrative constructions. Locating and analyzing this juxtaposition requires a consideration of the cultural reciprocal relationship between American and Italian cultures.

To make this clearer, I propose dividing contemporary Italian American writers into two categories: the "visible" and the "invisible." Those Italian American writers who choose to deal with the Italian American experience through Italian American subjects I will call the visible. Italian American writers who choose to avoid representation of the Italian American as a major subject in their works can be referred to as the invisible. To illustrate these concepts I will refer in this chapter to the narratives of Helen Barolini, Tina DeRosa, and Carole Maso as representative of the visible; and in Chapter 5 I will discuss the work of Don DeLillo and Gilbert Sorrentino as representative of the invisible.[6] The invisible Italian Americans create works that are more implicitly Italian American; the visible Italian Americans are more explicit in their Italian Americanness. Let us now turn our attention to this recovery of ethnicity and the role it plays in the novels of self-discovery produced by three contemporary American authors of Italian descent.

Helen Barolini and the Epic Quest for Self

If creating an American identity was difficult for Italian American men, the process for Italian American women, as Helen Barolini explains, would prove even more difficult: "The displacement from one culture to another has represented a real crisis of identity for the Italian woman, and she has left a heritage of conflict to her children. They, unwilling to give themselves completely to the old ways she transmitted, end up, in their assimilationist hurry, with shame and ambivalence in their behavior and values" (Introduction to *The Dream Book*, 13). "Shame and ambivalence" often become the building blocks of Italian American women's writing. In spite of her parents' attempts to turn their backs on their Italian heritage, some of her experiences raised questions of identity in this granddaughter of immigrants:

I knew very little of my Italian background because it had always been played down. There had been the early confusion in grade school when I didn't know what to fill in on the form when nationality was asked: was I Italian because my name sounded strange, or was I American because I was born here? By the time I was in high school, it was simply a matter of embarrassment to be identified with a people who were the dupes of that great buffoon, Mussolini, and the war intensified our feelings of alienation from Italy and the efforts to be thoroughly American. We didn't want to be identified with the backward Italian families who lived on the North Side and did their shopping in grocery stores that smelled of strong cheese and salamis. Neither the ethnic nor the gourmet age had yet dawned in the states; it was still the time of the stewing melting pot and of being popular by being what everyone else was or thought we should be. ("Circular Journey," 111)

However much the young girl wanted to disassociate herself from her Italian identity, there was always the female figure in black, her immigrant grandmother Nicoletta, "who didn't speak English and had strange, un-American ways of dressing and wearing her hair" ("Circular Journey," 111), reminding Helen of her family's Italian origins. However, in leaving home to attend college, Barolini ran not away from but right into an Italian identity. It was at Wells College, in a Latin course, that she was "first awakened — to unsuspected and deep longings for the classical Mediterranean world, and for an Italy from which after all I had my descent" ("Circular Journey," 111).

Later, on a trip to Italy, Barolini met the man she would marry, Italian poet and journalist Antonio Barolini. At first, the marriage upset her parents, "who felt that in marrying an Italian I had regressed in contrast to my brothers, who had married Irish" ("Circular Journey," 112). After settling into an Italian life, the couple soon found themselves back in New York, where Antonio was employed as consul general for one year. Antonio's career required frequent relocation between America and Italy. While the frequent travel to Italy of writers such as Mangione served to develop and strengthen an American identity, Barolini's experience was the opposite. Her life in Italy served to re-create and nurture her Italian identity, as she explains: "I had to make the long journey to Italy, to see where and what I came from, to gain an ultimate understanding and acceptance of being American with particular shadings of Italianita. To say that was at odds with the dominant American culture is an understatement. It is the essence of lifelong psychological conflict" ("Becoming a Literary Person Out of Context," 269). This conflict surfaces in her first novel, *Umbertina* (1979), an American saga that dramatizes the lives of three generations of Italian American women. Because the first generation turns its back on the past and looks only forward, it influences the second generation to do the same; the third generation looks back into the past for keys to its identity.

Umbertina is a novel of self-discovery, a bildungsroman that spans four generations and can be read as the historical evolution of the Italian woman into the American woman, as the feminization of the Italian woman as she becomes the Italian American woman. The novel is divided chronologically into three parts, each focusing on a female character: Umbertina, 1860–1940; Marguerite, 1927–1973; and Tina, 1950–. Significant is the absence of the second-generation female figure, Umbertina's daughter Carla, whose life is presented only through her relationships as the daughter of Umbertina and the mother of Marguerite. The female character named in each part is in search of what turns out to be her self. In "The Novel of Self-Discovery: Necessary Fiction?" Rita Felski provides a context in which to understand the importance of Barolini's narrative. Felski defines the novel of self-discovery as "a quest narrative tracing a protagonist's search for self-knowledge, a positive transformation expressed through a number of binary oppositions: from ignorance to knowledge, from speechlessness to language, from alienation to authenticity" (132–3). Barolini adds to Felski's binary oppositions by including Italian American. Felski identifies the novel of self-discovery by its redefinition of the heroine as an acting subject — one who no longer views herself through a male-defined perspective (133). Felski divides the novels of self-discovery into two categories: the bildungsroman and the novels of awakening (137). *Umbertina* is an example of the bildungsroman because "self-discovery is portrayed as an historically determined process occurring through dialectical interaction between self and society and articulated in a chronological and linear narrative structure" (137).

The opening of *Umbertina* presents Marguerite, the granddaughter of the immigrant Umbertina, in a male psychiatrist's office recounting a dream. This Jungian analyst interprets her dream, saying that it reveals her ethnic anxiety as to "whether you are American, Italian, or Italo-American" (*Umbertina*, 16). He suggests that she might begin her search for self by digging into her family's past. This encounter leads her to thoughts of her grandmother: "I always fantasized about my grandmother. I always thought I wanted to get back to her elementary kind of existence . . . her kind of primitive strength. I've always felt that my life was wasted on abstract ideas rather than being rooted in reality; even a brutal reality would have been better than the vagueness I've been floundering in. Naive my daughters call me. What they mean is soft, mushy. My grandmother, though, was tough. You know, I've always suspected it was my grandmother Umbertina who brought me to Italy in the first place" (17). This fiction parallels Barolini's actual experiences of the third generation's return to the past and recovery of an *Italianità* that establishes a historical context for her present-day self. As we saw earlier, in the career of Jerre Mangione, this odyssey in search of self took Barolini back and forth from Italy to America. By turning these experiences into writing, Barolini historicizes the Italian American woman, an act that John M. Reilly says revolutionizes our way of reading: "Giving voice to the women who have usually been given minor roles in realistic fiction and setting them in the center of interwoven narratives so that their experiences and thoughts form the substance of the novel is to define the women as historical actors and to modify our understanding of other texts in which the women were not subjects" ("Literary Versions of Ethnic History," 193). The central figure in this novel is Umbertina Longobardi, an Italian immigrant who becomes the matriarch of an Italian American family. She is the Eve of Barolini's Italian Americana, the mythical mother of Italian America whom later female figures must psychologically search out and confront on their journey to self-identity. Umbertina is a product of nineteenth-century southern Italian culture, which relegates women to the margins of male-controlled society. In part 1, Barolini presents Umbertina in the context of Italian history. The natural way of peasant life and its belief in determination by destiny is juxtaposed to the artificiality that ensues when men challenge that destiny by leaving home. Under the natural order it is the place of the woman to marry, to have children, to take care of the home. This is impressed on Umbertina early on when she saves her brother Beppino from losing money on the sale of a pregnant goat. In spite of her saving him, Beppino, though younger than she, scolds her, "It's not your part to interfere in the bargaining. . . . When I set the terms for the sale of the goats that's what it is. I am the man" (30).

Barolini uses Umbertina to re-create the object of male dominance and to illustrate the effect of the social norms and constraints placed on women by southern Italian culture. This reconstruction enables her to set up the source of the Italian American woman's identity crisis. By immigrating to America, which she decides to do after marrying the man chosen by her father, Umbertina gains a public power unknown to most peasant women of her ancestral region. Through her guidance and perseverance her family thrives in America, but she, in spite of her accomplishments, never receives the recognition she deserves. All the family's success is appended to her husband, Serafino, as evidenced by his obituary's reference to Umbertina as "his good companion" (123). She is never recognized as the force through which the Longobardi family gained its power in America. At the end of her life, Umbertina is left with a success story that she cannot communicate to the very ones who have benefited most from it: "She had won, but who could she tell her story to?" (139). By leaving Umbertina's story untold to future generations, Barolini sets up her next character for the identity crisis that faces many Italian American women.

Marguerite is constantly looking for her place in the world, for an environment where she can become an independent individual whose identity does not depend on a man. She tries to accomplish this by first leaving behind her American family, whose "talk was always in words of commercial transaction. Children *owed* parents respect; children *paid back* what was done for them by studying hard and leading good lives; children had to *capitalize* on their talents; doing so bore *dividends* in life; you didn't go around with certain people because there was no *profit* in it. The family motto could have been 'Money Talks'" (148). Her first attempt to leave the family ends in a bad marriage which her parents have annulled. Her next attempt to leave home finds her searching for a world in which material goods are not seen as the ultimate symbol for success. Her search leads her to Italy, where she falls in love with an Italian poet, fulfilling a prediction she had made earlier in her life. All along, Marguerite is searching for her place, following the advice Umbertina gave her daughters: "The important thing . . . is to find your place. Everything depends on that. You find your place, you work, and like planting seeds, everything grows. But you have to be watchful and stick to it" (133). In Umbertina's world, that place is with a man. While Marguerite's instincts tell her she will not find her place with a man, her social conditioning is stronger than those instincts and she constantly moves from man to man, never finding her place. In Italy she translates her husband's work but never does her own. She would like to be a photographer but cannot. Even when she thinks she is in control in an affair with an aspiring Italian novelist, she ultimately realizes that she is only being used by him to get him closer to her husband, a judge in a national literary contest. Marguerite dies in a car accident, pregnant with the young novelist's child, never having resolved her identity dilemma.

The journey is continued by her daughter, Tina, short for Umbertina, who completes the journey to self-fulfillment begun by her immigrant namesake. Born in Italy, half Italian and half Italian American, Tina succeeds in ways that her mother never could. Her success is due, of course, to the path laid out for her by her mother, Marguerite. Unlike her mother, Tina learns to feel at home in America, but she still faces the problem of how to define herself as Italian American. Also unlike her mother, Tina is determined to find her place without the assistance of men. Growing up during the rise of 1960s American feminism, Tina accomplishes what her mother could not by opting for a career in academia. Having solved her dilemma of gender oppression, she becomes free to deal with her ethnic dilemma. Tina's character represents the resolution of the conflict faced by the immigrant generation: "Your mother was never happy, married or not. . . . Your mother, Tina, never knew what she wanted. But you're more like *my* mother, the Umbertina for whom you're named. She was a strong person and she stuck to her guns" (380). Tina's strength, while self-derived, owes its existence to her ability to incorporate the past through memory, a process symbolized at the end of the novel by Tina's planting of a rosemary plant. "For remembrance?" her husband asks. "'Well, yes,' she laughed, 'maybe that, too, but actually for old Umbertina. It's the family women's quaquaveral plant—wherever one of Umbertina's clan descends, there also will be rosemary planted, for where it grows, the women of the house are its strength'" (403). Never having learned her great-grandmother's story, Tina has had to invent it in a way her mother never could. Tina travels to Umbertina's birthplace, but finds nothing there she can relate to. It is not until later, after she resolves her own identity as a woman by taking control of her body through an abortion, that she can concentrate on solving her ethnic dilemma. At the end of the novel Tina has decided to keep her own name and thus maintain her identification through a key Italian signifier.

Through these three characters Barolini sketches out the dilemmas of ethnic identity and gender oppression, as Anthony Tamburri points out in "*Umbertina*: The Italian/American Woman's Experience." However, while Tamburri reads each generation as a separate character, I see them as three stages of one character in the process of feminizing Italian American culture. Umbertina's success is never acknowledged, in spite of her control over her family's destiny. Marguerite dies, pregnant with the possibilities of finding her own place; and Tina is the self finally realized. By reading these three characters as the evolution of the Italian American woman, we can see, through Rita Felski, that Tina has recovered "an identity which is complete and self-contained, rather than contingent and historically and socially determined" ("The Novel of Self-Discovery," 141). And she has done it by going backward in her identity quest, a direction that Felski says is "mythical rather than historical" (141).

Through the symbol of the rosemary plant, Barolini enacts Gans's notion of symbolic ethnicity; the symbol becomes necessary only after the original signified disappears. However, there is more than mere symbolism in Tina's planting of the rosemary. Barolini has reinvented *Italianità* to serve her purpose of creating a feminist identity that transcends the constraints placed on women by Italian and Italian American cultures.

Tina will "plant humanism" the way her great-grandmother planted pepper plants. She has evolved beyond her great-grandmother's role of fulfilling material needs and can attend to the spiritual and psychological needs of self in a way that her namesake never could. Having constructed a strong self, Tina can then attend to the needs of the larger community, of women, of ethnics, which she can affect through her teaching. It is no accident, then, that the novel moves from one Umbertina to another through two stages (Carla and Marguerite). With this novel Barolini has created an Italian American woman's myth of origins in which future generations can find solace and a source of strength.

By writing this story Barolini fulfills the first generation's wish to be able to tell its story; she defies the traps of the second-generation women, who struggle to find a place where their identity is not determined by men; and she succeeds in having an impact on future generations through her self-generated art. Barolini's mythic tale of epic origins feeds the future and fuels a reinvention of ethnicity that while imprinted with the past, suggests real possibilities for the future. As Barolini's own critical work points out, for Italian American women, writing became not only a means of discovering an American identity but also a means of discovering and creating a human identity. It is this dual requirement that makes writing extremely challenging work for Italian American women as they attempt to reconcile past and present, Old World and New: "If not the immigrants, then their children and grandchildren are pre-eminently in the process of becoming something else, of making themselves over, of reinventing themselves as an amalgam of old and new elements. They must do this for themselves because there is no fixed and tested pattern for them in the new environs; the old tradition is not perfectly viable or transmittable in the new world no matter what the sentimental folklorists of Little Italies say" (Ahearn, Interview, 47). In her preface to *The Dream Book*, Barolini describes the demand that identification with *Italianità* places on the Italian American writer: "I believe that the superabundant tradition that we derive from has given us identity, has bequeathed both strengths and inhibitions, has presented problems as well as passions. No matter how encompassing our themes or broad our views, overtones of who we are and how we feel, as formed by our values and history, show up in our work" (x).

The Dream Book was awarded the American Book Award for best anthology of 1985 by the Before Columbus Foundation. This first-ever anthology of Italian American writing is a valuable and important contribution to American culture because it brought attention to many gifted women writers. Barolini knows the importance that creating and reading literature play in self-development, and she calls for Italian American women to begin writing their own stories: "Quite missing, as yet, are the honest and revealing stories of women's inner lives. . . . Redefining the self not as mirrored by society's expectations but in one's own authentic terms is essential for an integrated literary expression. Autobiography, when it is honest and not a camouflage, can be a powerful declaration of selfhood and a positive step toward establishing an incontrovertible voice" (Introduction to *The Dream Book*, 51–2).[7] Barolini's comments on the desire of second- and third-generation Italian American women to emulate and adapt to a more "American" way of life tell us much about the conflicts they experienced: "We wanted the look of tweed and tartan and not the embroideries of our grandmother's Italian bed linens; we wanted a Cape Cod cottage for our dream house, not some stuccoed *villino* with arches and tomatoes in the back yard" (Introduction to *The Dream Book*, 20). Italian immigrant families, in spite of embracing the freedoms America provided that Italy did not, kept up the traditional male/female double standard. Women were not expected to go on to college; when they did go, it was often with their parents' hopes that they would find husbands. Part of challenging that male-created standard would require fighting the image that the larger society had created for her to emulate. Helen Barolini took it upon herself to recast the public image of the Italian American woman in her own likeness. By doing so, she provided a model of self-exploration for future women writers.

Tina DeRosa's Lyrical Self-Awakening

Born in Chicago's Taylor Street Little Italy, Tina DeRosa started writing down stories of her youth at the urging of Michael Anania of the University of Illinois at Chicago, where she was working on a master's degree in English in the late 1970s. The work led to her first novel, *Paper Fish*, which tells the story of a young girl who comes of age in a dying little Italy.[8] Unlike Barolini's integrated, epiclike bildungsroman, Tina DeRosa's *Paper Fish* (1980), composed of fragmented lyrical segments, is an example of Felski's second category of the novel of self-discovery, the novel of awakening. This category "emphasizes spatial and symbolic patterns rather than the temporal and open-ended dimension of narrative; it is mythical rather than historical. Self-discovery is understood as "the 'awakening' to an essential female self" (Felski, "The Novel of Self-Discovery," 137). While Barolini chooses to present the journey in a more epic fashion, DeRosa fractures her tale into segments that move in the manner of human memory, resulting in the more complex style usually associated with high modernism. It is a style unlike any previous narrative by an Italian American writer. This lyric of origins, according to Mary Jo Bona, contains a metaphorical journey motif that "de-emphasizes the literal migration to the new world and instead legitimates the uses of memory in retelling the tale of beginnings" ("Broken Images," 96). The story of Umbertina's life, something the immigrant was unable to pass on to her children and grandchildren, is successfully transplanted into the mind, and thus the memory, of Carmolina, *Paper Fish*'s protagonist. These stories, much like the stories that Grandma Doria heard from her own mother, enable Carmolina to "metaphorically and literally resume the journey her grandmother wanted to take as a young, imaginative girl" (Bona, "Broken Images," 97). In essence, they enable her to awaken to the ethnic dimension of her identity.

DeRosa's novel mixes aspects of the historical novel into Felski's category of "awakening"; however, unlike Barolini, who anchors her story in historical time (by giving the life dates of her protagonists and by including many references to historical events that take place in the world outside the Longobardi family), DeRosa achieves a timeless quality through her creation of a world unaffected by any history beyond that of the personal history of the family. DeRosa, who can only imagine the southern Italian culture into which her grandmother was born, disconnects her characters from historical time and suggests that the journey toward self is a continuous quest, uninterrupted by the passing of generations. Carmolina's self-discovery is a "subjective and intuitive experience, a question of stages of spiritual growth; the social environment appears in a generalised and symbolic light, an exemplification of an inner state of mind

rather than a challenge to it" (Felski, "The Novel of Self-Discovery," 140).
The narrative's point of view shifts from the subjectivity of the protagonist's mind to that of an omniscient third-person narrator able to span
generations. This strategy meets Felski's definition of awakening as a "subjective and intuitive experience." The environment in which the novel is
set is symbolic. As the material world of a little Italy is destroyed, its
spiritual ghost survives in memory. Memory, and the stories that create it,
can rebuild a stronger self-identity. When Grandma Doria leaves the material world of southern Italy, her past life there is transformed into memory,
which enables her to rebuild her past in America. By telling her granddaughter Carmolina the stories of her past, Doria is preparing her for the
time when Carmolina will leave the little Italy into which she was born
and make her inevitable journey away from her family and into her self.
The strength needed to accomplish this lies in achieving the ability to
survive without the family. To help her reach this goal, Grandma Doria
teaches Carmolina to turn memory into strength.

Paper Fish is divided into eight segments, each depicting a vital stage in
the protagonist's awakening. A prelude opens the narrative with a meditation on the formation and dissolution of a family. Shifting among past,
present, and future, the prelude cryptically summarizes the entire narrative in miniature and comes to the reader as through a kaleidoscope,
providing a prehistory of the protagonist's life. In Part 1, "The Memory,"
Marco, the father of the family introduced in the prelude, is courting
Sarah, the mother. This part covers a number of years and includes the
stories Grandma Doria, Marco's mother, would tell of her past. Grandma
Doria's memory becomes the stage on which Carmolina begins to shape
her own self-consciousness.

And Grandma was making the world for her, between her shabby old fingers. She
was telling Carmolina about Italy, about the land that got lost across the sea, the
land that was hidden on the other side of the world. When Grandma said how
beautiful Italy was — how it was near blue waters which were always still and how
she could watch wooden sailing ships coming so close to her house that one day
she jumped on one and sailed away — Carmolina wondered, why did Grandma
do that?, but she was glad Grandma did, because otherwise she wouldn't know
Grandma, and that would be strange. (*Paper Fish*, 21)

Doria communicates her sense of destiny as well as the value of uniqueness to her granddaughter by passing on a belief she gained from her own mother: "It was true according to Doria's mother that each man is given a secret when he is born. He is meant by God to protect his secret, to hide it like a jewel throughout life. Each secret is different, and only God knows them all. The telling of secrets is forbidden. They must be held close to the body all through life, because they are the only treasure. Without them, a man is a snail" (29). Much of part 1 is told in the present tense, suggesting the immediacy of memories as they unfold in the mind.

Part 2, "Summer, 1949 Late July," recounts events chronologically by opening with a brief sequence that finds Carmolina away from home, outside the safety of her little Italy. This short sequence is followed by a longer one in which her father, a Chicago policeman, is searching for her in his car. The news of Carmolina's disappearance moves through the community and becomes the focus of talk and the prayers of the women in church, who believe that she has been kidnapped by gypsies. We do not learn until later, in part 4, that Carmolina has run away from home out of fear of being institutionalized along with her mentally retarded sister, Doriana. This is the beginning of Carmolina's journey into the world outside little Italy where she experiences the type of prejudice that her immigrant grandparents faced. To non-Italians, Carmolina becomes "the dago kid come to dirty up our street" (35).

In Part 3, "The Family," the narrative shifts into the remote past when the BellaCasa family settled into the neighborhood, back when the now "rusted red" streetlight poles were silver, a world yet to be tarnished by time (49). These are the days in which the family grows. Sarah marries Marco (54). From the wedding the narrative leaps ahead in time to Marco's funeral (56), then back in time to recount the fire that nearly destroys Marco and Sarah's home (60), which Grandma Doria sees as the cause of Doriana's mental retardation. Doria maintains that her namesake's condition is the result of Sarah's leap from the burning building while she was pregnant with Doriana.

Part 4, "Summer, 1949 Early June," returns to a chronological unraveling of the events that lead up to Carmolina's disappearance. This part opens with gypsies, the mysterious "other" in Grandma Doria's childhood in Italy, moving into a vacant storefront. The young Carmolina, who is out shopping for her grandmother, is fascinated by them. At a family meeting called by Grandma Doria to discuss the future of Doriana, the grandmother argues against institutionalizing Doriana. In Italy, she believes, things would have been different (74). Carmolina overhears the discussion and fears that she, like her sister, will be taken away from her family.

Part 5, "Summer, 1949 Late July," carries on the chronological time of part 4 as Carmolina leaves to do her grandmother's shopping. Her grandmother has tossed her coins tied in a handkerchief from her upstairs apartment window, inadvertently providing her with the means to escape. Carmolina takes the money and, instead of shopping, runs off to a part of the city she has never seen before, a place in which she finds out that she is Italian, where she faces discrimination and hatred and for the first time experiences ethnic anxiety. She becomes the "dago kid" (89) who is cheated out of her money in a diner. Much of the novel, especially this section, is written in an impressionistic style reminiscent of Henry Roth's *Call It Sleep*, as evidenced in the passage recording Carmolina's first experience outside the boundaries of her Italian neighborhood: "Night. A blink. An eye moving. Whose eye? A twist of the hand, fingers grip the dark, the dark has the hands of a skeleton. Hair falling into her eyes. Flash of red tennis shoes on hot pavement. This door is strange. That lamp is too bright. A head turning. Hair falling into place, out of place. Skin of rough objects. What was that? The hand of a dead man. The skin of a ghost reaching out to steal you" (104). This fragmented and impressionistic style is juxtaposed with the more lyrical presentation of the stories told by Grandma Doria to Carmolina so that she can understand her sister's illness.

"Doriana she get lost in the forest. . . ."
"Where Grandma?"
Grandma held her white head high like a proud horse; she would not look at Carmolina. "We no know where. We try to find her. We still try to find her. We never stop looking. . . . In the forest the birds are. Ah such beautiful birds. White birds. Blue and pink. Doriana when go into the forest to look at the birds and the birds they sing in the trees, they sing, they turn into leaves. Doriana she have a key to the forest. It a secret. Only Doriana know where she keep the key. One day Doriana go

into the forest. She forget the key. She get lost in the forest. She get scared. Her face it turn hot like a little peach and she scream and try to get out of the forest. . . . She try to come home from the forest. She no find her way." (111–12)

Grandma then explains that the reason Doriana is so beautiful is because she must "fight to come home. When you fight to come home, you beautiful" (112). Like Doriana, Carmolina becomes lost, but she has the key to return home, which she employs by going up to a policeman and screaming at him (117). But when she is returned to her home, she feels that her real family has been replaced by strangers. She is put into bed with a high fever, and her father tells her she is never to leave again. She replies, "When I grow up . . . I'm going to leave forever" (119).

In Part 6, "Summer, 1958," nine years have passed and we find Carmolina awakening to herself as she receives from her grandmother what Bona calls "the legacy of selfhood" ("Broken Images," 96). Felski explains:

Awakening is first and most obviously an internal and private act taking place inside the consciousness of the individual. Secondly, awakening marks a threshold; it is a circumscribed moment, a point between two states, and cannot in itself generate any sequential process. It is in this sense outside history, a point and not a temporal continuum. Finally, awakening signals a qualitative shift, a move from one mode of being to another (sleep/waking, alienation/authenticity), and hence implies an erasure of the past. The act of sleeping does not contribute to nor form part of the waking state — on the contrary, the latter negates the ontological reality of the former. Awakening, in other words, is a metaphor which suggests an essentially dualistic and disjunctive conception of experience. ("The Novel of Self-Discovery," 141)

DeRosa represents this dualism through her use of the mirror and re-creates the disjunctive conception of experience through her narrative structure. The entire novel revolves around this crucial section, in which the protagonist's mythical quest for archetypes is ended. The archetypal figure to whom DeRosa has led Carmolina is not Carmolina's mother but her Grandma Doria, who becomes her "Lost Mother," whom the desire to find, Felski tells us, "has been identified as a central theme in contemporary feminist fiction; the novel of self-discovery frequently describes the heroine repudiating her past history, her existence as a social individual, in order to discover a mythical identity" (141). Carmolina's achievement of this mythical identity is suggested through the sequence in part 6 when Grandma Doria is carried up the stairs to see her granddaughter in a wedding dress. Although Carmolina is not about to be married, Grandma Doria, knowing that her own death is close and that she will not live to see her granddaughter married, asks to see her dressed as a bride. In Italian tradition, the daughter (and quite often the son) does not leave home until she is married. Marriage is the ritual through which a young woman establishes her independence from her family. However, it also means shifting from an identification with family to an identification with a male who then becomes her new patriarch. DeRosa's presentation of this scene signifies a defiance of the Italian tradition. Carmolina achieves her adult identity not by attaching herself to a man, but by taking it from her grandmother, who acknowledges it through the blessing she gives her granddaughter.

In preparation for the visit, Grandma Doria dons her blue dress, the one she always wears on special occasions (123). Blue is the color traditionally associated with the Madonna, and it is fitting that the blue-eyed matriarch of the BellaCasa family wears it as she is carried up to see her granddaughter. As she is dressing, Doria looks into a mirror and sees "the face of her mother, there in the lines around her mouth . . . which hung in a picture in her own bedroom" (124). Her mother, Carmella, is the namesake of Carmolina. The scene then shifts to Carmolina dressing before a mirror in her room across the alley from Grandma Doria's house. Carmolina's brown eyes are "rimmed in blue" (124). While she dons her first long dress, a string of pearls that were "meant for her to wear as a bride," and kisses a cameo ring that "had belonged to her great-grandmother Carmella and her great-great-grandma," Carmolina whispers to herself, "they won't ever let us go, will they?" (125). Through this process Carmolina acknowledges her debt to the past and accepts her place in the chain of the BellaCasa lineage.

The family forms a line behind Doria's sons, who carry their mother on a chair up to Carmolina's room in a scene that re-creates the traditional procession of the Madonna, a staple in Italian culture, through which the people receive the blessing of God's mother. Carmolina, who is playing this masquerade "for the family" (127), views almost the entire scene through its reflection in the mirror. First she sees "the soft lines which she loved in her grandmother's face" (127), then sees her sister Doriana's reflection as a purple shadow. Grandma Doria enters and sees in the mirror "not one but two brides in white dresses with heavy dark hair and heavy dark eyes" (128), one of them is herself dressed as a bride; then, as she stares at the mirror, she watches Carmolina grow up. Doria hands her granddaughter a handkerchief tied around three coins, reminiscent of the shopping money she gave Carmolina nine years ago when Carmolina ran away from home. "This time," she says, "I give them to you on purpose" (129). The purpose is part of Doria's blessing to Carmolina. Grandma then forces Carmolina to look into the mirror. Carmolina first sees herself with her grandmother behind her. Her grandmother then moves back to the chair: "'Carmolina mia,' Grandma said from her place in the chair. 'Bambina,' she said softly. 'Now it you turn. You keep the fire inside you.' Carmolina looked into the mirror's silver face. It gave back to her her own face" (130). The legacy of selfhood that Grandma Doria passes on to Carmolina in this scene cannot be passed on to Doriana, Grandma Doria's namesake, and Carmolina cannot get it from her mother, who withdraws further and further away from her daughters and her family. Instead Carmolina looks to Doria, whose experience she re-created nine years ago by running away and then returning to the responsibility of securing her place in the world.

This important scene is followed by an epilogue that is divided into six segments, all illustrating different angles of the disintegration of the Italian neighborhood. More than describing the destruction of her old neighborhood, DeRosa re-creates the experience through an imagistic language that uses repetition, a technique that echoes the oral tradition from which she comes and underscores the folktalelike presentation of the narrative.[9]

Underneath, the street is brick, brick that is no longer whole and red, but chipped and gray like the faces of dead people trapped under lava. The street heaves up bricks, the guts of the street spit up brick. The face of the street cracks open and reveals its belly of brick, the gray faces. Squads of men in white t-shirts and hard hats with pickaxes in their hands chew into the street's cement face and the face cracks and there is no body under the bricks, only the cracked cement face. Then the street explodes, explodes in the faces of the men with pickaxes who come to take the streetcar line away. . . .

The people of the neighborhood sit on wooden benches, eat lemon ice in fluted cups, their lips are wet from the ice. The look at the clean steel bones of the tracks. (133)

The excavation of the city streets, like the archaeological diggings at Pompeii, might reveal layers of past life, but the observer of this scene sees nothing beneath the surface of this American setting. What has made this site sacred is not the life that came before, but the lives that are being destroyed as the workers remove the streetcar line. It remains for the observer/writer to transplant all this into memory, where it can live forever. The value of the writer to a culture is that she can create illusion out of reality and reality out of illusion, both of which affect human memory. DeRosa renders this idea through the poetry of the final segment, which finds Carmolina seated next to her grandmother at a circus, watching a clown sweeping away a spotlight.

Carmolina, Grandma whispers, you hear the magician? He still there?
He's there, Grandma?
Faccia bella, Grandma says.
The clown sweeps the light away.
The music stops.
It's only a trick, Grandma, Carmolina says. Don't let it fool you. (137)

Earlier in the novel Grandma Doria had told Carmolina that, unlike Doriana, Carmolina has a magician who watches over her and will bring her "good luck like gold" (110). The magician, however, also has the ability to create illusions, the ability to entertain people by making things seem to appear and disappear. For Carmolina, that magician is the story's narrator, who combines imagination and memory to bring life to the characters in Carmolina's life. Little Italy and the human forces that once gave it life may be physically transformed, but psychologically they remain forever, mentally preserved in the identity of Carmolina as she has fashioned it out of the stories of Grandma Doria.

While the novel ends with that image of a disintegrating little Italy, Italy will remain inside Carmolina as long as the memory of her grandmother is kept alive. This experience, the death of place and the inevitable dissolution of an accompanying culture, is recorded by DeRosa, an eyewitness, in a language that she has said was impossible for her ancestors to articulate. "Our grandparents and parents were bound to survival; we, on the other hand, have become freer to use our own talents and to rescue the talents of those who came before us. Because we have passed through more time, we have a perspective that gives us the ability to look back and to judge their experiences as treasures that we cannot throw out" (Gardaphé, "An Interview," 23). For DeRosa, the immigrant's story is one of the many myths the young learn as they interact with earlier generations: "Because I grew up with such a rich heritage, I can see how myth and reality in your imagination become so confused. We grow up with myths . . . your grandparents carry that mythology with them and try to pass it on so that it becomes a part of you" (Gardaphé, "An Interview," 23). For many Italian Americans who have never traveled to the country of their ancestors, Italy is an imaginary country. Though she has never been there, DeRosa uses the images that were presented to her through her immigrant relatives' recollections to create the *Italianità* of her novel, an *Italianità* that comes not from research, not from travel, not from reading, but from memory and imagination, a memory and imagination that, she says, "is as fragile and as beautiful as one of those Japanese paper fishes" (Gardaphé, "An Interview," 23). DeRosa's sense of *Italianità* came full circle in 1987 when she completed her second book, *Father to the Migrants*, the life story of Bishop Giovanni Battista Scalabrini, founder of the Missionary Fathers of Saint Charles, whose sole mission in the nineteenth century was to follow Italian immigrants to the Americas and tend to their Roman Catholic faith.

When I asked her to define *Italianità*, DeRosa replied:

On any level, *Italianità* is religious. When we look at our Italian American writers we get a different sense of religion from all of them. The work of di Donato, is religious in the deep sensual or pagan sense. The religion he presents is that of family, of father, and of food; religion of the body. I mean, think of the image of his father frozen in concrete. The work of [Jerre] Mangione represents a more refined, educated, aristocratic and intellectual sense of religion. Someone like Bishop Scalabrini represents something closer to a Christ-like version of religion; his work brings the body of di Donato together with the intellect of Mangione. And it is this sense of *Italianità* that I've tried to capture in the biography. (Gardaphé, "An Interview," 23)

The recovery of her ethnic heritage, both through the research she conducted for the nonfiction book and through the re-creation of the immigrant grandmother in the novel, has strengthened DeRosa's sense of *Italianità* and has contributed to the development of her self-identity as a woman and as an American writer of Italian descent.[10]

Carole Maso and the Art of Myth

La memoria è la stessa che la fantasia.
Memory is the same as imagination.
Giambattista Vico, *The New Science*

In 1986 Carole Maso made an impressive debut as a novelist. *Ghost Dance* tells the story of a third-generation ethnic American who, unlike earlier generations, has the option of picking and choosing from the many traditions that make up American culture. What Italian characteristics the protagonist, Vanessa Turin, has not inherited directly through experiences with her grandparents, she imagines and reinvents to fulfill her needs. Few novels capture so well the effects of the fragmentation that occurs when solid cultural traditions are fractured. In *Ghost Dance*, Maso reinvents an *Italianità* through her recovery of the myths that make up her ancestral past. Her father's mother immigrated from Sicily, and her father's father was from Genoa. Her mother is of German, English, and Armenian ancestry. Out of these diverse cultural roots Maso has fashioned a unique perspective on life and art.

Of her six novels, only *Ghost Dance* deals with visible Italian American subjects. Throughout this work runs the theme of creating a self out of the myriad stories one is told and those one tells. *Ghost Dance* dramatizes the effects of the submergence or loss of ethnicity based on Old World notions and illustrates attempts to reinvent the past so that it serves the present. Stylistically, this novel is a bridge between the mythic and the philosophic modes of narration as it documents the fall of the modern and the rise of a postmodern movement of Italian American narrative. Like DeRosa's *Paper Fish*, *Ghost Dance* is a novel of self-awakening that records the efforts of a young woman to achieve her own identity amid the chaos that accompanies her family's disintegration during her own coming of age. Vanessa Turin is the granddaughter of Italian immigrants on her father's side, and of Armenian and German ancestry on her mother's side. Without a strong sense of an Italian or Italian American cultural tradition, Maso's protagonist, more like DeRosa's than Barolini's, must depend on the fragments she can gather from those around her to piece together the puzzle of her identity. Throughout the novel, Maso's narrator examines the constraints that ethnic identities create for her characters. Vanessa's parents remain very distant from their own immigrant parents. After what he believes is his failure to achieve the American dream, Vanessa's Armenian grandfather changes his name back from Frank Wing to Sarkis Wingarian, leaves his college-aged daughters, and returns to the old country, where Vanessa imagines he might say he is "worth his weight in gold. In America I would look like an old man, but here old men are respected. Old age means wisdom" (*Ghost Dance*, 212). Her Italian grandfather, determined to make himself American, attempts to erase all his *Italianità* and replace it with Native American beliefs.

The novel is divided into four parts, each composed of narrative fragments, some of which are single sentences, that follow no chronological order. Many of these are repeated elsewhere in the novel. This structure mirrors the uncertainty and incoherence inside Vanessa as she attempts to build an identity out of the fragments of history and myth she picks up from her family. Most of these fragments are created through what she imagines might have happened in the past. *Ghost Dance* is all about the remaking of the self out of the remnants of competing myths of origin. In an attempt to find the sources of those myths, Vanessa and her brother, Fletcher, turn first to their parents: Michael, a father who doesn't say much, and Christine Wing, a mother whose "mind could not be trusted completely" (37). In an effort to get their father to speak, Vanessa and Fletcher invent a homework assignment of writing their autobiography. Their father tells them to make up anything they like and goes out for a walk. Denied access to her father's story, Vanessa and her brother study a mail-order family tree. But the names only bring questions, the answers to which Vanessa fabricates out of her imagination. Later, when she does get the autobiography assignment in ninth grade, Vanessa turns in her family fiction, to which her teacher responds, "This is good, but it lacks authenticity" (30).

Unlike Carmolina of *Paper Fish*, Vanessa grows up without an extended family. Her mother, Christine Wing, is a famous poet who leads a life that keeps her shuffling back and forth between Sabine, her lesbian lover, and her husband, Michael. Michael is a stockbroker who remains detached from his children; Vanessa characterizes him as "so remote" (17). Without a sense of who her relatives are, Vanessa relegates them to the status of "movie characters . . . distant, too easy to love." She is certain that if they could communicate to her, they would say nothing that her father would want to hide (30). Eventually Vanessa and her brother learn about their ancestry, and the reason their father won't talk about his past, through their father's immigrant parents, Angelo and Maria. Without a sense of how she acquired this story—that is, whether someone told her or she made it up—Vanessa presents a scene in which her father watches his father destroy the family's garden of tomatoes, peppers, and eggplants with an axe, "insisting that they [the family] are Americans now, not Italians" (74). This attempt to destroy the Italian signifiers leads Vanessa to a question: "Is this what my father means when he says there are things it is better to forget? Is this what he is forgetting—his own father out in the garden chopping the tomato plants into pieces. . . . Did his father announce that there will be no more Italian spoken in his house? No more wine drunk with lunch, as he burned the grapevines? Did he tell his wife there would be no more sad songs from the old country? How much she must have wept, hugging her small son to her breast!" (74). Vanessa imagines that this experience terrorized her father. Since she never gets an explanation from him, that can only remain speculation, but it leads her deeper into her search for ancestral roots.

In a similar scene, whose source again is uncertain, Vanessa re-creates the scene in which Angelo tells Maria that they have to erase their ties to the Old World. "'Maria,' my grandfather said one day long ago, 'today your name is Mary. Today I change my own name from Angelo to Andy. Today we are real Americans'" (76). The grandmother refuses to change her given name but does accompany Angelo to English classes. "'The accent must go,' he said each night before bed. 'The accent must go,' he said in the morning to his small son, Michael. 'An accent is no good in this new country.' Maria sighed, exhausted by so much enthusiasm. He was a teacher's dream, not a wife's. She felt lonely. The village where she was born and had lived her whole life welled in her stomach; she had to eat a lot of bread to keep it down; she had to sleep under heavy blankets" (77). Reluctantly, Maria goes along with her husband's idea of remaking themselves into Americans, but her Italian identity remains alive inside her, repressed by her husband and capable of surfacing only after his death.

To accomplish his transformation into an American, Angelo decides to adopt a more appropriate fashion of dress: "Meticulously my grandfather observed the dress of the people on the neighboring farms before going out to get his own blue jeans and work shirts and books. He especially noted the dress of the Negroes whom he considered the most authentic Americans. They were new and exotic like America itself. And above all they were not Europeans. Europe became 'for the birds.' 'Oh, Mary,' he would say, 'Italy is for the birds'" (77). Abandoning the old country's food, language, and dress leaves Angelo without a life philosophy. And so, as part of his effort to Americanize himself completely, he travels off to a Black Hills Indian reservation, a destination that came to him in a dream (91). There he speaks with an Indian named Two Bears in the language of hands, in which Angelo was "fluent from the moment he raised [his hands]" (78). Angelo returns with "the secret of rain, the dances of the sun, and the earth's songs" (79) as well as with new names for the family: Maria becomes "Wonderful Thunder," his own name becomes "Dreams of Rain," his son's name is "Moves on Water," and Christine's is "Brave Ghost."

Angelo becomes obsessed with the idea of rain and predicts that a terrible drought will come, "a fear that he had held in check for nearly seventy years; in Italy as a little boy, then as a young man, his whole life, it had been the same fear" (87). He takes his grandchildren out to record cloud formations and to study animal behavior and anything relating to rain (87). He learns the secrets of Indians, which he passes on to his grandchildren through stories. Angelo instructs them in a ritual they are to perform after his death so that there will be "the proper relation between the living and the dead" (92). If it is not performed, the ghost of the dead "will attempt to lure away the people it loved in life" (91). Angelo also relates to them the history of the Ghost Dance religion and teaches his grandchildren how to perform the dance. He understands that people need ways of processing the most fundamental experiences in life and that these ways are connected to the environment they inhabit. While he has given up the ways of his ancestral homeland in Italy, he adopts those which he believes naturally belong to his new land. By teaching his grand-children about the Ghost Dance religion he hopes to sensitize them to the evils of industrial progress. Historically, the Ghost Dance religion was "led by the Paiute medicine man Wovoka, who taught that Indians would be reunited with family and friends in another world where there was no sickness, death, or old age, if they lived in peace and put away the old practices" (Ruoff, *American Indian Literature*, 33). It was "a messianic movement that swept across the Plains in the late 1880s and 1890" and represented "the last gasp of Indian resistance" against forced assimilation by the United States government. One of the results of this resistance was the massacre at Wounded Knee (*American Indian Literature*, 3–4). An-gelo's influence becomes stronger when Christine mysteriously abandons her family. Later, when their father does the same, Vanessa and Fletcher are left to find their own way through life. Without any useful instruction from their parents they must turn to their father's parents to learn how to live and to deal with death.

Throughout *Ghost Dance* Vanessa demonstrates the importance of knowing one's past, of discovering it and using it to form one's self-identity. A key scene in which this happens comes when Michael walks with his children through a field. He points to the leaf of a flower which his grandmother in Italy used to cook so that it would "taste just like veal. He smiled a great smile, the memory warmed him and the warmth spilled onto us. This was one of the happiest days of my life: clutching his hand, holding close the story of how his grandmother, who had never lived before this day, changed simple leaves for a young boy into veal" (93). This rare acknowledgment by Michael of his ethnic past intrigues Vanessa, and she continues to explore its relevance to her own identity in the novel's next section.

In part 3, Vanessa enrolls at Vassar, where her mother is a famous alumna. She re-creates her mother's childhood in Paterson and the death of her grandmother, imagining that her mother learned to cope with tragedy through language. For Christine, "words are medicine" (111) through which she can create, change, and escape reality (114). Through this sequence Maso juxtaposes the mother's world of words against the grandfather's world of actions. During a family visit to the 1964 World's Fair in New York, her father spent nearly the entire time viewing Michelangelo's *Pietà* in the Vatican Pavilion. Vanessa's mother walked through the fair alone. While Vanessa does not know what her grandmother did, she does know that her grandfather and Fletcher joined a civil rights sit-in outside the Ford Pavilion's "Progressland" exhibit and were among those arrested and jailed. After bailing out Angelo and Fletcher, the family returns to the fair and Vanessa imagines, "My grandfather thought, looking at this exquisite show, that we had traded something important for all this. Primitive man was better" (129). When they leave, she says, "My grandfather turned his back on the lights finally and shook his head with the tremendous sorrow of someone who has been betrayed at the core" (130). He then journeys back into the past, "to a simpler place, where he would live the last years of his life" (130).

Although her grandfather abandoned his Italian culture during his life in America, he returns to it on his deathbed, a scene Vanessa witnesses. With Maria next to him, they speak Italian, "I had never seen his mouth form such shapes. It was Italian. He was talking in the forbidden language; the language he had given up in this country now came streaming back" (139). As he dies he tells Vanessa to take care of her grandmother and to be sure that she and Fletcher perform the Indian cornmeal ceremony after his death. His dying words are, "Try to forgive them — as I have tried" (140). Vanessa repeats these words in the next segment as if her absent father, whom she imagines is in "Denmark or Sweden, or maybe Norway" (140), can hear them. Juxtaposed to this strange world of her grandfather are Vanessa's experiences at college. One day Vanessa is summoned by a written note to Jennifer Stafford, the college's "resident feminist" and "Women's Studies student par excellence" (146). She meets Jennifer's roommate, Marta, who tells her that Jennifer is "doing her thesis now on the history of the women of her family, starting with her long-lost relative Sarah Stafford, who came over on the God-speed or one of those" (145). The Stafford family history, unlike that of the Turin family, can be documented and analyzed objectively enough to serve as a legitimate thesis subject. Like Jennifer, Vanessa is involved in the recovery of her family history; however, Vanessa must depend on her imagination to create the historical contexts in which the fragments she knows can live.

Marta, who is from Venezuela, introduces Vanessa to drugs and tells her the tragic story of Natalie, a young woman with whom Marta had been in love, who died in Europe from a drug overdose. Marta keeps the memory of Natalie alive by re-creating that relationship through Vanessa. In this section Maso shifts to Angelo's retelling the story of the origins of the Ghost Dance, which came to Wovoka in a dream. "And the dream was this: Christ had come back to earth as an Indian. Indians from all over went to Nevada to hear the dreamer's story. 'The dead will all be alive again,' Wovoka said. 'The earth will be green with high grass. The buffalo and elk will return. . . . It will be like old times'" (197). Wovoka tells the people that they will be able to "walk and talk with our lost ones . . . if you do the Ghost Dance" (197). Angelo later tells his grandchildren of the massacre at Wounded Knee. What she has learned from her grandfather saves Vanessa from Marta's fate. Marta, continually haunted by Natalie, eventually kills herself to join her lost love. Throughout this part Maso intersperses selections from Black Elk and Chief Seattle along with fragments from new stories that tell of the inhumanity of industrial society.

In part 4, Vanessa is living with her grandmother on the farm. With Angelo gone, Maria attempts to pass on her knowledge to Vanessa as a legacy: "At night my grandmother stands over my bed and repeats things she thinks I should know — useful things like when to sow vegetables. . . . Life is understandable was what my grandmother was trying to say. You can understand your life" (175). As Vanessa prepares to return to school, she eats lunch with her grandmother, who wants Vanessa to take control of her own life: "She asks that I cut myself out from her, like a cookie from dough, like a dress from cloth, and that I be grown up about it and sensible and that I go quietly" (177). In this section Vanessa reconstructs the story of her Armenian grandfather and his marriage to her German grandmother, which "everyone had disapproved of" (180), and her grandfather's belief that his "American daughter," Christine, could become a movie star because "in America, it was true, anything was possible" (181). When the family's financial security is threatened, Grandpa Sarkis takes his daughter to Hollywood for a screen test, which she cries through and fails. Vanessa believes that this was the beginning of her mother's rejection of her father and the past he represented.

In a later sequence, Maso places mother and daughter together in the garden. Christine, in her attempts to rearrange the plants and bushes, inadvertently kills everything: "Let's clear out the roots, honey. Let's start over. . . . We'll get rid of the roots, it's the only way." "It's the only way," she keeps saying. "We'll get rid of the roots" (217). This scene is a metaphor for the way Christine deals with her own past. To start over as an American, she must destroy all that has grown from her ethnic roots. For Christine, ethnicity serves no role in the creation of her art, "the roots" only get in the way of the new growth. But the price she pays for this disconnection from the past is loss of the knowledge of how to live, the lack of which contributes to Christine's "illness." This scene is followed by one in which Grandma Maria's ethnicity resurfaces after her husband's death.

On July 4, 1976, America's Bicentennial, Michael takes Vanessa and Fletcher to visit Grandma at her nursing home. Vanessa drives the car, and as she approaches the nursing home she sees on the lawn "a bizarre image, a picture of such eeriness in the fog . . . what seemed to be an old, old woman, or the ghost of a woman" (221). What they witness is Italy exploding out of Grandma Maria—an *Italianità* that has been dormant for years. "A red rosary hung around her neck. She wore a long skirt. Beads and other trinkets were sewn into it—beads from necklaces my grandfather had given her and she had never worn: . . . She wore a white peasant blouse, made hurriedly from a sheet, probably secretly. She had pulled the hair away from her face, braided and pinned up on top of head" (222). Dressed in makeshift clothes that conjure the fashion of her childhood Italy, Grandma hums to herself and begins dancing a tarantella: "She moved more quickly now, having been bitten, I imagined, by the tarantula of Italian folklore, the spider with a venom so potent that it had made her people crazy for centuries with the irresistible urge to dance" (222). As if in a trance, from which Vanessa dare not disturb her lest "she turn back into the old Grandma," Maria speaks in a voice whose "giddiness we had never heard before": "We used to make our own pasta. We used to make our own wine and olive oil. There were mountains there" (222). Vanessa describes her as being surrounded by home, "not ours, but hers." In the background of this startling scene are heard "strains of familiar music . . . 'I'm a Yankee Doodle Dandy' and 'America the Beautiful'" coming from the nursing home. Vanessa asks her grandmother why she kept all this from them, and Maria replies, "He never let me" (223). Michael and his children all hug her, and then Michael breaks down in tears. Maria holds her son for a long time, then breaks away into a dance. But before returning to her tarantella she bends down and picks up a dandelion and says, "We used to like these very much. We ate weeds and we were happy" (224). As she dances, Vanessa imagines that Grandma is talking to her own mother about fish when she calls out "*Piccolini*" (little ones), but she is actually speaking to her grandchildren. Maso closes this scene with the image of Grandma smiling with her eyes closed, remembering the sweetness of an Italian pastry she once used to make. This recalls Angelo's deathbed comment, "It's got a strange sweet taste, Maria . . . this dying" (139). This is the last image presented of Vanessa's Italian grandmother. She is left, trapped forever in memory as a living sculpture.

In part 5, we learn that Christine has returned home, only to die in the backseat of her family's Ford Pinto when it is rear-ended at a toll booth. Christine becomes the victim of the very company that had built the Progressland Pavilion at the 1964 World's Fair where her father-in-law and her son joined the civil rights sit-in. Christine's lover attends the funeral, out of respect for Michael, and visits Vanessa. The two make love: Sabine calling Vanessa "Christine," Vanessa calling Sabine "Mother." Neither can let go of the dead, and they continue to try to keep Christine alive through each other. It is not until Vanessa visits Fletcher, at the end of the novel, and the two of them do the Ghost Dance against the enemy—Ford Motor Company and all the industrial progress it represents—that Vanessa is able to finally let go of her mother's spirit, an act that renews her sense of family and life.[11]

Through this novel Maso presents the experience of the third-generation ethnic who, unlike earlier generations, has the option of picking and choosing from the many traditions that make up American culture. What ethnic trappings Vanessa does not inherit directly through experiences with her grandparents, she imagines and reinvents to fulfill her needs. In *Ghost Dance*, Carole Maso depicts the results of stitching a self together out of disparate parts. In doing so she reinvents *Italianità* through her recovery of the myths that have made up her ancestral past and creates an ethnic literary version of the Ghost Dance that regenerates an ethnic identity and enables the protagonist to avoid total assimilation into the mainstream American culture.

Modern Proposals

Before Italian American writers could reach beyond history to merge with the present, they needed a materialization and articulation of the past.

Some have accomplished this by re-creating their own autobiographical pasts, through what Lyotard would call the master narrative, a staple of modernist literature. The Italian American subject in these master narratives serves as a means of recovering or reinventing ethnicity. This reinvention usually takes the form of the bildungsroman, which has until recently been the staple of the Italian American narrative canon.[12]

In spite of the fact that most of today's Italian American writers have more economic, educational, and social opportunities than their predecessors, and thus are in the position to become makers and shapers of American culture, the majority are engaged in what we can call modernist projects. Although they also come to the task of writing with a greater knowledge of the world outside their ethnocentric birthplaces, and in spite of the fact that they bring to their writing a more "Americanized" quality compared with the more localized, or village, quality of their predecessors, the majority are absorbed with the project of re-creating history and inventing myths through which the past can be used to produce a more meaningful present. Their advantages place them in a better position to examine their cultural makeup and use it in telling their stories. William Boelhower points this out when he says, "By interrogating the 'traditio' of his ancestors, the ethnic subject opens a new inferencing field in which he can re-present the crisis of cultural foundations in a critical light" (*Through a Glass Darkly*, 140). In essence, then, this is the work against which a distinctly postmodern Italian American literature will develop. In a 1987 interview published in *Fra Noi* (Gardaphé, "Parini's *Patch Boys*"), the celebrated novelist and poet Jay Parini reveals that his second novel, *The Patch Boys*, is a novel of recovery—one in which he used the Italian elements of his upbringing to tell a story, and by so doing regained aspects of his heritage which, for the most part, he had previously ignored or left untapped. Parini's recovery of his ethnic heritage is indicative of the efforts of many of today's younger Italian American writers who, in the process of telling their stories, of re-creating a past and recovering a heritage, create for their readers an Italian American "imago mundi" with signs peculiar to Italian American culture. More and more their work transcends the confines of little Italy as characters, along with their authors, interact with the physical and psychological main streets of American thought. The more "American" quality in their writing comes from the fact that their experience is rooted in America. They write about "old neighborhoods," not the "old country." They cover more cultural ground and gain more diverse perspectives, which enable them to include a larger American audience. They are also, like so many of America's best writers (Faulkner is a prime example), documenting a disappearing culture.

Sollors sees the move away from more parochial writing, what he calls "provincialism," as being "marked by a collective rebirth experience of a tradition, which literary historians (and sometimes the cultural participants) customarily term 'renaissance' (American and Harlem) and renascence (southern) or describe with the ominous epithet 'new' (as in 'American drama,' 'Negro' or 'ethnicity')" (*Beyond Ethnicity*, 241). Today we are experiencing a virtual renaissance in Italian American literature. Contemporary Italian American writers are not linked as strongly with their descendant ethnic group, and, as Sollors has pointed out, earlier, distinctively ethnic writing was "equated with parochialism, and ethnic writers who were not parochial are simply classified not as ethnic but as 'wholly American'" (*Beyond Ethnicity*, 243). Now that their writing is no longer restricted to being distinctly ethnic, their identification as ethnic writers is more a factor of self-determination, or what I call the postmodern prerogative.[13]

Sollors has advanced this shift to self-determination of ethnic identity by offering a new definition of ethnic literature, one that enables the ethnic writer to be connected to the developments of modern literature,

works written by, about, or for persons who perceived themselves, or were perceived by others, as members of ethnic groups, including even nationally and internationally popular writings by "major" authors and formally intricate and modernist texts. Even ethnic writers who seem to be "traditional" may have been brazen inventors of these traditions. In any event, much thinking has been done about the affinities of ethnicity and modernity; and there is no reason why readers of ethnic literature should not benefit from these efforts in their own interpretations. (*Beyond Ethnicity*, 243)

By linking ethnicity and modernity, Sollors explains why some of these writers may have returned to using their ethnicity in their work: "Literary forms are not organically connected with ethnic groups; ethnicity and modernism form a false set of opposites; and the very desire to transcend ethnicity may lead writers back to the most familiar territory of ethnogenesis and typology" (258). Out of this familiar territory emerge the ethnic signs that are Italian. The recovery of *Italianità* has become vital in the production of recent Italian American fiction.

Whether they have stumbled or have consciously directed themselves into Boelhower's "world of signs — the world of absence," Italian American writers of the third generation have established a presence in American literature. Unlike Fante, Mangione, and di Donato, Barolini, DeRosa, Maso, and younger writers are free from the chains of the immigrant's memory and reality. Perhaps because they have had to rely on imagination — the fuel of true fiction — their writing reaches into the more mythic qualities of the Italian American experience, thus creating literature that transcends a single ethnic experience and reaches out to a wider audience of readers.

Other important American "mythic" novels flavored with *Italianità* are Anthony Giardina's *A Boy's Pretensions*, Josephine Gattuso Hendin's *The Right Thing to Do*, and Tony Ardizzone's *Heart of the Order*. These novels present the coming of age of the children of immigrants and their attempts to forge an identity separate from those of their families. This process is initiated by the protagonist's leaving home (and the little Italy neighborhood) to pursue a college education. The separation between family and child is fostered by the protagonists' relations with non–Italian Americans. It is this interaction with those from outside their ethnic background that creates characters' greater realization of what their ethnic background has done to make them different. Beyond simply telling the stories of their characters, these novels also represent the coming of age of Italian American literature. Perhaps now that we are well into the literature produced by third-generation Italian Americans such as Barolini, DeRosa, and Maso, we can look forward to more novels that can, in Boelhower's words, "hold . . . ground against the map of national circulation" (*Through a Glass Darkly*, 143). Only now can we look back with answers to the questions raised by Rudolph Vecoli and say that Italian American writing has matured to the point where it can command the attention that its earlier creators were denied.[14] For both in quantity and quality, the literature of the third generation has provided the long-awaited Italian American renaissance. This renaissance plays an important role in delaying the return descent into barbarism that Vico says is inevitable after a nation reaches the philosophic level of the cycle of history.

Five

Narrative in the Philosophic Mode

The mythic mode (Vico's Age of Heroes) inevitably shifts into the philosophic mode (Vico's Age of Man). According to Vico's conception of historical cycles, the Age of Man comes with "the decline of the power and reality of Heroes . . . [when] thought and language begin to order experience in terms of abstract or intelligible universals" (Verene, *The New Art of Autobiography*, 85). During this age, men destroy the myths that rule them and replace them with narratives based on their own superiority.

This destruction of the rules and regulations that order society is akin to the dismantling of the boundaries between disciplines that has been attributed to postmodernism. Vico claims that this is the stage that precedes a nation's descent into barbarism, its return to primitivism, which signals the end of a *corso* and the beginning of a *ricorso*. The ultimate descent into barbarism can be forestalled by recapturing the fundamental truths that originated the founding of the society. This, as we observed, was the function of the narratives produced in the later mythic mode that I referred to in Chapter 4 as forming a renaissance of Italian American culture. The American writers of Italian descent who choose not to use their Italian American cultural heritage in their narratives move their culture into the philosophic stage of Vico's cycle of history. During this stage, Vico tells us, a nation decays and falls into barbarism. This is precisely what the narratives written in the philosophic mode represent. This assimilation into the mainstream American culture and its depiction in their narratives foreshadow the descent into barbarism that follows a culture's decay. While the works in this mode may retain aspects of the poetic and the mythic modes, they distinctly distance themselves from both the poetic and the mythic modes.

(In)visibility: (Ex)tending or Escaping the Italian American Tradition

In Chapter 4 I proposed that literary representation of their own ethnicity by Italian Americans has become a matter of choice, a postmodern prerogative that was not available to earlier Italian American writers. The choice, once again, is whether or not to visibly identify self and / or subject in writing as Italian American. Richard Alba's notion of the "twilight of ethnicity" and Michael Fischer's notion of the "re-invention of ethnicity" posit two ways of reading the condition that sets up this prerogative. According to Alba, traditionally stable signs of Italian American ethnicity diminish over time, inevitably disappearing entirely. In contrast, Fischer sees ethnicity as "something reinvented and reinterpreted in each generation by each individual . . . something over which he or she lacks control" ("Ethnicity and the Post-Modern Arts of Memory," 195). I argue that Fischer's is the more accurate way of reading literature produced by contemporary Italian American writers. Fischer tells us that ethnicity "is not something that is simply passed on from generation to generation, taught and learned; it is something dynamic, often unsuccessfully repressed or avoided" ("Ethnicity," 195).

Gilbert Sorrentino and Don DeLillo are two contemporary writers of Italian American descent who can be read as either extending or escaping from the Italian American literary tradition I set up in the previous chapters. Both are accomplished writers who seem to have passed into Alba's "twilight." However, twilight has a way of obscuring signs that are visible during other times of the day; neither writer, as we will see, totally transcends his ethnic background to melt invisibly into American culture. One reason Sorrentino and DeLillo have not been read as proponents of an Italian American literary tradition is that their work has yet to be read for signs of *Italianità*.[1] In this chapter I present readings of narratives by Sorrentino and DeLillo that suggest that aspects of their experience of American life as Italian Americans have placed them in positions of liminality, positions which, according to Victor Turner, occasion "the freedom to imagine alternatives" (Daly, "Liminality and Fiction," 76). Analyzing the function of the Italian signs found in the works of these (in)visible ethnics and reading their narratives through these Italian signs can enhance the contributions they have made to American literature. In most of their work, these writers relegate visible signs of their ethnicity to the margins or under the surface. While DeLillo and Sorrentino rarely choose to deal with distinctly Italian American subjects, and thus are more easily read through the more mainstream American aspects of their Italian American culture, ethnicity and cultural difference underscore all of their work. These authors may have avoided or suppressed dominant ethnic traits in their attempts to transcend ethnicity, but, as I will show, their work contains signs of *Italianità* that can be connected to an underlying philosophy which is informed by their ethnicity.

Gilbert Sorrentino's (Art)ificial *Italianità*

There are no lies in art. The only lies in art lie in falsification of
structure. Art selects and orders experience. It is not history. It is not
what "really happened."
Gilbert Sorrentino, in John O'Brien,
"An Interview with Gilbert Sorrentino"

The key to assimilating into American mainstream culture is to become available to influences outside one's home culture. In the case of Gilbert Sorrentino, and many contemporary American writers of Italian descent, escape from the old neighborhood led to encounters with many social and cultural influences of the larger world beyond the family. These encounters not only enabled him to move in new and exciting directions as an artist, they also challenged him to establish an awareness of how his background differs from that of other writers and artists. This experience affected the way he would view his ancestral heritage and how he would use it in his art.

After high school, Sorrentino went to work as a clerk in New York City, and enrolled in and then dropped out of Brooklyn College to join the Army Medical Corps. He recalls saying to himself on his return home, "I am going to be a writer or I am going to be nothing" (O'Brien, "Interview," 7). However, "given the kind of working-class background that I came out of, there was literally no conception in my mind that I could become a writer, a serious writer, an artist. . . . I always thought of myself as perhaps becoming a journalist" (Alpert, 3). Sorrentino never became that journalist, the practical writer who chronicled reality. While he did write a realist bildungsroman based on his childhood experiences, he never published it (Russo, "The Choice," 339). In 1956, three years after he was discharged from the army, Sorrentino founded *Neon*, a magazine that featured the work of artists who were not part of the literary establishment. During this period Sorrentino abandoned the idea of literature as documentation of reality and began his pursuit of literature as an art form.

In "The Choice of Gilbert Sorrentino," John Paul Russo argues that "literary modernism gave Sorrentino a way of becoming a writer that his personal background did not make easily available" (338). Russo suggests that the lack of a visible and vital Italian American presence in American literature, which might have offered Sorrentino models that could be imitated or deconstructed, led him to affiliate with modernist poetics. That affiliation, according to Russo, led Sorrentino away from producing realistic portrayals of the Italian American experience and toward a more experimental use of experiential material.

As a poet, novelist, and critic, Gilbert Sorrentino has acknowledged — both in interviews and in his own writing — the influence of his Italian and Irish background on his writing. While Sorrentino sees this "genetic coding" as the basis on which literary influences acted and were employed, however, Russo suggests that Sorrentino's explanations of the Italian influences on his work are neither "original nor accurate" ("The Choice," 351).[2] Russo takes Sorrentino to task for misreading Italian culture and suggests that Sorrentino's work shows a fear, if not a denial, of the past which, when he does confront it in his work, is transformed into "monsters, surreal agents," which he then "either castigates . . . or waves his magic wand to make disappear" (345). Russo suggests that "Sorrentino fears emotion whenever the subject of peasant tradition emerges" (349). Indeed, one of the fears Sorrentino has expressed about depicting any aspect of his past in writing is the fear of reducing it to the sentimental.[3] Russo argues that the alternative to late modernism for Sorrentino was "*history*" (354). However, in an early interview, Sorrentino explicitly states that he is not at all interested in recording history. What interests him is creating fiction that cannot be mistaken for reality. The only way to do this, says Sorrentino, is to avoid plots and characters that pretend to be real: "Fiction should work in a fictional way. Fiction is not real, fiction is art. And art, to me, starts with rigorous selection" (O'Brien, "Interview," 9). And so Sorrentino makes no attempt to create narratives that meet conventional expectations; nor does he interpret his work for his reader, the way journalists do by hiding behind the "myth of objectivity." Sorrentino, like his contemporaries of the 1960s John Barth, Donald Barthelme, and

Robert Coover, is more concerned with the process of creating fiction than he is with the product that is produced and so has turned his energies toward creating forms for fiction that challenge traditional schools of writing and reading. In this effort, he writes, his ethnic background has served him well: "The Italians and the Irish hold reality cheap, and the brilliance of the art produced by these peoples is, by and large, the brilliance of formal invention used to break to pieces that which is recognizable to the quotidian eye. . . . The hallmark of the art of both these peoples is a relentless investigation into the possibilities of form, a retreat from nature, a dearth of content" ("Genetic Coding," 264). These attitudes toward form were "lying in wait for me . . . spoke to my genetic memories and permitted me to see my possibilities as an artist" (265). Sorrentino, whether mistakenly, according to Russo, or not, according to himself, uses his ethnic legacy to meet his artistic necessities, which he says are "an obsessive concern with formal structure, a dislike of replication of experience, a love of digression and embroidery, a great pleasure in false or ambiguous information, a desire to invent problems that only the invention of new forms can solve, and a joy in making mountains out of molehills" ("Genetic Coding," 265). This is precisely why, when reading Sorrentino's Italian signs, there can be no mistaking his Italians — who are almost always minor characters — for being anything like the Italians he or anyone else might have ever encountered. This idea keeps Sorrentino out of the business of creating ethnically "responsible" and representative writing and enables him to avoid the traps and burdens that history can place on those who produce narratives in the mythic mode. What places Sorrentino in the philosophic stage of the evolution of Italian American culture is his ability to reject the fiction of experience and renew the experience of fiction by creating novels, which in their anxiety to shed a modernist influence refuse the responsibility of reflecting life, of teaching lessons, of giving people the sense that there are truths out there that can humanize them. This is why we get no sense of the possibility of renewal of Italian American culture when reading Sorrentino. He constructs no myths of origins, and in fact so shatters the traditional methods of story making and telling that there is no mistaking the artifice he creates as a natural transmission of reality.

But how does one read the Italian signs that can be found in Sorrentino's fiction if they are nothing more than synthetic components of his fictional artifices? To those who would approach Sorrentino's narratives looking for connections to a "real" world, these signs would appear to function like the original signifieds to which we might assume they refer. In this case, the Italian signs appear to signify an underlying discomfort, if not a disgust, with Italian American culture; however, Sorrentino's Italian signs are so obviously inferior to any real world referent, and so artfully constructed, that they can only function parodically; his Italian characters are counterfeit caricatures through which Sorrentino some-times makes fun of the urban, street-bred Italian, and at other times shows the foolishness of the supposedly socially and culturally superior "Ameri-can"—the most obvious example of this usage being found in *Blue Pas-toral* (1983). Because Sorrentino has chosen to abandon conventional narrative techniques, thus avoiding the traps inherent in claiming to rep-resent nature with the artificial medium of language, he needs to be read as one would read Barth or Coover, as a word magician, a literary alchemist, and not as reconstructor of reality. In this light, the Italian signs in his work should be read as theatrical props or entertaining puppets, not as real-life actors who reflect the author's attitude. To understand this role of the Italian signs in his narratives, and to get a sense of the evolution of Sorrentino's use of Italian signs, I present a reading of a number of exam-ples found in his first eight novels, from *The Sky Changes* (1966) to *Blue Pastoral*. My reading applies Russo's observation of Sorrentino's poetry to his prose: "The Italian/American imagery is no mere local color, but at the very root of the poet's strategies and language" ("The Choice," 345). In fact, Sorrentino's Italian signs increase in their sophistication, and their role in his fiction becomes more complex and interesting. As we move from *The Sky Changes* to *Blue Pastoral* we can observe that the Italian signs surface slowly—almost from the depths of a lake in his earlier narratives, to riding atop the waters of his later narratives. The Italian signs evolve from the urban underground figures likely to be found in any city's alleys to respectable, if also ridiculous, assimilated members of mainstream so-ciety who might stroll with their pets down Park Avenue.

Counter to the mythic tales of immigration and the idea of the immi-grant as hero, Sorrentino's first novel, *The Sky Changes* (1966; rev. 1986), is, as he has said, about "unheroic loss. The loss of faith in oneself, the loss of friends, divorce. It's about a man's total lack of knowledge of his own desires, his own needs" (O'Brien, "Interview," 10). This novel is bleak and hopeless, and while it can be read as the dark side of Kerouac's *On the Road*, it can just as easily be read as a migrant novel that maps out a dead America from the perspective of a man who fits in nowhere. None of the characters have names. The protagonist is called simply "the husband." There is no sense of a plot; rather, the characters plod from one destination to another as the husband takes his family toward Mexico on a trip during which, he believes, he and his wife can "separate, with manufactured reasons that would never have proved efficacious in the stability of living, together, in one place, the stability of residence" (*The Sky Changes*, 62). The relationship between husband and wife, as the husband believes, has become stagnant through stability. The trip was "their exit, their opportunity" (62) to make it work. Initially he had hoped to enliven their marriage, to save it by moving to a new land where they could make a new life. The trip, characterized as "the tearing out of the rotting roots and the firing of them westward" (4), is financed by the legacy the husband inherited from his dead mother, money that his grandmother "would have laughed to know how [it] was being wasted, how it had brought, so far, only a floundering, and a stupid groping for happiness, away from that city that the money had been earned in, grappled for, starved for, that city where his grandmother had created a hell into which they had all been cast" (25). As the trip progresses it becomes obvious that there is nothing and no place in America that can help this marriage; the wife eventually runs off with the driver of the car, taking along the two children. The husband, alone at the end, purchases a train ticket back to New York, in essence returning to the hell of his past.

The novel is composed of segments that are labeled by the names of the various locations the family visits. Every place becomes an "objective correlative" that reflects the decaying relationship and the inevitable dissolution of the marriage: Washington, D.C., is "the mausoleum" (7); Indiana is a land of "dead, dried stalks" (17); a hotel in Newark, Ohio, smells of "must and rat shit and death that oozes out onto the street" (13); in Oxford, Mississippi (the birthplace of William Faulkner), the "[Negroes] seemed lifeless, crushed, they were concrete symbols of this country that had sullenly slashed its own throat and called the gesture magnificence" (43). Not realistic by design, the novel, as Sorrentino has said, "was simply a way of trying to structure the total degradation and destruction that befalls a family. . . . I tried to speak of that quality of banal disaster in such a way that it would seem complementary with the quality of life in this country" (O'Brien, "Interview," 10). While Sorrentino believes "there are no comic elements in the novel" (O'Brien, "Interview," 11), Russo suggests that there is at least one comic incident, and he links it to the possibility of representing the husband's Italian American background. It occurs in Jackson, Mississippi, when the husband, trying to make a spaghetti dinner, is unable to obtain the proper ingredients: "The store carried no garlic, no Italian sausage, no Italian tomatoes, no tomato paste, no oregano . . . as he looked for these things he found himself asking the manager about each item, and what completely angered him was the fact that the manager looked at him as if he were some sort of strange freak, some Martian. When he finally said, look doesn't anyone ever make spaghetti here, the manager said, look, boy, that ain't fewed" (47). This failure to create an authentic Italian meal denies the husband the possibility of backing up his boasts about "his magnificent spaghetti sauce" (46). The husband settles for American ingredients and is frustrated in his attempts to find wine. The experience also dissipates the lust he had been harboring for his female host. As Russo has suggested, the husband's frustration over locating the proper ingredients for a good Italian meal helps to accent his inability to feel comfortable in any place but the city he left.

The placement, in his first published novel, of this singular Italian American scene presents an interesting insight into Sorrentino's early sense of ethnicity. It suggests the inability of America to deal with "foreign" elements; like the totemic "spaghetti and meatballs," Italian American writing "ain't fewed" for the mind. The established American scene doesn't stock authentic Italian ingredients because it has no need for them. Sorrentino's relegation of Italian Americanness to a single incident in this first novel suggests an attempt (whether conscious or not) to cleanse art of the ethnic signs that might minimize its opportunities for acceptance as American.

In *Steelwork* (1970), Sorrentino creates a series of prose fragments of people who populate a single neighborhood (in Brooklyn) composed of many different characters, some of whom are obviously Italian. For this novel, Sorrentino avoids "telling stories for their own sake" (O'Brien,

"Interview," 12). By avoiding the short story mode through fragmentation, he succeeds in recalling the past without the sentimentality that often accompanies a writer's re-creation of his or her own past. Of *Steelwork*, Sorrentino has said, "If there is tragedy [in this novel], it is the tragedy of trying to live as a human being in this kind of milieu, which is not particularly degrading, but which is deadening" (O'Brien, "Interview," 13). To create this sense of death, Sorrentino never permits a fully developed character to emerge. Jack Byrne aptly refers to the characters of *Steelwork* as "cute little Italian three-wheeled, two-cylinder runabouts" ("Sorrentino's *Steelwork*," 171). One of these "runabouts" is Carmine, or "Carminootch," through whom we see effects of infatuation with jazz and sex. Another, and perhaps the most interesting, Italian American sign is presented in the figure of Artie Salvo (Art Savior, or a salvo at art, or arty salvo), through whom we see the frustration of the "born ballplayer" wounded by the streets, who has no way of connecting to the world outside the neighborhood once his dream of becoming a ballplayer is destroyed. Salvo is either too proud or too stupid to get the "Special Training" offered by the city for people with physical handicaps, and he is doomed to wander the neighborhood limping in and out of people's lives. Salvo, the most sustained Italian presence in the novel, is the kid that Gibby, himself a "dark kid" (and perhaps the character closest to Sorrentino's childhood self), must fight to enter the world of the street kids (120–1). In "Shining Green Coupe — 1938," Artie Salvo is sitting on the car of a "hero . . . fair of hair, blue of eye" (53). The hero throws Artie off the car:

It was the car; the very fact of it. In this year of the depression to have this vehicle. Symbol of home and regeneration, a sock full of golden eagles sewn into the mattress. Our hero had bought stock in America. No greasy haired Dago bastard was going to sully that. Later the hero was drafted and the block learned he was killed in Italy. Perhaps some distant relative of the Salvo family, jovially laughing in that well-known beloved Italian manner, full of wine and pasta, pictures of his curly-haired children in his wallet, dreaming of peace and his little fig grove, had put a Fascisti bullet through his head, relieving him forever of his American dream. (53–4).

Sorrentino uses this Italian American otherness not only to counter the image of the typical American hero, the blue-eyed blond, but also to present an ironic confrontation between the Italian and the American, a confrontation that is played out over and over again throughout the novel as characters identify each other by their ethnic or religious background. These encounters create a tension that pulses through the neighborhood like blood. "Dago, he said to Gibby, you're a Protestant Dago. Not, Gibby said, looking at Pat, bigger, older by three or four years. And he was born on this block. His block. *Not?* Pat said, not a wop? Not a Protestant, Gibby said. But a wop, Pat said. An American, Gibby said, he fumbled, American, like you. I'm *Irish*, Pat said. My mother's Irish, Gibby said" (94). The conflict between Irish and Italian comes to us again through the typical wiseguy, Fredo, a street tough who "never went to school" and "never went home." He steals merchandise from boxcars and change from newsstands, and he beats up Red Mulvaney because he hates the Irish, whom he equates with cops (99–100). This Irish Italian conflict appears in many Italian American novels. It represents the struggle that Italians experienced in their attempts to assimilate into American culture by moving up from the streets and into the penthouses, a process Sorrentino presents in the figure of Eddy Beshary.

None of the characters in *Steelwork* is fully developed, suggesting that the neighborhood does not foster the humanization of its inhabitants. Eddy Beshary, referred to as a "Joo bastid," is the closest thing to a philosopher that the neighborhood can produce. Beshary captures the plight of the novel's characters when he measures human progress in terms of an individual's position in a high-rise: "Menkind must get out of that basement to be happy, get away from these menial tasks he thinks are okay. . . . The improvement of the mind, the richness of reading the dictionary to express yourself. . . . All these things are the key to get you out of the basement and up to the higher floors — to the roof, the penthouse! Money is nothing without culture and learning, who cares about a new suit on a stupid back?" (172–3). If this is the philosophy that captures the neighborhood, then escape is the only recourse for those who want to succeed.

If *Steelwork* represents the world that Sorrentino escaped through the army and education (by following Beshary's advice), then the world re-created in his next novel, *Imaginative Qualities of Actual Things* (1971), presents the alternative to the stifling neighborhood as the world of those who have "culture and learning." In this world, the Italian signs are rare, but they are nonetheless interesting, as in the case of Emanuel Carnevali, who appears in a list of "some things Sheila Henry Grew to Care for: 1966–67" as "probably the most underrated prose-writer of his time" (11).

Carnevali, as William Boelhower tells us, was an avant-garde writer published abroad whose work did not reach the American public because of postal censorship. Carnevali served as an associate editor of *Poetry* and was published in *The Little Review Anthology*. He wrote *A Hurried Man* (1925) and died in 1941 as a result of the encephalitis lethargica he contracted in America, a disease Boelhower tells us was "diagnosed as 'intolerance of the spirit'" (*Immigrant Autobiography*, 138). A version of Carnevali's autobiography, compiled from unpublished chapters of a "novel" by Kay Boyle in 1967, is characterized by Boelhower as "a negation of the quest for a new American self" (*Immigrant Autobiography*, 141). Carnevali, unlike Sheila Henry and most of the writer-characters who populate *Imaginative Qualities*, was not a hack writer but a true literary artist who "was welcomed into the pantheon of revolutionary poets" (Mangione and Morreale, *La Storia*, 361) and then died in oblivion.[4] He is a good example of one immigrant writer who became an accepted artist, the exact opposite of all the pseudoartists that Sorrentino creates in *Imaginative Qualities*.

The only other reference to anything Italian in this novel comes to us indirectly through the character Dick Detective, who marries April, a Catholic whore (*Imaginative Qualities*, 224), who "studied accordion under Mario Cazzo [Italian for "penis"] in Schenectady" (231). As a priest, Dick becomes a follower of Pope Joseph, who gets to throw out the first ball on opening day at Yankee Stadium, and whose speech is represented by an Italianized broken English (230). Dick seduces Sister Rose Zeppole (a *zeppole* is a Sicilian cream puff–type pastry) and later writes a letter to her apologizing for leading her into sin (231–2). These brief and stereotypical uses of Italian culture contrast with the placement of Carnevali and begin to demonstrate Sorrentino's interest in juxtaposing aspects of Italian American popular culture, for which he has an obvious and warranted disdain, with aspects of Italian high culture, which he draws from in creating his narrative strategies and forms.

In his next narrative, *Splendide-Hôtel* (1973), there is one chapter, "M," that contains a few Italian signs, but which, more interestingly, also might shed some light on Sorrentino's attitude toward sentimental abuse of one's ethnic heritage:

One of the clichés of the time is that the very best men — one speaks of course of men who are "in the news" — are those who have not denied their roots. Wearying columnists with souls of excelsior, blank university presidents, distinguished dull-ards in every field — all are constantly battering one concerning the splendors of some lackluster politician who still retains traces of a Jersey City accent, who bravely lays into a huge order of scungilli at some restaurant on Elizabeth street, who puts on a hard hat and screws in a plumbing fixture (badly, of course, as he did when he *was* a plumber). Roots, roots! They address groups of drunken Norwegians in Bay Ridge, tell you of the finer points of bocce, remember fondly those days hustling freight on the North River piers. Somehow, these tenuous connections with their drab backgrounds are commendable. (32)

Years later "M" rediscovers his heritage, an act about which the narrator says, "As soon as he became real, he became false" (32). If there is no sincere way of returning to one's roots, then the only alternative is to distance oneself as much as possible from them. To achieve this distance, Sorrentino often opts for Italian signs when he creates a comic effect, such as his list of the hotel's famous clientele: Giovanni Cazzo (John Prick); "Tab" Jazzetti, the critic; Leroy Calamari; Curzio Sciaccatano; "Tiger" Marconi; Ishmael Melanzana (Ishmael Eggplant);[5] Lance Del Rio; Rocky Polenta; and Brad Cannoli (45). There is also a restaurant named Culo (Italian for "ass" [53]), a name no real Italian restaurant owner would ever use.

The comic use of Italian signs is magnified in Sorrentino's next novel, *Mulligan Stew* (1979). In this novel of "absolute artificiality" (O'Brien, "Interview," 17), Italians are constructed to destroy any notion of mimetic representation that might realistically relate to Sorrentino's ethnicity. Anthony Lamont, the protagonist who is a novelist (and who could be Italian American), has the books in his home inventoried by the characters in his fiction.[6] Among his books are a number by Italian American authors: "*Stolen Fruit*, by Jymes Vulgario" (Hymen Vulgar); *The Dry Ranges*, by Gilford Sorento; *The Model House*, by Iolanda Puttana (Iolanda Whore); *Schultz Is Dead*, by Una Cazzo (A Prick); *Born to Be Italian*, by Myles na gCopaleen (a *cupolino* is a small knitted hat; in Italian American slang it can signify a prophylactic); *Confessions Can Be Fun*, by Vito Calzone, S.J. (31); *My Most Memorable Lunches*, by E. D. Martini; *Those Happy Laughing Sicilians*, by Ruggiero Lupara (a *lupara* is a gun used by Sicilian shepherds to keep wolves away from their sheep; it is also a weapon identified with the Sicilian Mafia); *Directing Plays for the YMCA*, by Giovanni Simone; *A Bridal Idyll*, by A. Bandonado (33); *Venetian Bird*, by Venezia Uccello (the author's name is the same as the book's title); *Life Becomes an Acid*, by A. Dardinella (34). And among Lamont's periodicals are *Italo-American Cafone* (The Italian-American Idiot), *Sicilian Boffs* (*buffo* is Italian for "fool," but *boffs* can also signify "slaps" or "fucks"); *Scaffatune* (35; this could be a variation of the Italian American *schoff*, or "slap"). These signs, while representing the author's desire to have fun and play with the sounds and ambiguities of using a foreign language, also serve to characterize Anthony Lamont's selection of what he consumes of Italian American culture. By doing this, Sorrentino reinforces his notion that fiction is not real and that these Italian signs are evidence of pure invention.

In a segment entitled "Chats with the Real McCoy," an interview that appears in the novel, we get a comical commentary on Italy from the point of view of an American literary figure who imposes his standards on a foreign country, and a reduction of Italian culture to its essential stereotype: "Italy is an impossible country, he insists. He is always outraged by the wild, fruitless gesturing of the people and the continual noise. And the unbelievable food! Nobody can spell *anywhere* in Italy, he decides, except at the Hotel Melanzana. 'Not even Dante — a ridiculously overrated author — could spell. I've been thinking of writing a letter about my researches into this to *The New York Review*, but one hesitates for fear of becoming embroiled in a literary feud with outraged Italians. That city is chockablock with greaseballs'" (38). Such "greaseballs" appear later in the novel in "Flawless Play Restored: The Masque of Fungo," first published by Sorrentino in 1974 and inserted in *Mulligan Stew* as something one of Lamont's characters is given to read. Among the outrageous cast of characters are Signorina Rigatoni, Peter Boffo, Vinnie Pachisi, Italo-American toughs, Ant'ny, and the Audience, which functions like a Greek chorus. While the parody of Italian American popular culture is obvious, Sorrentino also reminds us how artificial these stereotypes really are, as when the Audience calls out: "Sing 'Sorrento'! Sing 'Mama'! Sing 'I Met

Maria in the Pasticceria'! They begin to toy with their gold earrings and to twirl their mustaches" (182). Sorrentino uses Italian characters and Italian American culture to highlight the differences between high culture and popular culture. He uses popular culture to (re)write and thus revitalize high culture. He also plays with the hilarious and musical sounds that the Italian language can produce, sounds Italian American children grow up imitating, often without knowing what the words mean. These signs point to a major change in Sorrentino's attitude toward the role that Italian American culture is allowed to play in his fiction. He invents song titles, such as "My Cazz' Has Got the Hots for Only You" (183) and "My Mamma's Cannoli Was Holy to Me!" (193), and characters like the bawdy Signorina Rigatoni, who calls out, "Zom'body do me, no? Oo wan's do me?"

The most significant use of Italian American presence in *Mulligan Stew* is the Audience of *The Masque of Fungo*, which responds to characters like Susan B. Anthony: "Sing 'Oh, Marie,' you fuckin' puttan'!" then, "*eat large caponato sandwiches and exude great waves of ethnic warmth.*" "Hey, wotta pair o' tits on that broad! Hey baby, trow some up here" (188); their response to a character named The Fuckin Whore is: "'Ey! Trow the fuckin' whore out! Wot kinda fuckin language is dat? I got my mudder's pitcher in my wallet" (189)! Sorrentino's Italians, while used for comic relief, also present an irony of which they themselves are unaware. When Vinnie Pachisi hits Harry the Crab, he says: "I gotta hand it to you mockie basteds! You really take advantage of an education" (197). Eddie Beshary steps in to interpret: "This equine cockaroach wishes to bask in the reflected glow of true scholarship as exemplified by the Job-like figure cut by Mr. Crab. It is unworthy of a Son of Italy," and the Audience responds: "What's that son of a bitch talkin' the Sons of Italy? [the largest fraternal association of Italian Americans in the United States] What is he crazy? He looks like a melanzan' to me!" (*Melanzan* is Italian slang for "black" or "nigger.") "He don't have no goddam respect." They disappear into semi-detached brick houses (198).

When Senator Street, a notorious anti-Italian figure, has a heart attack on Mulberry Street, the Italian characters comment as follows:

Vinnie Pachisi: But the basted wouldn't except the axpirations of the Italo-American community.

Audience (worshipping a bas-relief frieze depicting Mario Lanza, Julius LaRosa, Al Martino, Dean Martin, Lou Monte, Jimmy Roselli, Steve Rossi, Jerry Vale, Frank Sinatra, Enzo Stuarti, Tony Bennett, and Sergio Franchi as the twelve disciples, strong teeth flashing, caught for posterity's delight in an eternally joyous tarantella): How come he never talked up guys like Enrico Fermi?

Jimmy Durante?

Cesare Cazzobianco? (201)

Here, Sorrentino pokes fun at Italian Americans' worship of American crooners of Italian descent. At the same time he raises the question of alternative heroes, such as Enrico Fermi, whom the mainstream rarely, if ever, equates with Italian American culture. Sorrentino then moves back to pop culture Italian with Durante, and concludes with a made-up and quite vulgar name in Cesare Cazzobianco (Caesar Whiteprick). At the ball game where Foots Fungo is playing, the Audience calls out, "'Why don't the bitch at the organ play some Italian songs?' Sniffling, they gaze at photos of Joe DiMaggio. Mothers and aunts in black carry in Bath Beach and hoist it to the ceiling where it becomes a giant tomato plant" (210). Here, a whole section of Italian Americana, Bath Beach, is reduced to the totemic tomato plant, a rich symbol in Italian American culture and one used by many writers.[7] This transformation recalls the use of the tomato plant in Sorrentino's poetry.[8]

Besides the play, a number of Italian signs can be found in the novel in sections such as "Lamont's Scrapbook," in which the answer to "Who Killed Cock Robin?" is "Mafia hit men" (219), and in which there is a line that parodies the popular song "That's Amore" with "When the moon makes you feel like you just et scungill'" (289). All these signs point to Sorrentino's parodic use of Italian culture and are reminiscent of the parody at work in Giose Rimanelli's *Benedetta in Guysterland*. Both writers use Italian culture to create narratives about literature, and not to create narratives about the Italian experience in America. This similar use joins them in ways that separate the two from the romantic and realistic versions of narratives produced in the mythic mode. In the view of Linda Hutcheon, "it both legitimizes and subverts that which it parodies" (*Politics*, 101). Indeed, it seems that Sorrentino can have his connection to Italian American culture and negate it too.

In his next novel, *Aberration of Starlight* (1980), Sorrentino creates his first important protagonist who is partially of Italian descent and expands his use of Italian signs. In fact, the major conflict that Billy, the young protagonist, exhibits is the battle between the Irish and Italian sides of his family. The boy's Italian father, Tony Recco, has abandoned his wife and child. The mother, an Irish American, takes up with a proto-American suitor by the name of Tom Thebus. One of the only stable truths maintained in this novel is that Irish Americans and Italian Americans are incredibly incompatible.

John Paul Russo has pointed out the stereotypical use of the Italian father, who is "associated with sexuality, the unpredictable, anarchy, liberality and betrayal" ("The Choice," 351). This stereotyping appears in another Italian, Guido Pucci, the kid who teaches Billy about sex. But beyond serving as the conduit of Billy's early awareness of sex, Guido provides Billy with the "real" Italian against whose identity Billy can gain his own identity as an American. Guido "was a real greaseball because he was born in Italy." In the school Christmas play, Guido becomes the stereotype "Happy Tony, the fruitstand man. . . . He waved an Italian flag" and sang, "I love to sing and dance and my favorite dinner is spaghetti and meatballs! I come from sunny Italy's pleasant land where grapes and olives grow" (43).[9]

In this novel, the criticism of Italians is left to the Irish characters, who call them "guineas" (45) and "greaseballs" (82). Much of this happens in an extended description of Billy's parents' wedding reception, at which all the Recco brothers are present: Tom, who "talked until he foamed at the mouth" (99); fancy dancing Tony, capped in "that beautiful white Borsalino and [wearing a] tropical suit" (99); Angelo, "as strong as a bull, drank a cup of fresh blood every morning at the slaughterhouse" (99); and Caesar, the intellectual. Marie could have had any of the brothers. Here, Sorrentino exaggerates the cultural differences between the two groups that lead to insurmountable obstacles that the marriage cannot overcome. Later in the novel, the reader is presented with a letter that Tom Thebus has written to Billy's mother in which he says he won't hold her earlier marriage to a "dago" against her. "Did I ever tell you my ex, Janet was also of Italian blood and heritage" (120).

Billy cannot relate well to either side of his family. His grandfather "was blind and he couldn't understand what he said to him, they'd sit together in the backyard while the old man smoked licorice twists Uncle Angelo said were cigars. 'Pop talks that damn Chinese to him all day long'" (42). To later generations, Italian might as well be Chinese, for they are unable to understand it. This inability of one culture to accept the other and of one generation to understand the other appears again in Sorrentino's next novel.

Crystal Vision (1981) is inscribed at the opening with an epigraph from Dante's *Inferno* that tells of the souls who inhabit the first circle of Hell, those who lived lives worthy of reaching heaven but who were either born before Christianity or were not baptized. The epigraph, symbolic of Italian high culture, is juxtaposed with the zany, pop culture figures found in the Italian American caricatures of Ticineti, a gigolo; Santo Tuccio, a consumer and student of pop culture; Cheech (a nickname commonly given to those named Francesco); and a produce man and his helper. The novel is a surreal return to the Brooklyn neighborhood of *Steelwork*. Ticineti, "the famed, the mysterious, the fixer" (*Crystal Vision*, 30), is a man of disguises, rumored to be the produce man, who "often sported a golden earring in his left ear and sometimes wore a long drooping mostachios. Red bandanna. Straw hat. Your usual ginzola starotype. He sang, 'Sorrento' and 'Ciel la Lun'? 'Mamma'? The Drummer asks" (32). Ticineti is the street figure who can turn his ethnicity on and off as he needs to.

Through Mrs. Glynn, née D'Amato, Sorrentino begins to bring up some of the more positive qualities of Italian and Italian American culture. Glynn goes to see Ticineti about her son, who has taken to drinking and hanging out with a bad crowd. She is "deeply upset by all this, especially the drinking. Alcoholism seems to her, as it does to all Italians, totally incomprehensible, as puzzling as parents who don't care about their children" (139). A character named the Arab responds, "Must we again tolerate with benignous good nature and bonhomie in the extreme these clichéd and unfounded mindless cracks about Italians" (139)? The Arab is the first character who comes close to providing Sorrentino's readers with the voice of ethnic consciousness. The Arab's challenge, albeit a fictional challenge in a fictional world, nevertheless enables us to question the superficiality of the Italian signs used by Sorrentino's narrators. Chapter 45, "Cheech's Composition," is an essay entitled "My Favorite Childhood Holiday." It is a nostalgic reminiscence about how Cheech's extended family ("with three Aunt Roses") celebrated Easter Italian style (160). This fond reminiscence of Italian family life is countered by a hilarious street encounter in which young Italian Americans mock Italian immigrants. This juxtaposition of sentimental attachment to an ethnic culture with a contemptuous mocking of it keeps us from determining Sorrentino's real attitude toward his Italian American culture.

In Chapter 67, "The Perils of Advertising," Sorrentino presents the dilemma of misunderstanding between two generations of Italians and points to the cultural conditioning of the children and grandchildren of Italian immigrants by dramatizing the impossibility of their understanding the immigrant generation. This is done through an encounter between several boys and Salvatore, the produce man's helper, "the guy off the boat" who is calling out, in broken English, the names of the fruits and vegetables from atop the horse that is pulling the produce man's wagon (235). Cheech, Fat Frankie, Richie, and Santo Tuccio goad Ticineti into talking to Salvatore in Italian. Ticineti says, "O.K. We'll *all* talk to him in Italian. Hey Salvatore . . . Cosi di Salvatore, hah? Che s'dice the acorn-a squasha? Tutti squasha? Che s'dice 'spesh'" (235). The boys all shout back to Salvatore in a mocking broken English that mimics him. The fruit man, in defense of his helper, calls out, "Faccia di brutto," telling the boys they are making *malafigura*, a bad public show. This only eggs the boys on, and they call out, "DiMaggio calamari e sopresatta . . . Dante Aligheri . . . Camilli rizzuto an' cul'." When the fruit man calls them crazy ("Tutti pazz'") Cheech yells back, "Pazz' your ass. . . . Pasta! you mean. Pasta cicc'! Pasta fagiol'! Galento graziano la motta di pair o'balls-a!" (236).

In this segment Sorrentino captures the later (more Americanized) generations' attitudes toward those who represent the Italians with whom they are often derogatorily associated. Their defense against this association is to publicly offend the greenhorns. The mocking episode, a common occurrence in my own childhood in an Italian community, separates the Italian American from the Italian. It also reveals the shallowness of the Italian culture that remains to these young Italian American street kids. Their sense of speaking Italian is yelling out names of food, sports figures, and pop culture heroes, all incomprehensible to the immigrant produce man and his helper. The result is a nonsensical exchange which to outsiders might seem to be communication, but to those who know the Italian language is easily identifiable as an idiotic dialogue. In this segment, Sorrentino makes his Italian American heritage work for him. The intraethnic conflict points to a major intracultural obstacle that occurs during the process of assimilation, especially when two generations are educated or have come of age speaking different languages. The inability of the street toughs to communicate and thus relate to the immigrants reduces any attempt they might make to understand to nonsensical vocalizations of gibberish. The result is a public display of disrespect that violates the code of *bella figura*. Such behavior is indeed is one of the perils of advertising. This episode is one of the most telling uses of Sorrentino's *Italianità*; while ostensibly comic, it is also culturally tragic. But it also suggests that Sorrentino is both seeing and using the Italian elements of his experience in his narratives with crystal clarity.

In *Blue Pastoral*, Sorrentino presents his most interesting Italian American sign and his most powerful fictional Italianate character in the figure of the dentist Dr. Sam Ciccarelli. Dr. Chick, who can play the stereotype at will and to a purpose, is the produce man of *Crystal Vision* transformed into a respectable professional. Ciccarelli is the one who claims he sent the protagonist, Serge Gavotte, a.k.a. Blue, on a wild-goose chase in quest of the perfect musical phrase. Ciccarelli can turn his Italianness on and off, as evidenced by his ability to shift from "stage 'greaseball' accent, direct from the beloved Hollywood 'films' of the 30s and 40s" (7) to a mainstream use of English. Ciccarelli says his

golden-earring-and-drooping mustachio accent . . . works wonders with idiot WASPs from the clamorous plains and environs, especially when employed at sidewalk feasts like those of St. Anthony, San Gennaro, and Santa Rosalia, by Italo-Americans, all of whom are Ph.D.s. With the accent, a few shrugs and hand talk, and that white smile preceding the well-known and beloved infectious laugh, my countrymen get rid of mountains of eighth-rate "food" that would ordinarily be used to bait rat traps. . . . It is my warm accent, my winning accent, my I-am-so-grateful accent, my great-big-family accent. It is the accent used when some poor contadino is queried by the police as to the source of a few hundred grand in cash found in an old AWOL bag. You get the idea, right? Works something like that other famous speech tic, the brogue. (7).

Ciccarelli is also the figure through which a crazy critique of WASP culture is delivered to the novel's narrator, Dr. Vince Dubuque: "My Christ! You give somebody a monicker like Clark or Mercer or Shuttleworth and he takes to wearing reticent navy-blue ties and talking about economics. That's a joke, solemn one. Can't you stop thinking about your bible-black

Mercedes even for a minute? Ever notice how the WASP face gets like old leather? Sort of like the visage of a debauched Tom Sawyer carved in a white prune?" (8). Ciccarelli ends his talk with *"facciabrutto"* (ugly face) in response to the narrator's comment that it is "odd how, despite our enormous superiority in all things—the criminal and ignorant histories of our forebears, for instance—we find you oddly amusing" (11). Ciccarelli, the first Italian American character in Sorrentino's work who can hold his own in the world of the WASPs, represents the pinnacle of the evolution from the vaguely ethnic husband in *The Sky Changes*. Like Sorrentino, Ciccarelli can do what he has to do to survive in America. He is evidence that Sorrentino has become more reflective of his relationship to his own sense of *Italianità*. Ciccarelli reflects the experience of having two very different worlds to draw from in fashioning a self-identity; he can play the Italian or the American.

Sorrentino's artificial Italians encapsulate aberrant values and behaviors; while caught in the mainstream of American culture, they swim against the current. At times, they represent those who lack the desire, if not the means, to become civilized in the traditional American way— those who live in neighborhoods out of which the only escape comes through "earning a lot of money, joining the army or dying" (O'Brien, "Interview," 11). They are the people Sorrentino had to run away from in order to become an artist, but also those he has returned to throughout his career to prop up his art. Sorrentino, unlike the writers who work primarily in the mythic mode, draws what he needs from his ethnicity to create a body of literature that transcends the confines of little Italy and reaches into the imagination of an entirely different and larger group of readers. While his work has escaped the tradition set up by earlier Italian American writers, he actually extends that tradition by recycling signs of *Italianità* into his narratives.

Don DeLillo's American Masquerade: *Italianità* in a Minor Key

Bill was not an autobiographical novelist. You could not glean the
makings of a life-shape by searching his work for clues. His sap and
marrow, his soul's sharp argument might be slapped across a random

page, sentence by sentence, but nowhere a word of his beginnings or
places he has lived or what kind of man his father might have been.
Don DeLillo, *Mao II*

Unlike the authors I have discussed to this point, Don DeLillo has kept an
almost eerie silence about his Italian American past. In the few interviews
he has granted, DeLillo has surrendered precious little information about
his Italian American upbringing. Once, when asked why so little information is available about his personal life, he replied, "Silence, exile and
cunning, and so on. It's my nature to keep quiet about most things"
(LeClair and McCaffery, "Interview," 80). One interviewer tells of being
handed "a business card engraved with his name and [the sentence] 'I
don't want to talk about it'" (LeClair and McCaffery, "Interview," 79).
The "it," I believe, does not refer so much to his work, as the interviewer
suggests, as it does to DeLillo's name and all that goes with it. In that 1979
interview, DeLillo constantly refers to his desire to "restructure reality," to
"make interesting, clear, beautiful language," and to "try to advance the
art" (LeClair and McCaffery, "Interview," 82). These desires, combined
with the pressures many ethnic Americans face to assimilate into mainstream American culture by erasing all but the most acceptable signs of
their culture, can help us understand the absence of self-referential ethnicity in all but DeLillo's earliest writing.

The absence of literary reference to DeLillo's own ethnic background
both in his interviews and in his writing has been discussed by only a few
critics. In his essay "How to Read Don DeLillo," Daniel Aaron writes,

I think it is worth noting that nothing in his novels suggests a suppressed "Italian
foundation": hardly a vibration betrays an ethnic consciousness. His name could
just as well be Don Smith or Don Brown. His ethnic past does not serve for him as
an "intoxicant of the imagination" (Allen Tate's phrase) in the way New England
Puritanism did for Hawthorne and Emily Dickinson or the experience of being
Jewish did for several generations of Jewish writers. DeLillo can be very funny, but
unlike black and Jewish writers who have sucked humor from their humiliations,
there's nothing particularly "ethnic" about his dark comedy unless we imagine that
traces of the uneasy alien or of ethnic marginality are discernible in his brand of
grotesque parody, his resistance to the American consensus, and his sympathy and

respect for the maimed, the disfigured, and the excluded people in his novels. (68–9)

There is an "Italian foundation" in DeLillo's work, however, and it is a vital basis of the philosophy on which he constructs his narratives. This Italian foundation is more obvious in his earliest narratives. That it rarely surfaces in his later work can be attributed both to DeLillo's growing mastery of the writer's craft and to his ability to mask it by using WASP protagonists. That this masquerade is seldom acknowledged by critics is the result of their inability to construct a culture-specific code for reading the Italian signs that appear rarely, yet consistently, in nearly all DeLillo's published narratives. While Aaron identifies a notable absence of Italian Americanness, and while he points to places where we might find it, he makes no attempt to read the ethnic "traces" that can be located in De-Lillo's work. This is what I will do through a discussion of the Italian signs that appear in two of his earliest published stories and in his first novel. I will conclude my discussion of DeLillo by pointing out the Italian signs that appear in a number of his later works and demonstrate how aware-ness of these signs can generate new readings of DeLillo's writings.

From the little that DeLillo has revealed about his personal life, we know that he was born in 1936 to Italian immigrants, and that he left his working-class, Italian American home to attend Fordham, a Catholic uni-versity in New York.[10] His early life was spent in the urban settings of the Bronx and Philadelphia, where he most likely experienced the type of neighborhoods he describes in a few of his early stories. Of his entire body of published work, only two of his earliest stories are set in a little Itay, and these are the only works that use Italian American subjects as protagonists. The Italian American signs that emerge in DeLillo's later writing are al-most always relegated to the margins of his narratives in the same way that his characters are relegated (or relegate themselves) to the margins of their societies. Of the ten novels DeLillo has published to date, seven contain characters that can be identified as Italian Americans. However, the novels contain any number of ethnic characters who have traits that DeLillo suppresses and at times even erases (or his characters try to erase).[11] Frank Lentricchia reminds us that "DeLillo's heroes are usually in repulsed flight from American life" ("American Writer," 5). Indeed, there is almost always an obvious ethnic character in DeLillo's narratives whose very presence undoes or attempts to undo the knot of American identity. A consistent thread that runs throughout his work is the posing of the question, What does it mean to be American? It is often through the ethnic characters that DeLillo delivers his strongest social criticism. Although Lentricchia is one of the few critics able to read the ethnic signs in DeLillo's work, he never refers to any of the Italian American traces there.[12] In his essay "*Libra* as Postmodern Critique," Lentricchia perceptively points to DeLillo's characterization of Jack Ruby as "an escape hatch back to the earth of the robust ethnic life" (212). Ruby's private world remains "outside the subterranean world of power . . . whose only exit is blood" (213). Countering Ruby's self, which is found in the private world of ethnicity, is Lee Harvey Oswald, whose historical self is lost in the public world of political action. America can make us all Librans, as Lentricchia suggests (210), because it enables us to constantly re-form our selves. For DeLillo, ethnicity and a loyalty to it represent the maintenance of an autonomous selfhood; to maintain a strong ethnic identity is to remain in the ghetto, on the margins of society.

DeLillo is among the most prolific of the writers I examine in this book. Indeed, an entire book could be devoted to analyzing the ethnic signs in his ten novels. In order to demonstrate the effect of his ethnic sign production on his narrative development, I will present readings of his stories "Take the 'A' Train" and "Spaghetti and Meatballs" and the novel *Americana*, along with brief references to aspects of his later work in order to demonstrate the new readings that can be generated when those narratives are contextualized within an Italian American literary tradition.

As is the case with so many writers, DeLillo takes the content of his earliest stories, especially the two I examine here, from his own ethnic "home." In later stories and in his first novel, the content comes from the homes of "others." The primary home in these later works is that of the white, Anglo-Saxon, Protestant American that we find as the protagonist of his first novel, *Americana* (1971). On a formalist level, DeLillo's writing moves from an experience-centered to a language-centered focus, from creating a single, modernist version of truth to the depiction of versions of truth. Accompanying this is a freedom to be whatever one wants by having the ability to reinvent one's self. By not writing a typical bildungsroman,

DeLillo, working in the tradition of high modernism, is able to avoid the burden of history, of one's personal and social histories, which lead to a reification of tradition, the propensity for repetition and the enshrinement of forms. By asserting his individuality through art, DeLillo moves away from the family and the identity gained from it. This movement toward assimilation (certainly a decentering experience), out of little Italy and into big America, expands DeLillo's artistic horizons and enables him to fashion an escape from the bonds of loyalty often demanded by one's filiation. Free from the burden of his own personal tradition, DeLillo can more easily affiliate with the works of Joyce (who, interestingly, also used the Jew to represent social alienation), for example, than with those produced by such Italian American writers as Pietro di Donato. In the eyes of mainstream American readers, this affiliation with Joyce is a far richer intertextual relationship. In the eyes of many marginal readers, however, this may be read as selling out. It is not known whether or not DeLillo was familiar with the narratives of earlier Italian American writers when he wrote his earliest stories, but a look at these reveals that he shares much with his predecessors. "Spaghetti and Meatballs" and "Take the 'A' Train" are heavily loaded with Italian American geography and time and are focused on the burdens that history and family place on the Italian American individual. These burdens, as these early stories suggest, hinder successful participation in American society. Much of DeLillo's work, as Judith Pastore has noted, is colored by his ethnic heritage, even as it reveals his movement away from it.[13]

In her discussion of DeLillo's attitude toward marriage, Pastore never gets specific about how DeLillo's heritage affects, or "colors," his narrative presentations. While she perceptively observes that DeLillo uses divorce to present the decay of family-centered society in America—equating the strong family with Italian American culture—and while she points to the central role that food plays in Italian American culture, Pastore never gets beyond these two stereotypical "ideals" in her analysis. Thus, while she is on the right track in hunting down the Italian signs in DeLillo's work, she never gets to a culture-specific reading of their significance. While many of the self-specific signs of ethnicity found in his earlier work are lacking in DeLillo's later fiction, this early work can be read as rehearsal for some of the more interesting aspects of his later work.

In "Take the 'A' Train," published in 1962 when DeLillo was twenty-six years old, the author portrays the inability of a son to be a son in the traditional Italian way. Angelo Cavallo is a man on the run, like the horse that his surname means in Italian. Cavallo leaves the little Italy where he was born and raised because he is in debt to loan sharks for his gambling. At the opening of the story he is told by his landlord, to whom he owes rent money, that "two men was here to looka for you. Tree times they come today" (9). Knowing that he is a dead man if he stays, Cavallo leaves his "garlic-and-oil Bronx tenement" and hits the streets of a "dead" neighborhood. He sees a subway entrance and heads underground where he plans to "stay . . . and sleep" (10). Angelo is an angel cast out of the paradise his parents had come to from Italy. His pride keeps him from going to his father for help. His only alternative is to spend his time in exile, riding the New York subway system. This scene, in miniature, reappears as the opening scene in DeLillo's *Libra* (3–4), his most controversial novel and the novel that, as Lentricchia points out, helped to draw DeLillo out of his early obscurity ("American Writer," 3).

For days Cavallo rides the underground trains, knowing that it is only a matter of time before he becomes a "bum sleeping on the subway like the bums you see all the time in bars and in the street sprawled like dead men" (10). Cavallo must "stay down . . . down in the dark" (10), where "a man could live his entire life . . . in this compact civilization beneath the earth" (14). Cavallo, in an interesting way, prefigures the characterization of Lee Harvey Oswald that DeLillo creates in *Libra*. Like Cavallo, Oswald believes that "there was nothing important out there."

The language and imagery created in this section of the story create obvious allusions both to the fall of Lucifer and to the fall of Adam and Eve. Banished from his life in little Italy, Angelo is able, for the first time, to really think about his life there. No matter what he encounters on the trains underground, it reminds him of his life in the old neighborhood. When he awakens the next day during rush hour, the people going to work remind him that he can never return to his job as a maintenance man in a Bronx department store because his salary "wouldn't even begin to get him out of the hole" (11). The sight of a blonde woman reminds him of his ex-wife, Helen, the non-Italian, non-Catholic woman he met in 1945 while he was a soldier stationed in England. Angelo married her, much to the dismay of his father, who made life miserable for the couple whenever they visited. And one day, after nine years of marriage, Helen left him for another man. On the train in the present, his thoughts shift back to his wedding reception, which he recalls as "a smiling snapshot of everything he wanted his life to be: a good big slow meal with the wife, then maybe some of the family coming over to play lotto or cards or something; good wife, good family, lots of laughs, lots of beer. . . . No, he would never forget that night. It was one of the few things left to remember" (12–13). Once Cavallo enters the underground, he has nothing left but memories like this one. Throughout the story, his thinking shifts back and forth between consciousness of his present degraded condition and reveries of his past. In an attempt to connect his present condition to the events that led him to this state, he speculates that it might have all begun with his father. "Maybe his father was the beginning of sleeping on trains, and he was saving thinking about him until now, until he had something to hate him for" (15). First of all, Cavallo's father never welcomed his wife, and would taunt them both when they'd come over for dinner: "For why you come here. . . . For you mama's spaghetti because your wife no can cook? Or for your old man's money because you no can find good job? Some son, my Angelo. This country big country. Lots jobs. Even carpenter like me make so much money in one week that in old country I dropa dead joost to look at it" (15). In this exchange DeLillo captures the failure of the son to take advantage of what his father came to America for and suggests that while the meaning of America changes with each generation, the earlier generation has a tremendous influence on the way later generations live their lives. As much as Angelo fears his father, he tolerates the old man who sits "at the head of the table, the throne" (16) because he needs to borrow money from him. It is Helen who cannot take the old man's criticism: "She a stranger, that woman. She is not of us. She no belong here. Why she no give you kids? A woman is to give you kids. She no give kids, she no woman. She no even smell like woman. A bar of soap you are married to, Angelo. She is to wash hands with, that woman. Where you find her; on shelf in English supermarket? I do not make joke. You want to come-a this house anymore, you leave her home" (16). No matter what he does, Cavallo cannot gain his father's approval. He stays away from his parents for three years and tries to forget his father, but he can't.

How do you forget the man who is your father? This was the thing he thought about more than any other during the time of not seeing him; this was the thing he could not do, the forgetting, because too many years went into the making of the memory, too many times of love and hate and fear and love again. This is a turning away that some people can make, he thought . . . a turning away that starts when they are six and sent to some camp on some mountain every summer until they are thirteen when they are sent to something called prep school which lasts until it is time to be sent to college and then to the army and then to marriage; and this is why they never have a mother or father, only a two-headed thing called parents who are only to write letters to, never to touch. There is no love without touching and feeling, he thought. (17)

Cavallo cannot turn away from his parents, just as he cannot deny his dependency on touch even when it hurts. Cavallo recalls his thirteenth birthday, when his father's present was a strange dramatization of the facts of life:

"In this country they read it to their young ones from books with long words. No book I need to tell you this. Take down your pants." . . . His father took the boy's organ in his coarse hand. It hurt. "This is what makes you man. It is not just to go to bathroom with. It is to put into woman. When you are close to woman and touch her and move your hands over her, it will get hard as fist, and burn red like torch. That is all you must know. . . . Remember this day, Angelo. It is the day of your becoming man. It is the day your father made you man." (18)

Cavallo's relationship with his parents is based on a sensuality that his wife is unable to share. After she refuses to make love one night, he returns to his parents' home; a year later Helen leaves him. The overwhelming presence of his father, the patriarch in an oppressive culture that needs no books to transmit knowledge, follows Cavallo through his marriage like a shadow and accompanies him in his flight underground. Cavallo's past tortures him into contemplating suicide, but he can't do it: "For Angelo. Kill myself and I kill them all, all forever, the ones who danced one night for me. No, he could not die that way" (22). He surfaces for a brief period and joins the Saturday night street crowd in Times Square only to realize that he no longer fits in with them. Cavallo, by leaving his past, finds that there is nowhere he can go; he is a man out of place aboveground, and so he returns to the subway. The story ends on "Sunday: the end of the world" (24) with Cavallo recalling his long-ago realization that he could no longer have sex with his wife "without knowing that the old man was coming in too" (25). The presence of his father is so strong that he can never run away from it. DeLillo ends the story with Cavallo on the wrong train, one that moves out of the underground and into the sunlight. Frantically Cavallo runs through the cars toward the rear, with "an immemorial desolate shriek unbending in his chest. As he ran, his right arm was stretched forth, high in the air. The hand was open, fingers straining, as though he were trying to seize one final handful of a darkness black as the universe" (25).

DeLillo reduces Angelo to "nothing but a mind thinking" (24), a man reaching for darkness. Angelo Cavallo, literally an angel on the run, is a man who belongs nowhere, who must remain in perpetual motion, like many of the characters who permeate DeLillo's later fiction. Critic Charles Molesworth notes that "DeLillo's novels begin, again and again, with a solitary man being propelled headlong in a sealed chamber. . . . Many of his characters find their destinies shaped by or expressed not only in place — a room, a hole — but in movement. One way to read a typical DeLillo agent/scene ratio is to see the encasement of young Oswald [Lee Harvey in *Libra*] as that of a bullet that will eventually smash through the dark of America's nightmare" ("Don DeLillo's Perfect Starry Night," 143–44). In running away from the burden of his father-haunted past, Angelo Cavallo is doomed to spend the rest of his life hurtling forward into the light while he gropes for the darkness that grants him the safety of anonymity in the security of belonging somewhere. But what DeLillo suggests in this story is that one can never remove the impact of the past on one's mind, even if one physically removes oneself from the environment that shaped that mind. Read alongside *Libra*, "Take the 'A' Train" can help us to unmask the characters of DeLillo's later American masquerade.

In "Spaghetti and Meatballs," published in 1965, DeLillo paints a classic Italian American still life out of a conversation between two Italian immigrant men. The story opens with Rico Santullo, age fifty-five, sitting out in the street among his belongings. He has been thrown out of his apartment, and his wife has gone off to live with her cousin. Old Man D'Annunzio, age seventy-nine, comes upon Santullo and the two sit and talk. D'Annunzio recounts the story of Mazzoli the chestnut man, who faced a similar situation and tried to kill himself only to be saved by the police. Santullo laments the fact that there is no privacy anymore: "Whatever you try to do there's a priest or a cop to save you" (245). The issue of privacy is one that reappears in DeLillo's later work, but in this story Santullo is the man who has nothing, the homeless man who sits in public among his material goods. Santullo has no plans but to "smoke my guinea stinker" (245). When lunchtime rolls around, Santullo and D'Annunzio hail a neighborhood kid and send him to a grocery store to fetch salami, cheese, pickles, and olives. As they wait for the boy to return, they discuss food and Rico asks D'Annunzio, "What would you eat if you could only have one thing to eat for the rest of your life" (248). The old man answers that he would eat bread, cheese, and wine: "It's simple and yet it is everything. That is all I would need" (248). Rico says his choice would be spaghetti and meatballs and wine mixed with soda. Their choices of typical Italian and Italian American meals reveal both their unfamiliarity with the other foods of America and their dependence on their own culture for sustenance. They, like the father of Angelo Cavallo, remain trapped in their culture of origins, which, while continuing to offer people like Santullo respect even when he has been dispossessed of his home, does not prepare them for life outside their ghetto.

As they eat their lunch, Santullo remarks, "Is this happiness or is this happiness?" (249). But as Santullo turns on a portable radio to soft music, his attitude toward all this changes, as evidenced in his remark, "But this kind of beauty never lasts" (249). D'Annunzio tells him to "think of the present. Of now" (249), and not to worry. Santullo continues his lament, and D'Annunzio urges him to "eat the lunch, enjoy" (249). When Santullo asks what is to become of him, D'Annunzio responds, "Is too complicated. Don't think about it. Eat, eat" (249). But Santullo doesn't take his advice. Instead he offers, "Life is politics. It's politics and no money" (249), to which D'Annunzio adds, "And being alone" (249). Through this interaction DeLillo reveals that these men are trapped by a mentality that was formed by the politics that kept them poor in Italy, that forced them out of their native country; the difference between being poor in Italy and being poor in America is that in America the poor are alienated even from each other. In spite of the fact that America has offered them a better opportunity to earn a living, it still offers them hardly any opportunity to control their destiny. D'Annunzio, content to enjoy the moment, is juxtaposed with Santullo, who stops enjoying it once the radio has been turned on.

As they talk about their lunch, D'Annunzio says that it was good until the end, meaning until Santullo brought out his worries. They smoke a cigar, and the old man falls asleep. The music stops and the stock market report comes on. The story ends with Santullo smoking his cigar as he listens to the announcer summarize the market's action for that day. DeLillo offers no resolution to the story, no Maupassantian twist that points to a moral. Instead, he leaves his characters trapped at the end, like Cavallo in the subway train. This trap juxtaposes the Italian man of the Old World, sitting still and smoking, with the disembodied voice of technology in the New World proclaiming the status of the stock market, which represents the mechanism created by those who control the forces that evicted Santullo and sent him onto the streets. Against the forces that control his destiny, Santullo can only sit still. By ending the story in this way DeLillo is suggesting that a clash of two different cultures has occurred and that the culture of the New World has Santullo worried.

In both stories DeLillo characterizes the Old World–shaped Italians as unable to connect to the world outside their culture. They are limited in their abilities to control their own destinies and thus change their positions in society. The only hope for the immigrant and the immigrant's children is to leave that world behind and forge a new identity that will enable them to thrive in modern society. Cavallo, who escaped the labyrinth of his little Italy, finds that his only option is to remain alone in the maze of the New York subway system. Santullo, who has realized that the reality of the life he has lived is "politics and no money," is unequipped to challenge the world that comes to him from inside the radio, and so must remain just a listener. These Italian characters, unable to actively make their way in the world outside their ghetto, remain frozen in the past. It is no wonder that in his later work DeLillo abandons these Italian prototypes for more American characters able to achieve the power they need to shape the content disseminated by the media. This is the major theme of his first novel, *Americana*.

Before his first novel appeared, DeLillo published a number of stories that reveal his movement away from his ancestral culture and toward the larger, mainstream American culture. In "Coming Sun. Mon. Tues.," published in 1966, DeLillo sketches the antics of a 1960s couple who run away from home. "Baghdad Towers West," published in 1968, tells the tale of a man whose wife left him to "run off with an enforcer for the Mafia" (205). The man sets up house with three women — a sculptress, a model, and an actress — in an apartment complex called Baghdad Towers West. "The Uniforms," published in 1970, features a gang of terrorists who kill, among others, a group of WASP golfers; this story reappears as the opening of DeLillo's *Players* (1977). In "In the Men's Room of the Sixteenth Century," a story that appeared the same year as his first novel, DeLillo creates an undercover cop who, disguised in drag and known on the streets as Lady Madonna, attempts to bring law and order to Times Square nights. These stories suggest DeLillo's movement away from little Italy and out onto the streets of mainstream America. Yet, while he has abandoned the "foreign" protagonist, he has retained the philosophy that underscored that protagonist's presence in his work.

Tom LeClair points out that while DeLillo did not write an obviously autobiographical first novel, he nevertheless drew on his experience as an ethnic American: "If first novels, especially family novels, are commonly autobiographical, a seemingly 'natural' form, *Americana* is intentionally detached from DeLillo's own experience as the son of Italian immigrants living in the Bronx. Rather than offering an account of ethnic assimilation, DeLillo composes a narrative of mainline 'desimilation,' an account originating in leisure and alienation, a life that stands for American middle-class values" (*In the Loop*, 34). The American middle-class values that DeLillo infuses into David Bell, his protagonist, are the very values that the ethnic who wishes to become American must acquire. By exploring the other, DeLillo presents a warning to those who covet Americanness and attempt to remake themselves in the image and likeness of the stereotypical American. DeLillo uses his WASP protagonist to deconstruct the media-made and -controlled myth of the American dream. The natural move for the child of immigrants, as we have seen in the works of Fante, Mangione, and di Donato, is away from the world of the parents and toward the larger world of mainstream America. As DeLillo takes these natural steps away from the immigrant world, he turns his attention away from the past and toward the present and future. By concentrating his creative and critical sensibilities in this direction, he becomes involved in the choices and challenges that face the ethnic self confronted with the dilemma of abandoning the Old World of his or her ancestors for an accepted place in the New World. Unlike John Fante, DeLillo does not wholeheartedly embrace the possibilities of the American Dream. More like Pietro di Donato, he scrutinizes it carefully. In a move that takes him beyond di Donato's outright rejection of the American Dream by the Italian immigrant's child, DeLillo, through his American protagonists, dramatizes the effects of living life the American way. He also redefines America through what he presents as the most American of protagonists. Unlike earlier novelists who present the dangers of assimilation, such as Garibaldi LaPolla (*The Grand Gennaro*, 1935), Guido D'Agostino (*Olives on the Apple Tree*, 1940), and Michael DeCapite (*No Bright Banner*, 1944), DeLillo makes the same point more effectively by using a mainstream persona. By suggesting that becoming/being American is destructive even for the w a s p, DeLillo implies that the idea of the ethnic's desire to assimilate into American culture is ludicrous.

LeClair perceptively identifies DeLillo's invisible ethnic background as contributing to his ability to capture and analyze the effects of contemporary American culture:

Although no ethnics have central roles in DeLillo's fiction, the social distance of his upbringing contributed, I believe, to his double view of American life, its promises and mythologies, an appreciation of its rich potentialities and an ironic sense of its excessive failures. Raised in a world of work and family, DeLillo is in his novels fascinated by the seductions of American leisure and privacy, the needs of entertainment and connection produced by these "achievements," the violence and secrecy that fill the voids of needs unmet. American success for DeLillo also means education in abstraction and technology, preparation for a highly mediated and digitalized life, producing . . . methods for wide understanding and for floating alienation. DeLillo's early social distance may also be partly responsible for his split attitude toward literature: his self-confessed obsession with writing and his recognition of its punishing isolation, his desire to reach a general audience and his suspicion of any entertainment's effect, his need to insert himself into yet remain alien from American life. (*In the Loop*, 14)

The idea that the ethnic American brings a dual view to his experience is one that Jerre Mangione analyzes with particular attention to the Italian American writer in his 1981 essay "A Double Life: The Fate of the Urban Ethnic": "Cultural pluralism means, of course, a quest for identity, a way of resolving problems of duality. But it also has economic implications — that is, the effort of the poor trying to get their fair share of the capitalistic pie. . . . To a greater degree than their parents, the children of the immigrants were truly victims of circumstances, born to live a double life, caught between two sharply differing cultures — that which their parents had brought with them from the Old World and that which was thrust upon them outside the home" (171–2). That DeLillo does not use Italian American characters to make his point does not necessarily disconnect him from an Italian American literary tradition. In fact, his philosophy of America, as expressed through his WASP protagonist, David Bell, is as critical as any put forth in the works produced by Italian American writers using Italian American characters, and it reflects an approach to the question of American identity similar to that employed by earlier American writers of Italian descent.[14] DeLillo manifests this sense of a double life as a struggle between the private and the public, the mob (meaning crowds) and the individual, personal anarchy and public culture, in nearly all his novels.

Americana is David Bell's record of his journey in search of an America other than the New England WASP society into which he was born. Bell is very much at home in mainstream America, whose power structure is populated by WASPs. He is able to rise to a position of power at a young age because he has always fit in with mainstream Americans like those "nice people" who would come to his parents' parties, those who "had no scars or broken noses. They dressed more or less the same. They talked the same way and said the same things, and I didn't know how dull they were or that they were more or less interchangeable. I was one of them, after all. I was not a stranger among them" (*Americana*, 189). While the WASP world might be dull, it represents the realm of success that everyone seems to aspire to. The pressure of fitting into this WASP society is presented through a number of minor(ity) characters in the novel. At a party near the opening of the novel, the host, Quincy, entertains his guests by "telling a series of jokes about Polish janitors, Negro ministers, Jews in concentration camps and Italian women with hairy legs" (5). Enlightenment is demonstrated by how loudly one laughs: "It was meant to be a liberating ethnic experience. If you were offended by the jokes in general, or sensitive to particular ones which slurred your own race or ancestry, you were not ready to be accepted into the mainstream" (6). At the same party, a nondrinking Pakistani Muslim holds a glass so that others will not "think me too solemn and undeviating an individual" (8). The only people free to be individuals are WASPs like David Bell, who became a high school sports star by "being first in scoring, last in assists" (91), that is, by being an individual.

David has been groomed for success by his father, Clinton Harkavy Bell, a success in the world of advertising and himself the son of Harkavy Bell, "one of advertising's early legends" (132), who knew how to take advantage of "a good American name" (197). David's father studies television commercials at home with his children. It is through him that David learns of the American Dream, which requires that "you save, you finagle, you invest. You work yourself up to x-amount of dollars and if you plan well and get lucky in the market you can begin to build something for your family. That's what makes a democracy worth all the sweat and corruption. Security for your wife and children after you're gone. . . . That's your job as head of a family in a free republic" (152). But the world Clinton lives in keeps him alienated from much of America. He cannot understand why his train home from work is attacked by Puerto Rican and Negro kids from Harlem and Italian kids from the south Bronx who pelt the train with rocks. He asks, "What did we ever do to them?" His daughter answers simply, "You moved to the suburbs" (155). What Clinton does not realize is that he represents what those kids have been conditioned to want and what they are kept from having by the very system he has helped to create. As Ken Wild, David's friend from college, says later in the novel, "Systems planning is the true American artform" (265). David reconstructs the key to the system used by the electronic media in the section of his autobiographical film that represents his father. The actor playing his father tells the camera that advertising and TV create a system that makes a person "want to change the way he lives" (270): "It moves him from first person consciousness to third person. In this country there is a universal third person, the man we all want to be. Advertising has discovered this man. It uses him to express the possibilities open to the consumer. To consume in America is not to buy; it is to dream. Advertising is the suggestion that the dream of entering the third person singular might possibly be fulfilled" (270). America's greatest achievement, as David's script reads, is that it has "exploited the limitation of dreams" (271).

On his graduation from a California college where he studied film, David is offered the choice of three jobs arranged by his father: two in advertising and one in the mailroom of a television network. David chooses the mailroom job to avoid "following too closely in his [father's] footsteps" (34). He moves up from the mailroom in near-record time and enters a work environment that is populated by employees with hyper-Anglo-Saxon names like Weede Denney, Richter Janes, Quincy Willet, Grove Palmer, Jones Perkins, Reeves Chubb, and Theodore Francis Warburton. This monolithic crew of WASPs controls the programming of the network. David creates *Soliloquy*, a network television show that "consisted very simply, of an individual appearing before the camera for an hour and telling his life story" (24). After the show is canceled without reason, David prepares to produce a documentary about the Navajo Indians. On his way out to meet the film crew, David gathers a woman sculptor, known only as Sullivan; an alcoholic named Jack Wilson Pike, whom Sullivan describes "as American as a slice of apple pie with a fly defecating on it" (47); and novelist Bobby Brand, a Vietnam veteran who is trying to eliminate the slang from his vocabulary because "it's insidious. It leads to violence. . . . I want to be colorless" (113). David is drawn to these people because he wants to become an artist; however, he learns that Brand is a "novelist" who has written nothing, although he talks of a novel-in-progress called *Coitus Interruptus*, which features a WASP ex-president who is turning into a woman. The new president is black, "hip and magical." "The theme is whatever you want it to be because appearance is all that matters. The whole country's going to puke blood when they read it" (205).

The group halts its westward trek in Fort Curtis, a midwestern town in which David begins to make his autobiographical film using the town's residents as actors. He gets so caught up in the enterprise that he fails to meet the network's television crew and is subsequently fired. From Fort Curtis he begins hitchhiking west and is picked up by Clevenger, a Texas entrepreneur who drives a lavender Cadillac. Clevenger drops him off near a "sci-fi oriented" (357) community consisting of white kids who refuse to become "part of the festival of death out there" (355) and so live near eleven Apache Indians, "exiles from an Apache tribe, who refused to become ranchers like the rest of their people" (355). The group has no idea what the Indians do other than play poker. The group's founder is a tall white man with blue hair called The Incredible Shrinking Man, who describes their philosophy as conservative: "We want to cleave to the old things. The land. The customs. The words. The ideas. Unfortunately wilderness will soon be nothing but a memory. Then the saucers will land and our children will be forced to embrace the new technology" (358). Clevenger returns to carry David back to civilization and offers him a job testdriving tires for his company, which is organized so that "the Mexicans did most of the driving, the blacks most of the tire changing, the whites most of the balancing and measuring" (370). When David tells Clevenger that he wants to drive and change tires, Clevenger just looks at him "in anger at all dumb-ass northern guilt and innocence" (370). David leaves Texas after witnessing a drunken orgy performed by Clevenger and two of his white assistants with three Mexican women. After a series of strange rides he uses his American Express card to fly back to New York.

Americana is a novel about language and its role in representation. On the one hand, language conditions as it creates consumers; on the other hand, when analyzed carefully, it can be used to deconstruct ruling myths that create, organize, and control mass realities. The same country that has made David Bell enables him to remake himself in the likeness of those who are different. In this novel DeLillo may have abandoned the use of Italian American characters to talk about such themes as alienation, difference, and relationship to family and history, but he has simply found a different way of presenting the same issues he worked with in his early stories.

In *Americana* we find two representations of Italian Americans who, while both minor characters, set up ways of being that challenge the w a s p experience in David's America. The first is Tommy Valerio, Bell's best friend, whose "mother would squeeze my cheeks and rub her knuckles on my head" (134). This touching "embarrasses" him and makes him uncomfortable around the Valerios, so that he "soon found excuses to stay away" (134). Tommy introduces David to the police chief's daughter, "who was available for experiments of all kinds" (134). The two "take turns" with her in the back seat of Tommy's car. Tommy appears in one other scene, hitting fly balls for David to catch. The experience, David recalls, was one of being "nobody. I was instinct and speed and a memory that extended back for no more than seconds. That was all" (199). There is a similar scene at the end of the novel, when David plays catch with an Indian boy, an experience of which he says, "I could not recall feeling this good in many years" (359). Later, when David tries to contact Tommy, he learns that Tommy was killed in the Vietnam War and that his family has accepted the death and is impressed by a letter the president sent to Tommy's mother.

The second representation of an Italian American is Arondella, a mysterious character who could be a racketeer (the likes of which Richard Conte plays in the film *Cry of the City*), with whom David's sister runs away from home. Arondella, as Mary tells David, is a hit man she met in Boston. She is running off with him because "there are different kinds of death. . . . And I prefer that kind, his kind, to the death I've been fighting all my life" (163). Mary encourages David to leave home because the place is "haunted" and their mother, who is deathly ill, will "try to take you with her" (164). Arondella is re-created in David's autobiographical film through Mary, who is played by Carol Deming, a Fort Curtis woman.

His sense of insult was overwhelming. If someone used an obscene word in my presence, he demanded an immediate apology. He always got it, of course, his reputation being what it was. He was prepared to kill, quite literally to kill, in order to avenge the honor of someone he loved. He was always swearing on his mother's grave. In his company of men, there was no greater promise or proof of honor than to swear on your mother's grave. . . . He told me about a friend of his called Mother Cabrini. Cabrini got a lot of mileage out of his mother's grave until it was learned that his mother was not dead. Telling this, he managed to be both outraged and amused. They were all children, of course, but not in the same way the rest of us are children. We have learned not to be afraid of the dark but we've forgotten that darkness means death. They haven't forgotten this. They are still in the hills of Sicily or Corsica, wherever they came from. They obey their mothers. They don't go into a dark cellar without expecting to be strangled by a zombie. They bless themselves constantly. And us, what do we do? We watch television and play Scrabble. So there it is, children of light and darkness. (278)

What David and Arondella have in common, despite their different up-bringings, is the "instinct that death is without meaning unless it is met violently" (280). Arondella represents a world that is dark and full of superstition, an in-your-face world that knows how to deal with death, and thus with life.

Through Tommy Valerio and Arondella, David creates identities that serve as alternatives to his WASP world. They represent the sensual other toward whom David moves as he "de-similates." These characters, like the other non-WASPs that David encounters, offer alternative philosophies. Like the Indian Black Knife, of whom Sullivan speaks; Dr. Hiroshi Oh, David's college professor of Zen; and the Mediterranean woman he and Brand run into at an A&P (206–7), these people represent salvation to the systematized American. As Sullivan says, "America can be saved only by what it is trying to destroy" (256). By the end of the novel David believes that by turning away from corporate America and toward art he has achieved his ultimate goal of becoming "an artist as I believed them to be, an individual willing to deal in the complexities of truth. I was most successful. I ended in silence and darkness, sitting still, a maker of objects that imitate my predilection" (347). Thus, the solution for David Bell lies in creating art and through the process re-creating a self that can be separated from the past. DeLillo, like Sorrentino, sees becoming an artist as a way out of the history that attempts to shape his protagonist's personality.

Signs of *Italianità* and references to identification with other cultures surface in some way in nearly all of DeLillo's later work, more often than not through minor characters. *Great Jones Street* has a writer named Carmela Bevilacqua and Azarian, who is into soul music and the Black experience (a version of Norman Mailer's "white nigger"?). In *Ratner's Star* there are characters such as Lepro, who uses a word that means both "why" and "because" (as does the Italian word *perchè*), and Lo Quadro and Consagra. In *Running Dog* there is a cop named Del Bravo and the Talerico brothers, Paul and Vinny the Eye, who as members of organized crime belong to families, and "families know where they belong" (220). The narrator's identification of Italians with families and the CIA with organization replicates the dilemma presented in *Americana* of the system versus the family. In *The Names*, Volterra is an artist-filmmaker who serves as the protagonist's alter ego. In *White Noise* there is Alfonse "Fast Food"

Stompanato, the head of a college's Popular Culture Department, and Grappa, both of whom represent assimilated Italian Americans. In *Libra* there is the mafioso Carmine Latta, and again DeLillo refers to the CIA as the company and the Mafia as the family. DeLillo uses these minor characters — who often appear more as caricatures — as foils against which he creates an identity for his protagonist. Although the Italian American signs seem to have disappeared altogether from his latest novel, *Mao II* (1991), and his latest short fiction, *Pafko at the Wall* (1992), a novella published in *Harper's*, and "The Angel Esmeralda" (1994), a short story published in *Esquire*, he continues to present the struggle between the private and the public, the individual and collective life, as the great challenge that faces every American.

In much of DeLillo's writing there is reference to the breakdown of family and the subsequent cultural fragmentation that forces people to forge identities out of materials that are presented to them from outside the family. Without the family, the Italian American can become a cultural chameleon, affiliating with whatever he or she chooses.[15] In terms of Italian American culture, DeLillo's abandonment of the Italian American as a subject of his writing suggests the decline of a distinct *Italianità*, which has assimilated into the larger American culture that in the Vichian scheme of nationalism is in decay; it is a culture that leads nearly all of his protagonists to search for a better life in the margins of society.

Though DeLillo has successfully left behind the Old World and the myths that immigrants have created in the New World (for, as Lentricchia says, "writers in DeLillo's tradition have too much ambition to stay home" ["American Writer," 2]), his departure is guided, if not haunted, by proverbs such as *Chi lascia la via vecchia sa quello che lascia ma non sa quello che trova* (Who leaves the old way for the new, knows what is left behind but not what lies ahead), and he may belong more to the Old World than one might think, especially if one recalls some of the proverbs that guided public behavior in southern Italian culture: *A chi dici il tuo secreto, doni la tua liberta* (To whom you tell a secret, you give your freedom); *Di il fatto tuo, e lascia far il fatto tuo* (Tell everyone your business and the devil will do it); *Odi, vedi, e taci se vuoi viver in pace* (Listen, watch, and keep quiet if you wish to live in peace). Looked at in this light, DeLillo's writing is perhaps more closely aligned with the traditional southern Italian idea of keeping one's personal life to oneself, an idea that Dante proposes when he writes in his *Convivio* that speaking of the self is improper.[16] Strategically, DeLillo avoids breaking a personal and an ancestral *omertà* by employing the narrative strategy of speaking through the persona of the other, by creating a masquerade in which his ethnicity can enter the mainstream without detection.

While the Italian signs are not always visible in the works of writers in the philosophic mode, these authors do represent the struggles that occur within a national culture that has reached its decadent period in the Vichian cycle of history. Although the narratives of Gilbert Sorrentino and Don DeLillo do not replicate the historical experience of Italian Americans, they nevertheless contribute to our understanding of the process by which Italians have assimilated into American culture and by which they have gained a cultural authority that enables them to choose how they relate to and reform the artist's relationships to Italian and American cultures. While both authors have managed to avoid being labeled as ethnic writers, they have achieved their American status by different means. Sorrentino reaches into his experience as an Italian American and pulls out the stereotypes, the clichés, and the signs of Italian Americana and uses them to inscribe his narratives in comedic ways that might have drawn flack from Italian American antidefamation organizations had his work reached such an audience. By employing such techniques, Sorrentino effectively places himself between the Italian and the American worlds. While DeLillo projects some of the same Italian American elements onto the page, he does so by attributing these to marginal characters who are not easily identified with the Italian American experience. DeLillo's subtlety comes as characters attempt to become other through such acts as changing names, as his characters so often do.[17] What these two authors share are narrative strategies that employ a more philosophically formulated content which reminds us that fiction, like criticism, is as much about concealing the visible as it is about revealing the invisible.

Epilogue

Mary Caponegro: (Re)forming *Italianità*

While traditional signs of *Italianità* might be more difficult to detect in the work of contemporary writers who do not use Italian American characters, settings, or themes, Italian signs have not yet disappeared altogether from their work, and until they do, if ever, these signs require codes by which they can be read. As the following look at the narratives of Mary Caponegro demonstrates, there are contemporary writers whose narrative work is informed by a reformed sense of *Italianità* based on, among other things, new encounters with contemporary and historical Italy.

The short stories of Mary Caponegro represent the effects of advanced assimilation on the contemporary American writer of Italian descent. Lacking early influence from the Italian half of her heritage (she is Italian American from her father's side, and German American from her mother's side), Caponegro's writing, not surprisingly, contains few signs of *Italianità*. Unlike Sorrentino and DeLillo, she did not grow up in an Italian American urban ghetto. Her education at Bard College and Brown University extended her distance from possible connections with Italian American influences. She has studied with the likes of John Hawkes, Robert Coover, and Robert Kelly, and thus is more likely to reveal a connection to the work of Sorrentino and DeLillo than to that of the other writers discussed in this book. Her stories have earned a number of major awards: a 1988 General Electric Foundation Award for Younger Writers, and in 1991, the prestigious Rome Prize from the American Academy of Arts and Letters in New York, which enabled her to return to the land where her father's parents were born, where she reconnected with the Italian heritage she says her father did his best to suppress.[1] According to Blossom Kirschenbaum, who is currently completing a study of Rome Prize winners, Caponegro is the first Italian American woman to be awarded the prize.

On the surface, the fiction of Mary Caponegro has much in common with that of Gilbert Sorrentino and Don DeLillo. Like Sorrentino's, her fictions are strongly antimimetic and often contain unreliable narrators. Like DeLillo, she creates characters who have uncomfortable and ambivalent relationships to the past. In "Materia Prima" she deals with a major theme in her writing thus far, a child's difficulty connecting to her past and the establishment of a strong sense of identity as an individual through intellectual and sexual development. As her protagonist, Clara, remarks, "how important for development of one's own self is the way we grow away from one another, declare ourselves other, apart, so as to have the means to craft within ourselves our own identity" ("Materia Prima," 71). Clara attempts to connect herself to her extended family's ritual Thursday gatherings, at which the past was often discussed. The presence of the children was tolerated, but less so their participation. The child narrator recalls, "The maxim that stipulated children be visual nonaudible entities ruled our home, and if it was less the case in my cousin's, when in Rome they did as we did" (49). Her failure to participate in the creation of family memory leads her to "devote myself to the study of the natural sciences," which would provide her with "a factual foundation, inviolate against them, to compensate for my failure to achieve participation through the more subjective element called memory" (55).

In much of Caponegro's work, the mind is or becomes a mirror of the body. Her use of a Maurice Merleau-Ponty quote, "The perceiving mind is an incarnated mind," as an epigraph to her *Tales from the Next Village* (1985) is a signpost that points the way to reading much of her work. For Caponegro, body is soul. In "The Star Café" and "Sebastian," intellectual activity is often a form of sexual foreplay, and sexual activity is often depicted as a field for intellectual games. This treatment of the relationship between mind and body, intellect and sex, recalls the writing of Pietro di Donato, especially his novel *This Woman*. Caponegro has unknowingly rewritten di Donato's macho male–dominant philosophy by reversing the traditional roles of men and women. As Kirschenbaum points out, one reviewer has juxtaposed her fiction to the visual antics of the pop figure Madonna and comes to the conclusion that Caponegro's fictions "don't quite serve, they break off; they shiver, like Madonna, in disembodied lust" (Eder, 9). While the connection to Madonna might seem facetious and au courrant, that reviewer, Richard Eder, has stumbled onto what could be the most useful way of viewing Caponegro's connection to a new development in Italian American culture. Caponegro's fiction, Kirschenbaum notes, "incorporates a new paganism of magic, animism, and folk

wisdom with hints of cargo-cult and fire-next-time sci-fi religion, bursting
through conventions to explore relationships between man and woman as
well as other primary ties" ("Mary Caponegro," 8). In effect, Caponegro's
fictions evidence something that we often find in the autobiographical
work of Italian American women, a struggle to forge a free self in a
patriarchal system. The first major autobiography by an Italian American
woman was *Memoirs of a Beatnik*, by Diane di Prima. Published in 1969,
Memoirs opens with the violation of two traditional taboos based on the
two social codes *bella figura* and *omertà*: she *talks* about *sex* in public.[2] This
text represents the definitive fracturing of *omertà* that, as Helen Barolini
explains so well in her introduction to *The Dream Book*, has been the
cultural force behind the public silence of Italian American women. While
Memoirs does not constitute a traditional autobiography, it can serve as
an urtext of sorts through which we might read the sexual personae of
women like Madonna and Camille Paglia. It is in this light, then, that the
fictions of Caponegro, lacking in superficial signs of *Italianità*, can be
connected to the underlying philosophy of the writing of Italian American
women.

In her novella "Sebastian," included in *The Star Café* (1990), Caponegro plays with the Italian Catholic iconography created around Saint
Sebastian, the protagonist's namesake. As Camille Paglia points out in
Sexual Personae, the many depictions of Saint Sebastian are manifestations
of "the ancient chthonian mysteries [which] have never disappeared from
the Italian church" (33). Sebastian, a lapsed Catholic, is hounded and
haunted by the imagery of the seminude depiction of the saint filled with
arrows. The male-female interaction in this story happens between a couple engaged to be married: Sarah Zeidman, a Jewish American artist, and
Sebastian, an emigrant from England to America. Sebastian, a business-
man and would-be writer, is driving to the airport to fly off on a business
trip. On his way, he stops at the cleaners to pick up a pair of pants that were
not returned with a suit he had had cleaned (which Sarah had picked up).
The rest of the story takes place in Sebastian's mind, supported by Aristo-
telian philosophy and badgered by a strong sense of alienation, both from
American culture and from the ritualistic history of Jews. Sebastian plays
with language but can never make it work in the way that Sarah is able to
make everyday American materials work in her art. His accent, which

marks his foreignness and betrays his "invisible immigrant" status, is characterized as that which "seduces surface," as something Sarah "would reduce him to" ("Sebastian," 123). The struggle then becomes one between the accomplished American Jewish artist and the immigrant "would-be" artist whose past constantly interferes with his ability to consummate anything but the sexual level of their relationship. Sebastian, unlike Sarah, who is comfortable (and somewhat obsessed) with the Marianist Catholic imagery and the ideas associated with the historical depictions of the Madonna and Saint Sebastian, is uncomfortable during a trip, which occurs entirely in the maze of his mind — a "chthonic journey only Eros could redeem" — and is left trapped in an elevator between floors in the building that houses Sarah's studio. This struggle between Mediterranean-based and Anglo-based cultures is the closest Caponegro comes to depicting the conflict between the Italian and American cultures.

Caponegro is more interested in gender issues than in depicting the tensions and conflicts brought out by a character's relationship to his or her ethnicity. In fact, ethnicity is characteristically absent from nearly all of her stories: many of her characters are either nameless or are known only by first names. One exception is her placement in China of a series of "folktales" in her "Tales from the Next Village," tales reminiscent of the oral tales that foster the development of literary traditions in any culture. Caponegro creates very strong female archetypes, in the manner of Maxine Hong Kingston's "No Name Woman," in tales that are strange twists on ancient wisdom. In the tale "IV" a woman ties herself, with permanent knots she learned from studying flower arrangements, to a yew tree. Her lover first thinks she does it for attention and orders her to untie herself. When she refuses he tries but cannot untie her. While he frets about her, she chants to the tree, "O noble yew, I bind to you to make myself strong, let me become your firm-rooted majesty" ("IV," 7). After seven nights of troubled sleep, the man keeps a vigil "as one attends the loved one's death bed, to know the exact moment of transition" ("IV," 7). The next morning the village finds the man entwined among the tree's branches; the woman is no longer visible. Through these tales Caponegro reveals a keen sense of the function of the folktale in forming gender consciousness. Her use of the form suggests an attempt to reform contemporary attitudes toward women.

If it were not for her surname, an obvious Italian signifier, one would never suspect Caponegro's ancestral connection to Italy by reading her fiction.[3] However, while the writing she has published thus far reveals no visible signs of *Italianità*, her experience in Rome, which she says helped her reconnect with the Italian side of her family, has become the basis for a number of stories she plans to publish as her next collection. Caponegro, as Kirschenbaum points out, is one of "[t]hese new American Italians, acquainted with earlier achievements, [who] realize that Italy has been changing, the U.S.A. has been changing and the implications of being 'Italian' in America have been changing. They know how easy it is to travel between two countries; they may be at home in both and even have two *patrie*" (10).

If writers such as Mary Caponegro do not write narratives about the Italian American experience, they nevertheless signify a sense of *Italianità* in their writing. While it might be important to Italian Americans such as Gay Talese to see best-selling novels come out of the Italian American community, what is important for the American writer of Italian descent is simply to write. When Talese asks why Italian Americans have fared better in the motion picture industry than in the print media market, he is inviting an unnecessary and useless comparison with other ethnic and racial cultures. Creating art in America is difficult work. And when critics begin dividing writers into teams based on race, ethnicity, gender, sexual orientation, or regional identities, the result is a destructive mode of discourse that leads only to shouting matches and the disintegration of shared notions of artistic achievement. The fact that a number of American film directors and pop culture stars of Italian descent have "made it" in American culture has nothing to do with why writers from the same ethnic backgrounds have not. Certainly one could point to the stronger relationship between storytelling in the oral tradition and storytelling in the electronic media, and could note that Italians emigrated en masse to the United States during a period when the electronic media were revolutionizing the way Americans process information, to explain why there are so many Italian Americans working in the mass media. One could also point to the patriarchal dominant family, to the cultural code of familial *omertà*, and to the immigrant's distrust of public institutions and the written word to suggest why Italian Americans experienced a delay in developing their literature. But none of these excuses should matter to the individual writers. Directing attention to and rewarding artistic productions have never been the jobs of the artists. These tasks belong to social institutions. As Italian Americans begin to gain political power and to recognize their writers as necessary to the survival of their culture, then, perhaps, they will reward these writers by purchasing their art, by establishing centers for study, by creating publishing opportunities, and by preserving their papers.[4] In the meantime, American writers of Italian descent will continue to produce literature, either visibly or invisibly as Italian Americans, that will address anyone who takes the time to read it.

Some Final Thoughts

While the systematic approach that I have fashioned out of Giambattista Vico's evolutionary stages of culture indeed predicts the eventual conclusion to a *corso*, there are many ways to view the transition into the *ricorso* of Italian American culture, and any sweeping conclusions drawn at this stage in my work would be premature. I believe that the study of any ethnic culture, especially one's own, is part of an ongoing process of education. Such study needs to be done in ways that avoid ethnic chauvinism and promote what Richard Gambino has called "creative ethnicity." In *Blood of My Blood*, Gambino presents the dilemma that today's Italian Americans face: they can become "jelly fish Americans — transparent souls in surface pursuits," or they can become chauvinistically ethnocentric. His answer to this dilemma is creative ethnicity, which he defines as the "revitalization of Italian-American traditions and the contribution in a new form to an enriched American culture" (327). The creative ethnicist uses "his ethnic background as a point of departure for growth rather than as proof of his worth," and "gains insight into himself that gives a sense of meaningful, realistic self-control of one's life." Gambino calls for an "educated ethnic awareness that will provide the creative ethnicist with identity, energy and direction" (362).

I hope that in the preceding chapters I have answered Gambino's call by breaking new ground in the establishment of ways to historicize and read Italian American literature and its relationships to Italian and American cultures. There is a way to read the Italian signs found in the narratives of American writers of Italian descent. Whether consciously or not, these writers have fashioned a tradition of Italian American literature that will reward those who continue to examine it. There are many novelists and short story writers, both living and dead, whose work could have been used to illustrate my arguments. Michael Anania, Tony Ardizzone, Dorothy Bryant, Mary Bush, Diana Cavallo, George Cuomo, Michael and Raymond DeCapite, Rachel Guido de Vries, Albert DiBartolomeo, Robert Ferro, Rocco Fumento, Anthony Giardina, Daniella Gioseffi, Josephine Gattuso Hendin, Garibaldi LaPolla, Sal LaPuma, Frank Lentricchia, Susan Leonardi, Renee Manfredi, Carl Marzani, Kenny Marotta, Eugene Mirabelli, Anna Monardo, Ben Morreale, Joe Papaleo, Jay Parini, Lisa Ruffolo, Anthony Valerio, and Robert Viscusi have all produced significant narrative writing that could easily have been the subject of this book. Their absence here is perhaps the greatest reason why my work should be seen as the beginning of my contribution to the larger effort of establishing an awareness of the great and varied contributions that American writers of Italian descent have made to American culture. Similar studies are needed on the contributions to American poetry of Felix Stefanile, Diane di Prima, Lawrence Ferlinghetti, Gregory Corso, Gerard Malanga, Maria Mazziotti Gillan, Rose Romano, and Dana Gioia; and also on the cultural criticism of Louise DeSalvo, Luigi Fraina (Lewis Corey), Sandra Gilbert, Edvige Giunta, Barbara Grizzuti Harrison, Josephine Gattuso Hendin, Frank Lentricchia, Marianna DeMarco Torgovnick, and Camille Paglia.[5]

The challenge to contemporary American writers of Italian descent will be deciding not so much where their loyalties as intellectuals lie (Do they join Constantine Panunzio, Jerre Mangione, and Helen Barolini in politicizing their narratives by speaking for their culture, or follow Pascal D'Angelo, Pietro di Donato, Gilbert Sorrentino, Carole Maso, and Mary Caponegro and seek a place in American culture as artists?) but how to fashion an identity as artists out of influences provided by both Italian and American cultures. We can expect that as long as there is an Italy, as long as there is a memory flavored with *Italianità*, there will be American writers of Italian descent whose contributions to American letters will add new dimensions to what it means to be American and whose work will require critics able to negotiate the Italian signs found on these American streets.

Notes

Introduction

1. In *Proletarian Writers of the Thirties* (1968) David Madden does pay attention to Louis Fraina, also known as Lewis Corey. But Fraina, while he wrote some of the earliest Marxist cultural criticism produced in this country, concentrated his efforts on social, economic, and political analysis and did not write fiction. Paul Buhle has written on Fraina, *Dreamer's Paradise Lost.* I deal with Fraina's writing, especially his antifascist writing, in my article "Italian/American Literary Responses to Fascism."

2. See Fraina's obituary, "Lewis Corey, 1894–1953," *Antioch Review* 13.4 (1953): 538–45.

3. In one of his few directly antifascist articles, "Human Values in Literature and Revolution," Fraina speaks out against fascism and argues that the only good literature is that which concerns "itself primarily with consciousness and values, with attitudes toward life" (8). Of the literature of his time that does this, Fraina notes three types: "the literature of capitalist disintegration," "the literature of fundamental human values and defense of those values," and "the literature of conscious revolutionary aspiration and struggle." Fraina saw fascism as "the final proof" that "in any period of fundamental social change, particularly as the old order decays, there is an increasing degradation of human values" (8).

4. One key stage in the risorgimento of Italian American studies occurred in 1967 through the founding of the American Italian Historical Association, which, while not dedicated to literary studies (its founding members were primarily historians and sociologists), did welcome and encourage literary analysis and dedicated its second conference to the Italian American novel. It is through that association that some of Italian Americana's best literary criticism has come to be known, especially through the contributions of Robert Viscusi and John Paul Russo.

5. Olga Peragallo, a student of Giuseppe Prezzolini's at Columbia University in the 1940s, was the first to attempt to gather the names and works of Italian American writers. Her *Italian-American Authors and Their Contribution to American Literature* was edited by her mother and published posthumously in 1949. Prezzolini wrote the preface to this first attempt to historicize American authors of Italian descent.

6. Here I am thinking of critics such as Daniel Aaron and William Boelhower.

7. The indigenous critics who have dealt with Italian American literature include Helen Barolini, Frank Lentricchia, Robert Viscusi, Anthony Tamburri, John Paul Russo, Mary Jo Bona, Justin Vitiello, Thomas J. Ferraro, Louise Napolitano, Edvige Giunta, and Marianna DeMarco Torgovnick. In light of the exciting work being done today, more and more previously submerged American scholars, critics, and writers of Italian descent are surfacing on the pages of *Differentia, Italian Americana, Voices in*

Italian Americana, and at local and national conferences. In the publishing arena, more and more writers are being accepted by traditional and avant-garde presses such as Antonio D'Alfonso's Guernica Editions of Canada, which has become the leading publisher of Italian American literature.

8. Peragallo's *Italian-American Authors and Their Contribution to American Literature* is an encyclopedia of sorts that includes a list of American authors with Italian surnames along with brief biographical sketches and bibliographies for each. While an extremely valuable research tool, it is crudely critical.

9. For early criticism of Rose Green's study, see Francesco Cordasco's review "The *Risorgimento* of Italian-American Studies," *Journal of Ethnic Studies* 2.4 (1975):104–12.

10. Seminal works in this field include Houston Baker's *Blues, Ideology and Afro-American Literature*, Henry Louis Gates's *The Signifying Monkey*, Juan Bruce-Novoa's *Chicano Authors* and *Chicano Poetry*, Ramón Saldívar's *Chicano Narrative: The Dialectics of Difference*, Amy Ling's *Between Worlds: Women Writers of Chinese Ancestry*, and Gerald Vizenor's *Narrative Chance*. I owe much to these critics for helping me to realize the need for and the possibilities of creating a culture-specific approach to Italian American literature.

11. See Vico, *New Science*, book 1, no. 111.

12. Many critical studies of minority literatures include the word *margin* in their titles: Arnold Krupat's study of Native American Literature, *The Voice in the Margin* (1989), and Anthony Tamburri, Paul Giordano, and Fred L. Gardaphé, *From the Margin: Writings in Italian Americana* (1991), are two of the more recent ones.

13. Hayden White, in his essay "The Tropics of History," spells out the interaction between Vico's notion of social development and the prime characteristics of the accompanying languages:

1. The transition from primal metaphorical identifications by naming external reality in terms taken from the most particular and most sensible ideas of the parts of the body and the emotional states to metonymic reduction is analogous to the transition in society from the rule of the gods to the rule of aristocracies; 2. The transition from metonymic reductions to synecdochic constructions of wholes from parts, genera from species, and so on is analogous to the transition from aristocratic to democratic rule; and 3. The transition from synecdochic constructions to ironic statement is analogous to the transition from democracies rule by law to the decadent societies whose members have no respect for the law. (209)

14. Vico also calls this stage the incredible because it represents a deconstruction of the earlier myths and traditions on which the culture is based. I include my discussion of Rimanelli's work in Chapter 3 so that the reader can better observe the impact of Rimanelli's work in the philosophic mode in relation to the mythic texts produced by Puzo and Talese.

15. Vico's notion of *corso* and *ricorso* will help us not only in discussing national literatures but in examining individual authors as well. The careers of John Fante, Helen Barolini, Pietro di Donato, and others have moved through a type of *corso* and *ricorso*.

16. Stephen Greenblatt, a leading practitioner of New Historicism, explains how ethnography will work in reading literary texts:

Anthropological interpretation must address itself less to the mechanics of customs and institutions than to the interpretative constructions the members of a society apply to their experiences. A literary criticism that has affinities to this practice must be conscious of its own status as interpretation and intent upon understanding literature as a part of the system of signs that constitutes a given culture; its proper goal, however difficult to realize, is a *poetics of culture.* (*Renaissance Self-Fashioning*, 4)

Greenblatt draws on the work of anthropologist Clifford Geertz in creating his New Historicist approach and tells us that "we must, as Clifford Geertz [in "Art as a Cultural System"] suggests, incorporate the work of art into the texture of a particular pattern of life, a collective experience that transcends it and completes its meaning" (179). While Greenblatt produces an admirable reading of English Renaissance texts utilizing an ethnographic approach, clues as to just what anthropological elements he employs in his readings are difficult to ferret out.

17. This published talk was a revision of an earlier article of the same title that first appeared in the 1964 *Smith Alumnae Quarterly.*

One Narrative in the Poetic Mode

1. It was only in 1877, when the Coppino Law was enacted, that formal education was made mandatory for all children between the ages of six and nine. This law was vigorously resisted by inhabitants of the Mezzogiorno and was not enforced. For a discussion of the effects of illiteracy on Italian immigrants and their children, see Richard Gambino, "Childhood and Education," in *Blood of My Blood.*

2. Mario Puzo consistently makes this connection — most recently in a scene from *The Godfather III*, in which Don Altobello requests that an assassin's retarded son "do the donkey," an act in which the son contorts his face and brays. It also appears in his earlier novel *The Sicilian* (1984):

The Sicilian peasant has an affinity with his mule and donkey. They are hard-working beasts, and like the peasant himself have flinty, dour natures. Like the peasant they can work steadily for very long hours without breaking down, unlike the higher nobility horse, who must be pampered. Also, they are surefooted and can pick their way along the mountain terraces without falling and breaking a leg, unlike the fiery stallions or the high-blooded, flighty mares. Also, peasant and donkey and mule subsist and thrive on food that kills other men and animals. But the greatest affinity was this: Peasant, donkey and mule had to be treated with affection and respect, other-wise they turned murderous and stubborn. (58–9).

3. Though Italians have been part of America's history since Columbus's voyage, only in retrospect can we establish a distinct Italian American literary tradition that

begins with accounts of explorers, missionaries (Father Samuel Mazzuchelli's *Memoirs* [1967], Sister Blandina Segale's *At the End of the Santa Fe Trail* [1978]), and statesmen.

4. In her introduction to *The Dream Book* Helen Barolini explains why Italian immigrants did not encourage their children to write: "When you don't read, you don't write. When your frame of reference is a deep distrust of education because it is an attribute of the very classes who have exploited you and your kind for as long as memory carries, then you do not encourage a reverence for books among your children. You teach them the practical arts not the imaginative ones" (4).

5. Barolini, in her introduction to *The Dream Book*, points out that as late as 1949, the date of the first published survey of Italian American writers (Olga Peragallo, *Italian-American Authors*), the U.S. Census counted only a little over 4.5 million Italian Americans, fewer than a million of whom spoke English, a small number to expect many writers to emerge from (5).

6. We must keep in mind that the experiences of migration from northern and southern Italy have as many differences as similarities, especially in terms of sociopolitical development. Though the written tradition of the Italian autobiography can be traced back to Dante and continues developing through such prominent figures as Benvenuto Cellini, Giambattista Vico, and Benedetto Croce, these writers were *prominenti*, representatives of an Italian experience that differed greatly from that of the immigrant. Italian American autobiographers, then, can be seen as creating a new tradition and are often doing something that, in the minds of most Italian immigrants, is considered "American."

Giuseppe Pitre and Solomone Marino have both done important work on southern Italian folk culture that has yet to be translated into English. Their work can be found listed in an excellent bibliography on Italian folklore compiled by Italo Calvino in *Fiabe italiane*.

7. For example, in America *omertà* is often pointed to as an attribute of Mafia members, who hold their tongues under fear of death.

8. For a survey of the movement from an oral to a literate-based culture, see Fred L. Gardaphé, "From Oral Tradition to Written Word: Toward an Ethnographically Based Literary Criticism."

9. William Boelhower, in *Immigrant Autobiography: Four Versions of the Italian American Self*, presents the most thorough analysis to date on the subject of Italian American autobiography. Rose Basile Green's pioneer study *The Italian-American Novel* presents some of the earliest Italian American writing and examines autobiographical aspects of Italian American fiction. And in *The Ethnic I*, James Craig Holte provides valuable information on the autobiographies of Frank Capra, Edward Corsi, Leonard Covello, Lee Iacocca, and Jerre Mangione.

10. For an interesting account of Italians' and Americans' language encounters, see Robert Viscusi, "Circles of the Cyclopes: Schemes of Recognition in Italian American Discourse."

11. For excellent discussions of the similarities between early Italian immigrant autobiographies and the *Autobiography* of Benjamin Franklin, see James Craig Holte's

"Benjamin Franklin and Italian-American Narratives" and "The Representative Voice: Autobiography and the Ethnic Experience."

12. Panunzio had already received some education when he arrived in the United States. D'Angelo had none; he learned English on his own while trying to survive as an unskilled laborer.

13. Cavalleri was the surname given to Rosa by Ets; Rosa's legal surname was Cassettari. For an account of the publication history of *Rosa*, see Winifred Farrant Bevilacqua's "Rosa: The Life of an Italian Immigrant—The Oral History Memoir of a Working-Class Woman."

14. *Rosa* does not reveal the real names of those who played major roles in her life. She fears that what she says will somehow harm or anger those still alive at the time of her telling.

15. Ets tells us in her introduction that she lived at the Chicago Commons and worked as a social worker. She graduated from the University of Chicago Graduate School of Social Service Administration (3–4).

16. According to Bevilacqua, Ets's revisions were attempts to bring "the language closer to standard English and giving the narrative a less rambling quality" (547).

17. Bevilacqua notes that there is a book-length manuscript of Rosa's folktales entitled "These Stories I Know Them from Italia" on deposit at the Immigration History Research Center in St. Paul, Minnesota (547).

18. Bugiarno, the pseudonym given for Rosa's native village, can mean "no lie," *bugiare* being the Italian infinitive of the verb "to lie." Since Ets does not tell us whether or not she knew Italian, it makes us wonder whose choice this word was.

19. Cannaletto, or "cane bed," is the name chosen as a pseudonym for the convent where the wild young Rosa was sent for her education. Again, it is anyone's guess as to whether Rosa or Ets made up the name.

20. *Fantasio*

> As Night like a black flower shuts the sun within its petals of gloom,
> The silent road crosses the sleeping valley like a winding dream—
> While the whole region has succumbed under the weight of a primeval silence.
> The mountains like mighty giants lift themselves with a regal haughtiness out of the
>   ruling gloom.
> Across the dim jagged distances are pearl-gray wings flitting
> Flitting—
>
> The moonlight is a hailstorm of splendor
> Pattering on the velvet floor of gloom—
> The moon!
> The moon is a faint memory of a lost sun—
> The moon is a footprint that the Sun has left on the pathless heaven!
>
> Pearl gray wings are whirling distantly—
> Whirling!

A fever of youth streams through my being
Trembling under the incantation of Beauty,
Like a turmoil of purple butterfly caught in a web of
    light.

A black foam of darkness overflows from the rim of night,
And floods away the pearl-gray wings! (43)

21. *Night Scene*

An unshaped blackness is massed on the broken rim of night.
A mountain of clouds rises like a Mammoth out of the walls of darkness
With its lofty tusks battering the breast of heaven.
And the horn of the moon glimmers distantly over the flares and clustered stacks of
    the foundry.

Uninterruptedly, a form is advancing
On the road that shows in tatters.

The unshaped blackness is rolling larger above the thronged flames that branch
    upward from the stacks with an interwreathed fury.
The form is strolling on the solitary road
Begins to assume the size of a human being.
It may be some worker that returns from the next town,
Where it has been earning its day's wages.

Slowly, tediously, it flags past me —
It is a tired man muttering angrily.
He mutters.
The blackness of his form now expands its hungry chaos
Spreading over half of heaven, like a storm,
Ready to swallow the moon, the puffing stacks, the wild foundry,
The very earth in its dark, furious maw,
The man mutters, shambling on —
The storm! The storm! (75–6)

22. *Accident in the Coal Dump*

Like a dream that dies in crushed splendor under the weight of awakening
He lay, limbs spread in abandon, at the bottom of a smooth hollow of glistening
    coal.
We were leaning about on our shovels and sweating,
Red faced in the lantern-light,
Still warm from our frenzied digging and hardly feeling the cold midnight wind.
He had been a handsome quiet fellow, a family man with whom I had often talked
Of the petty joys and troubles of our little dark world;

In the saloon on Saturday night.
And there he was now, huge man, an extinguished sun still followed by unseen
  faithful planets,
Dawning on dead worlds in an eclipse across myriad stars —
Vanished like a bubble down the stream of eternity.
Heedlessly shattered on the majestic falls of some unknown shores.
And we turned slowly toward home, shivering, straggling sombre —
Save one youngster who was trying to fool himself and his insistent thoughts
With a carefree joke about the dead man.
Snow began to fall like a white dream through the rude sleep of winter night,
And a wild eyed woman came running out of the darkness. (117–18)

23. *Omnis Sum*

On the Calvary of thought I knelt, in torment of silence.
The stars were like sparks struck from the busy forge of vengeful night.
The sky was like a woman in fury
Dishevelling her tresses of darkness over me.
It seemed as if the whole universe were accusing me
Of the anguish of the deity. (119)

24. This is the same segment that Van Doren includes on page xiii at the end of his
introduction. Chances are, the "leading magazine" D'Angelo refers to is the *Nation*. See
Franco Mulas's *Le poesie di Pascal D'Angelo* for an account of the publishing of D'Angelo's poetry.
25. *The City*

We who were born through the love of God must die through the hatred of Man.
We who grapple with the destruction of ignorance and the creation of unwitting
  love —
We struggle, blinded by dismal night in a weird shadowy city.
Yet the city itself is lifting street-lamps, like a million cups filled with light,
To quench from the upraised eyes their thirst of gloom;
And from the hecatombs of aching souls
The factory smoke is unfolding in protesting curves
Like phantoms of black unappeased desires, yearning and struggling and pointing
  upward;
While through its dark streets pass people, tired, useless
Trampling the vague black illusions
That pave their paths like broad leaves of water-lilies
On twilight streams;
And there are smiles at times on their lips.
Only the great soul, denuded to the blasts of reality,
Shivers and groans.

And like two wild ideas lost in a forest of thoughts,
Blind hatred and blinder love run amuck through the city. (162–3)

26. His trials are summed up in the final poem he includes.

Light

Every morning, while hurrying along River Road to work,
I pass the old miser Stemowski's hut,
Beside which pants a white perfumed cloud of acacias.
And the poignant spring pierces me.
My eyes are suddenly glad, like cloud-shadows when they meet the sheltering
gloom
After having been long stranded in a sea of glassy light.
Then I rush to the yard.
But on the job my mind still wanders along the steps of dreams in search of beauty.
O how I bleed in anguish! I suffer
Amid my happy, laughing but senseless toilers!
Perhaps it is the price of a forbidden dream sunken in the purple sea of an obscure
future. (179)

D'Angelo's own personal life becomes the subject of this poem. His personal well-being, once comforted by nature, now depends on what is inside him.

27. William Boelhower devotes a chapter of *Immigrant Autobiography* ("A Shadow in the Garden") to Panunzio's autobiography. Panunzio's work is also discussed by James Craig Holte in "Benjamin Franklin and Italian-American Narratives," and in his "The Representative Voice: Autobiography and the Ethnic Experience."

28. This was a pose Panunzio would take throughout his life. As a professor at the University of California at Los Angeles, he contributed to the understanding of the plight of Italian Americans caught between loyalties to Italy and America during the 1940s through his article "Italian Americans, Fascism and the War," published in 1942 in the *Yale Review*. In it, Panunzio explains the relationship between Italian Americans and the government of the immigrants' native land. He argues that while Italian Americans might have nibbled at the bait of fascism "as mainly a diversion or a means of escape from the feeling of inferiority which the American community imposed on them" (782), they never swallowed the hook, and "now that the test of war has come, there is no question as to where almost one hundred per cent of our Italian immigrant population stands" (782).

29. There are interesting similarities between the autobiographies of Panunzio and George Copway. This section is a shortened version of "Two Versions of the Self Made American," a paper comparing the two autobiographies that I presented at the 1991 MELUS conference in Minneapolis.

30. Panunzio attended Wesleyan College in Middletown, Connecticut, after graduating from the Maine Wesleyan Seminary.

31. Like D'Angelo, Panunzio's model reader is the educated American who has power over his or her own life and also has the power to assist the immigrant. These two authors are very much unlike Rosa, who had no idea who her audience would be other than Ets, and who died before her narrative was published.

32. In his deportation study Panunzio never identifies himself as an immigrant. He merely states that he is a Methodist minister who has studied and worked with immigrants.

33. Panunzio followed his autobiography with *Immigration Crossroads* (1927), which continued his work as a cultural mediator between immigrants and American society.

Two The Early Mythic Mode: From Autobiography to Autobiographical Fiction

1. See "The Establishment's Solution to the 'Foreign Problem' (1914–1930)," in *WOP!: A Documentary History of Anti-Italian Discrimination in the United States*, ed. Salvatore La Gumina.

2. "Drive for Law to Deport 6,000,000 Aliens Will Be Organized All over the Country," *New York Times*, June 23, 1935, sec. 1, p. 1.

3. A more thorough description of this synthesis can be found in the introduction to *From the Margin: Writings in Italian Americana*, ed. A. J. Tamburri et al.

4. For a more detailed account of the relationship of these writers to proletarian literature, see Fred L. Gardaphé, "Left Out: Three Italian/American Writers of the 1930s."

5. While most scholars are familiar with Sacco and Vanzetti—two major figures and the objects of leftist writing of the period—documentation and close reading of Italian participation in American culture has been left out of most studies of the 1930s.

Italian American writers were left out of such anthologies as Granville Hicks's *Proletarian Literature* (1935), John Herbert Nelson and Oscar Cargill's *Contemporary Trends: American Literature since 1900* (1949), Louis Filler's *The Anxious Years* (1963), Harvey Swados's *The American Writer and the Great Depression* (1966), and Jack Salzman's *Years of Protest* (1967). Not a word can be found about Italian American writers in such major works as Joseph Warren Beach's *American Fiction 1920–1940* (1942), Alfred Kazin's *On Native Ground* (1942), Maxwell Geismar's *Writers in Crisis* (1947), Leo Gurko's *The Angry Decade* (1947), Walter Rideout's *The Radical Novel in the United States* (1956), Daniel Aaron's *Writers on the Left* (1961), and Michael Millgate's *American Social Fiction* (1965). Even Marcus Klein's *Foreigners* (1981), which includes many noncanonical writers of the period, only briefly quotes Mangione in reference to the WPA Writers' Project. This absence is quite characteristic of contemporary scholarship, which either ignores or outright dismisses the contributions of American writers of Italian descent. More often than not, these writers, if considered at all, are not read in the context of their Italian American heritage. And when their writing is recognized, these writers are usually read as members of the dominant white Anglo-Saxon culture. While this practice might please those who wish to erase the stigma of an immigrant past and thus pass as WASPs, it distorts (if it does not ignore or erase) the social and political problems encountered by Italian Americans and shadows the contributions they have made to American culture.

6. Fante, a loyal follower of H. L. Mencken, stayed out of politics and described his attitude toward party-line politics and Marxist aesthetics in a letter to his literary mentor:

I haven't sucked out on Communism and I can't find much in Fascism. As I near twenty-six, I find myself moving toward marriage and a return to Catholicism. Augustine and Thomas More knew the answers a long time ago. Aristotle would have spat in Mussolini's face and sneered at Marx. The early fathers would have laughed themselves sick over the New Deal. . . . If I get ahold of enough money, I may leave the country. Give me a few books, some wine, a girl and a bit of good music. The sheep will be stamped out and die anyhow. All I want is that they leave me alone. (Moreau, *Fante/Mencken*, 103)

Fante's "return to Catholicism" and his choice not to align himself with left-wing ideology hindered his reception and consideration by cultural critics who adhered to Marxist aesthetics. Fante never committed himself to any political cause. He registers his disappointment in those who mix politics and literature in one of his many letters to Mencken, in which he recounts his experience at the 1939 Western Writers' Conference in San Francisco: "My experience with writers is invariably disillusioning. The more I meet them the less I think of the profession. There is always the man's work — and then the man. That is excusable in hacks and to be expected, but it seems to me the messiah on paper should not step out of his role in real life. Mike Gold for example turns out to be a platitude carrying a cross. He's so god-awful paternalistic, and yet so unmistakably adolescent" (Moreau, *Fante/Mencken*, 106).

7. Bandini's treatment of Mexicans in *Ask the Dust* is the same as his treatment of Filipinos in *The Road to Los Angeles*. Though this has been read as racism, readers must realize the irony at work in the protagonist's attempts to achieve an American identity at the expense of denying other minorities their Americanness.

8. One impediment that continually keeps Fante's protagonists from identifying themselves completely with American culture is their strong connections to Italian Catholicism. More than half the stories of his collection *Dago Red* (1940) deal with this subject. The protagonist of *1933* believes he has been visited in the night by the Virgin Mary.

9. In the late 1970s and the 1980s Black Sparrow Press reprinted all of Fante's earlier novels and published his new novels. Charles Bukowski wrote the preface to the reprint of *Ask the Dust*. In 1989, *Wait until Spring, Bandini* was made into a film starring Joe Mantegna as Svevo Bandini and Faye Dunaway as the widow Hildegarde, and directed by Dominique Deruddere.

10. Di Donato's diction is the one aspect of his novels that has received the most criticism. See the critical work of Robert Viscusi; Franco Mulas, "The Ethnic Language of Pietro di Donato's *Christ in Concrete*"; and Luigi Ballerini and Fredi Chiappelli, "Contributi espressive delle scritture e parlate Americo-Italianie."

11. Viscusi's criticism of di Donato is as prolific as it is insightful. He has included di Donato's writing in nearly all of his major articles: "*De Vulgari Eloquentia*: An Approach to the Language of Italian American Fiction," "The Semiology of Semen: Questioning the Father," "Circles of the Cyclops: Schemes of Recognition in Italian American Discourse," "Debate in the Dark: Love in Italian-American Fiction," "*Il caso della casa*: Stories of Houses in Italian America," and "A Literature Considering Itself: The Allegory of Italian America."

12. Two critics have perceptively identified the pre-Christian strain in di Donato's work but unfortunately did not develop their readings of this element. Giovanni Sinicropi points to di Donato's language as "steering away from the logic of literature and into the logic of life" ("Christ in Concrete," 177), something Sinicropi sees as "one of the great causes for which the Futurists had fought" (177). And Rose Basile Green acknowledges di Donato's treatment of "'folk religion,' that substratum of faith that exists below the level of organized religion" (*The Italian-American Novel*, 155).

13. Di Donato's devotion to Catholicism prompted him to write two religious biographies: *Immigrant Saint: The Life of Mother Cabrini* (1960) and *The Penitent* (1962), which tells the story of Saint Maria Goretti through the point of view of the man who killed her.

14. Redemption through women is a theme that resurfaces throughout di Donato's subsequent writings: *This Woman, Three Circles of Light, Immigrant Saint, The Penitent*, and most strikingly in the unpublished *The American Gospels*. See *VIA* 2.2, which contains a selection from di Donato's *Gospels* in a section devoted to di Donato's contribution to American literature.

15. For an account of di Donato's life between the publication of *Christ in Concrete* and *This Woman*, see Michael D. Esposito, "The Travail of Pietro di Donato," especially pages 55–56. Essentially, di Donato toured the country promoting his novel, working in a camp for conscientious objectors during World War II, married, and started a family and a construction business.

16. Di Donato used to tell a story that his father was the illegitimate son of D'Annunzio.

17. For a reading of this theme as it appears in a collection of shorter works and excerpts of di Donato's books, see Anthony D. Cavaluzzi's "'Flesh and Soul': Religion in Di Donato's *Naked Author*."

18. For an interesting reading of the diplomatic function of Mangione's writing, see Viscusi's "*De Vulgari Eloquentia*" (37) and "Debate in the Dark" (147).

19. Malcolm Cowley, letter to Jerre Mangione, April 29, 1981, Jerre Mangione Papers, Rush Rhees Library, Department of Rare Books and Special Collections, University of Rochester, Rochester, New York.

20. This trip is also recounted in *An Ethnic at Large*. In the chapter "Afraid in Fascist Italy," Mangione recalls his fear that he, like other Italian American young men who had traveled to Italy, might be forced into the Italian military "as a reprisal for his [father's] having escaped army service by migrating to the States" (179).

21. While sympathetic to the Communist Party in America, Mangione never formally joined it because he recognized in it a constraining dogmatism that reminded him of Catholicism. His memoirs *Mount Allegro* (1943) and *An Ethnic at Large* (1978), along with *The Dream and the Deal* (1972) — a study of the Federal Writers' Project — present a very thorough accounting of the 1930s from an ethnic perspective. His interest in writing and his encounters with American avant-garde artists of the 1930s led him to dismiss the "art-for-art's-sake" cult and to realize that "no writer worth his salt can turn his back on social injustice" (*An Ethnic at Large*, 49). For a brief time he attended meetings of the New York John Reed Club and taught literary criticism at the New School in New York. Though uncomfortable with party-line politics, he became a dedicated antifascist and contributed to the antifascist cause through news articles, book reviews, and social and political satire published in the *New Republic*, the *New Masses*, the *Partisan Review*, and the *Daily Worker*, many of them published under the pen names Mario Michele and Jay Gerlando. In spite of his left-wing activities and his strong antifascist beliefs, however, Mangione's work has never been adequately acknowledged in histories of this period.

22. Mangione received the 1989 Pennsylvania Governor's Award for Excellence in the Arts; among his many awards are a Guggenheim fellowship (1946), a Fulbright fellowship (1965), two National Endowment for the Arts grants (1980 and 1984), and the prestigious Italian Empedocles Prize (1984). In 1971 Italy named Mangione Commendatore and awarded him the Star of Italian Solidarity. He has also received two honorary degrees: Doctor of Letters from the University of Pennsylvania (1980), and Doctor of Humane Letters from the State University of New York at Brockport (1986).

23. In "Finale," a new chapter to *Mount Allegro* added in 1981, Mangione laments the total disappearance of his old neighborhood. Today, a historic marker, dedicated in a ceremony by the City of Rochester, marks the site of the "Mount Allegro" area.

24. Against Mangione's wishes, *Mount Allegro* was first labeled by the publisher as fiction. In response to his publisher's demands, Mangione fictionalized his characters' names prior to publication; thus the Mangiones became the Amorosos, and Jerre became Gerlando (Mangione's actual given name). For a thorough account of the genre jumping *Mount Allegro* experienced — from novel to children's literature and finally to memoir — see Boelhower's chapter on Mangione in *Immigrant Autobiography*.

25. My application of Viscusi's house paradigm to Mangione's four autobiographical works is in "My House Is Not Your House: Jerre Mangione and Italian/American Autobiography."

26. In "Song of the Bicentennial," poet Joseph Tusiani expresses this duality: "Two languages, two lands, perhaps two souls . . . / Am I a man or two strange halves of one" (7). For an account of how a sense of this duality can be read in ethnic American authors, see Jerre Mangione, "A Double Life: The Fate of the Urban Ethnic."

27. Mangione's latest publication, *La Storia*, is the result of ten years of research and a lifetime of dealing with the subject of Italian Americana. In it, he and co-writer Ben Morreale re-create the story of the many stories that make up Italian America. For a comprehensive Mangione bibliography and recent articles on Mangione's career, see *VIA* 4.4 (1993).

Three The Middle Mythic Mode: Godfathers as Heroes, Variations on a Figure

1. While Italian American writers do sometimes note that they have read the work of other Italian Americans, and in some cases even review each other's work, Italian American writers rarely read each other.

2. In "Mari Tomasi's *Like Lesser Gods* and the Making of an Ethnic *Bildungsroman*," Mary Jo Bona presents what I believe is the first discussion of the literary use of a godparent figure in Italian American literature.

3. Puzo draws on his experiences prior to writing *The Godfather* in creating the character Merlyn in his novel *Fools Die* (1978); see especially pages 57–58.

4. See "Choosing a Dream" and "The Italians, American Style," in Puzo's *The Godfather Papers and Other Confessions*.

5. Puzo's representation of Italian language throughout the book is more often than not based on aural transcriptions of Italian words and words of Italian American dialect. His most peculiar signs are "putain" (15) for *putanna*; "consigliori" for *consigliore*; "boccie" (47) for *bocce*; "rajunah," which he uses to signify the Italian *ragione*, "reason," and which he falsely defines as "to rejoin" (47); and "gavones" (283) for *cafoni*.

6. My thanks to Michele Cheung for her insights into Puzo's use of traditional mythology in the novel.

7. For two of these readings, see Marianna Torgovnick's "*The Godfather* as the World's Most Typical Novel," in which she presents the novel as "a version of Homer's work [*The Odyssey*] for our time"; and Tom Ferraro's "Blood in the Marketplace," in which he argues that "the Mafia achieves its romantic luster not because Puzo portrays the Italian-American family as a separate sphere, lying outside of capitalism, but because the Italian-American family emerges as a potent structure within it" (193).

8. This does not happen in the film, which depicts Kay as the American power who can stop the growth of this Sicilian family's business.

9. Talese points out this connection when he writes, "A kinship of sorts probably did exist between these men [mafiosi] and the legendary American cowboy, Bill thought, impressed by the similarity beween the tales of the Old West and certain stories he had heard as a boy involving gun battles between mounted mafiosi in the hills of western Sicily. He had heard that his grandmother in Castellammare sometimes packed a pistol in her skirts" (59). Critics have also picked up on this connection. See Ronald Dworkin's discussion in "Views," *Listener*, August 24, 1972, 233–4.

10. See Talese, "Where Are the Italian-American Novelists?" *New York Times Book Review*, March 14, 1993, 1.

11. Ronald Dworkin writes: "The Mafia of the stories serves the role of a myth that denies change, but it serves another purpose as well. Americans who live in cities are desperately afraid of the black man with a knife who needs a fix, or the junkie who kills on a high, or, most of all, the radical with a bomb who threatens their life and their way of life as well. The Mafioso kills in a way that satisfies their taste for violence without fear; his murders are neither indiscriminate nor pointless nor political, and they threaten no one who does not live by choice in that world" ("Views," 24).

12. In Talese's exploration of the Mafia, he provides through Bill Bonanno a documentary of Michael Corleone. Bill receives a good education and is trained as a soldier through his college ROTC experience (59). The difference between Puzo's and Talese's Mafia sons is that Bonanno's experiences and voice were not constructed out of a writer's imagination, but instead were transcribed from audio tapes and reconstructed from a reporter's notebook. The story thus has a documentable referent in reality.

13. Reviewer Pete Hamill sees *Honor Thy Father* as "one of those sturdy Victorian novels that take us beyond the curtains to look at human lives" ("Bonanno and Son," 4).

14. It is interesting that Puzo has Michael Corleone move the family west to Lake Tahoe and the business to Las Vegas.

15. Lounsberry's page references are from the World Publishing edition of *Honor Thy Father* (1971).

16. Dworkin sees Bill's taking of a mistress as "part of his flirtation with an alien world" an act that ironically reunites the "divided family [as it] closes ranks in support of his wife" ("Views," 234). While Puzo's Sonny acts in a similar manner, he is never "sickened" in the way that Bill Bonanno is, nor does he ever philosophize about what his sexual antics might mean to his father, who does see Sonny's sexual transgressions as a weakness.

17. While this sequence mirrors Michael Corleone's fictional struggle, Bill Bonanno fails miserably to keep the tradition alive, while Michael succeeds.

18. The film *The Godfather Part III* makes a futile attempt at depicting the inability of the third generation to maintain the crime family's integrity. It fails where Talese succeeds in depicting the effects of the Mafia lifestyle on the later generations.

19. Talese published this segment in "Image of the Mafia," an op-ed piece for the *New York Times*, October 5, 1971. Here he touches on the reality of Mafia life that Puzo never presents.

20. Talese also reprinted this in "Image of the Mafia."

21. In some ways Bill Bonanno is Talese's alter ego. The writing of this book gained for Talese a power in the publishing industry equal in many respects to the power Joseph Bonanno once wielded.

22. Talese's presentation of Rosalie's perspective mirrors Kay Adams's questioning in Puzo's novel. Like Kay, Rosalie attempts to run away with her children.

23. Rimanelli's novels, such as *Tiro al piccione* (Einaudi, 1991), are again best-sellers

as they are being rediscovered and republished as classics. See Anthony Tamburri's "Giose Rimanelli's *Bendetta in Guysterland*" for an excellent discussion of Italian and American signs in the novel.

24. Long before he moved to America Rimanelli was examining the influence of America on life in Italy. In his *Peccato originale* (1954; translated by Ben Johnson and published by Random House in 1957 under the title *Original Sin*), the dream of a better life in America is a topic of debate among the villagers: "As far as I'm concerned, America is an illusion, one big illusion," says Scocchera in response to Nicola's suggestion that once settled there he will send for his friend, Scocchera. Scocchera then takes out a letter from one Vincenzo Rimanelli, "the one whose son's a writer, and who took it into his head to go to America with that busted leg he had" (the letter tells of the trials of life in America). Scocchera reads from the letter: "And then, I won't even tell you about the Italo-Americans. They're all hopping madmen, and if things keep on the way they're going we'll be off our heads too. And now, just thinking it over real good, America is a big fat bluff, they treat us like pack asses" (92).

25. I am thinking of Anthony Valerio's short fiction, especially "The Last Godfather," of Don DeLillo's portrayal of the Mafia through the Talerico brothers in *Running Dog*, and of Sorrentino's brief sketches throughout his early work.

26. Countless films, television shows, novels, short stories, etc., have used the Italian American subject in parodies. In many cases, as in such films as *I Married the Mob* and *Moonstruck*, the parodic elements are (mis)read as realistic portrayals of Italian Americans.

27. Rimanelli is as much concerned with preserving folk culture through his dialect poetry and songs as he is with creating new literature through his Italian and English language experiments.

28. As Rimanelli notes in his appendix (no. 4, p. 218), *Sexophone* was the title of a Curzio Malaparte revue produced in the mid-1950s. According to Luigi Barzini, the revue was a "vulgar and pointless challenge to the taste of a public" that might have existed in 1919, who would have been "alarmed at the notion of saxophones and sex and Negro Music" (*From Caesar to the Mafia*, 59).

29. Rimanelli's source for chapter 3 is *Honor Thy Father*, chapter 12, pages 181–200.

30. In chapter 25 (177) Rimanelli presents a conversation between Zip and Pimple Boy that is based on the DeCavalcante tapes presented in *Honor Thy Father* (379).

Four The Later Mythic Mode: Reinventing Ethnicity
through the Grandmother Figure

1. Mary Jo Bona explains, "The fact that ethnic writers choose the immigrant as literary protagonist compels a reformulation of the efforts made in gaining an identity in America, one which will finally embrace the immigrant's unique position" ("Broken Images," 91).

2. This notion of the cultural immigrant was first discussed in my essay, "Lo scrittore Italo-Americano è ancora un emigrante," *Bolletino della Fondazione Rimanelli* (1987):4 It is further developed by Gardaphé et al. in the introduction to *From the Margin* (5).

3. Mary Dearborn discusses the generational saga in reference to non–Italian American ethnics in *Pocohantas's Daughters*, 159–60.

4. In *Through a Glass Darkly*, William Boelhower remarks that to divide American fiction into ethnic categories is to diminish the importance of the work as representative both of the ethnic group and of the larger society. To such critics as Boelhower and Werner Sollors, all American writing is ethnic because that is the nature of the American experience. As Sollors says, "American literature as a whole can be read as the ancestral footstep or coded hieroglyph of ethnic life of the past and ethnic tensions in the present" (*Beyond Ethnicity*, 649).

5. Antidefamation groups prospered during the second generation, and much of the Italian American community's public presence was devoted to defending Italian Americans from defamatory remarks and unfair media representations. Removed from much of this direct discrimination, Italian Americans of the third generation are freer to concentrate on what I call profamatory productions.

6. The labels "visible" and "invisible" correspond in many ways to Edward Said's notion of "filiation" and "affiliation," and to Werner Sollors's notion of "descent" and "consent." All writers, I would argue, can be read as being somewhere along a continuum from one to the other; it is the purpose of my analyses to locate each writer's position, as well as to determine his or her ratio of visible to invisible.

7. An excellent article pointing to sources for study of the experiences of the Italian woman in America is Betty Boyd Caroli's "Italian Women in America: Sources for Study," *Italian Americana* 2.2 (1976):242–51. See also *Voices of the Daughters* (Princeton: Townhouse Publishing, 1989), a compilation of responses to questionnaires, face-to-face interviews, phone interviews, and oral histories of Italian American women colllected by Connie A. Maglione and Carmen Anthony Fiore between 1984 and 1989.

8. *Paper Fish* was nominated for a Carl Sandburg Award, and portions of the novel received Illinois Arts Council awards. Jerre Mangione praised the novel and wrote the back cover blurb: "*Paper Fish* is an outstanding literary event, a first novel that breaks through the barriers of conventional fiction to achieve a dazzling union of narrative and poetry. . . . Hers is a delightfully fresh voice, filled with ancient wisdom which is new and probing, miraculously translating the most ineffable nuances of human existence in a language that is consistently beautiful and vital."

9. For a more thorough discussion of the oral tradition evidenced in DeRosa's writing, see my "From Oral Tradition to Written Word: Toward an Ethnographically Based Literary Criticism."

10. Interestingly, DeRosa's ethnic heritage is only half derived from Italian culture. Her mother's side is descended from Lithuanian aristocracy forced out of Europe by communism.

11. Despite what Robert Viscusi has said, this dance, and not the scattering of the cornmeal, is the ritual from which Maso's novel takes its title. Viscusi was mistakenly

referring to a traditional burial ceremony, and not the Ghost Dance, which originated with the Paiute Indians and moved to the Plains Indians, and represented rebellion against assimilation into American culture. For a detailed account of the Ghost Dance religion, see James Mooney, *The Ghost-Dance Religion and the Sioux Outbreak of 1890*.

12. A few of these bildungsroman novels are Helen Barolini's *Umbertina*, Tina DeRosa's *Paper Fish*, Kenny Marotta's *A Piece of Earth*, Rachel Guido de Vries's *Tender Warriors*, Jay Parini's *The Patch Boys*, Carole Maso's *Ghost Dance*, Tony Ardizzone's *The Heart of the Order*, Anthony Giardina's *A Boy's Pretensions*, and Josephine Gattuso Hendin's *The Right Thing to Do*.

13. See my essay "Visibility or Invisibility: The Postmodern Prerogative in the Italian/American Narrative."

14. See Rudolph Vecoli, "The Italian-American Literary Subculture: An Historical and Sociological Analysis."

Five Narrative in the Philosophic Mode

1. The cultural reciprocity between their (in Edward Said's terms) filiative and affiliative cultures has yet to be considered. In *The World, the Text, and the Critic* (1983), Said presents an interesting way of analyzing the relationship of a critic (for our purposes we can also read "writer") to his or her tradition. Said's "filiation" and "affiliation" form two "formidable and related powers" that engage "critical attention": "One is the culture to which critics are bound filiatively (by birth, nationality, profession); the other is a method or system acquired affiliatively (by social and political conviction, economic and historical circumstances, voluntary effort and willed deliberation)" (24–5).

2. See "Genetic Coding," the last essay in Sorrentino's *Something Said*, a collection of his essays.

3. Frank Lentricchia expressed a similar fear in an interview: "I feel impelled to write an autobiographical essay once in a while about this stuff [his Italian American working-class background] and I've always held back, because I fear this goddam sentimentality about it" (Salusinszky, "Frank Lentricchia," 182–3).

4. For a brief sketch of the life and literary career of Carnevali, see Jerre Mangione and Ben Morreale's *La Storia* (360–62).

5. *Melanzana*, the Italian word for "eggplant," is also used to refer to African Americans.

6. Although the narrator(s) never tells us, there is a chance that Lamont could be perceived as an Italian. Joseph Beshary sends Lamont a letter addressed to Anthony LaMonti asking that Lamont back his gambling efforts (334).

7. One of the most famous uses is in *The Godfather*, in which Don Corleone dies in the garden while tending his tomato plants (408–9).

8. See "A Fixture" and "Ars Longa," and John Paul Russo's discussion of them in "The Choice of Gilbert Sorrentino."

9. Guido appears in *Mulligan Stew* as Mario, a kid that Halpin tells Ned Beaumont

he knew: "I knew a boy named Mario who wore his rubbers to school every day because of the enormous holes in his shoes. This was during the warm and wonderful 30s. This sartorial eccentricity did not negate the fact that he had been born in Sciacca" (*Mulligan Stew*, 429). Sciacca is the town where Sorrentino's father was born.

10. Giose Rimanelli has discovered that DeLillo's parents come from Montagano, a small town near Casacalenda (Rimanelli's hometown) in the region of Molise. Rimanelli believes that DeLillo's surname was originally DiLillo and was most likely changed when DeLillo's parents entered the United States.

11. While DeLillo's second novel, *End Zone*, lacks an identifiable Italian American presence, there is a strong ethnic presence in Anatole Bloomberg, a Jew who believes that "history is guilt" (45) and therefore attempts to "unjew" himself. Bloomberg spells out this process — really a recipe for assimilation, which requires (1) geographic relocation to "a place where there aren't any Jews," (2) the elimination of linguistic markers of ethnicity, and (3) acquiring a new way of thinking (46). Later, Bloomberg defends this process: "I don't want to hear a word about the value of one's heritage. I am a twentieth-century individual. I am working myself up to a point where I can exist beyond guilt, beyond blood, beyond the ridiculous past. Thank goodness for America. . . . I reject heritage, background, tradition and birthright. These things merely slow the progress of the human race. They result in war and insanity" (77).

12. For an interesting reading of ethnicity in DeLillo's work, see Judith Pastore's "Marriage American Style: Don DeLillo's Domestic Satire" and "Pirandello's Influence on American Writers: Don DeLillo's *The Day Room*."

What Lentricchia has been working toward in his theory and practice of American literary criticism is precisely what DeLillo does with American literature; that is, he keeps "readers from gliding into the comfortable sentiment that the real problems of the human race have always been about what they are today" ("American Writer," 6). For a more detailed analysis of the role *Italianità* plays in the development and practice of the cultural criticism of Frank Lentricchia and a discussion of Lentricchia's reading of DeLillo, see my article "(In)visibility: Cultural Representation in the Criticism of Frank Lentricchia."

13. Pastore notes that "if we look at what DeLillo is saying about marriage and divorce American style, we find that beneath his sophisticated postmodern format, his satiric voice is fairly conventional, moving away certainly from his Italian-American, Catholic origins, but still retaining enough of that heritage to color his presentation ("Marriage American Style," 2)."

14. This is especially the case with *Mao II*, the novel that earned DeLillo the prestigious Pen/Faulkner Award in 1992.

15. For a more detailed analysis of DeLillo's use of the family in his fiction, see Judith Pastore's "Marriage American Style."

16. "The established canons of rhetoric forbid anyone to speak of himself except for some compelling reason. The ground of this prohibition is that one cannot speak of someone without either praising or blaming him, and to let either of these pass one's

lips in regard to oneself would be to show a want of urbanity" (Dante, *The Banquet*, 14).

17. In *End Zone*, Norgene Azamanian is named for a brand of refrigerator (69). To become other is to rid oneself of old languages and to learn new languages — a major theme in *End Zone*, *Ratner's Star*, and *Great Jones Street*.

Epilogue

1. Caponegro's grandfather on her father's side comes from Cosenza in Calabria, and her grandmother on her father's side comes from Arpino, near Rome, where Cicero was born.

2. Di Prima has been publishing pieces of her autobiography-in-progress in such publications as *Mamma Bears News & Notes* out of San Francisco (excerpts appear regularly from volume 6 on), *Voices in Italian Americana*, and *Mother Jones*. In these excerpts she goes back to the troubled times before she left home (when *Memoirs* begins) and uncovers the family secrets that haunt her.

3. In a telephone interview (January 30, 1993), Caponegro told me she once considered changing her surname, which she thought was "too Italian."

4. It is unfortunate that as of 1994, there was still no center for Italian American studies anywhere in the United States. The papers of writers such as John Fante and Pietro di Donato remain in the homes of their heirs, unprocessed and unavailable to scholars, and there is still not a single endowed chair for Italian American studies.

5. As I plan to show in future work, Giambattista Vico's notions of the stages that occur during the rise and fall of nations can be fruitfully applied to the bodies of literature produced by American writers who belong to or are descended from other cultures.

Works Cited

Aaron, Daniel. "How to Read Don DeLillo." In *Introducing Don DeLillo*, ed. Frank Lentricchia, 67–81. Durham: Duke University Press, 1991.

———. "The Hyphenate American Writer." *Smith Alumnae Quarterly* (July 1964): 213–17. Revised for *Rivista di studi anglo-americani* 3.4–5 (1984–85):11–28.

———. *Writers on the Left*. 1961. Reprint. New York: Oxford University Press, 1977.

Adamic, Louis. "Muscular Novel of Immigrant Life." Review in the *Saturday Review*, August 26, 1939, 5.

Ahearn, Carol Bonomo. "Interview: Helen Barolini." *Fra Noi* 25 (September 1986):47.

Alba, Richard D. *Italian Americans: Into the Twilight of Ethnicity*. Englewood Cliffs, N.J.: Prentice-Hall, 1985.

Alfonsi, Ferdinando. *Dictionary of Italian-American Poets*. New York: Peter Lang, 1989.

———. *Poesia Italo-Americana/Italian American Poetry: Saggi E Testi/Essays and Texts*. Catanzaro, Italy: Antonio Carello Editore, 1991.

———. *Poeti Italo-Americani/Italo-American Poets: Antologia bilingue/A Bilingual Anthology*. Catanzaro, Italy: Antonio Carello Editore, 1985.

Alpert, Barry. "Gilbert Sorrentino: An Interview Conducted by Barry Alpert." *Vort* 2.3 (1974):3–30.

Ardizzone, Tony. *The Heart of the Order*. New York: Henry Holt, 1987.

Auerbach, Erich. "Vico and Aesthetic Historism." In *Scenes from the Drama of European Literature*, 183–98. Minneapolis: University of Minnesota Press, 1984.

Baker, Houston. *Blues, Ideology and Afro-American Literature*. Chicago: University of Chicago Press, 1984.

Ballerini, Luigi, and Fredi Chiappelli. "Contributi espressive delle scritture e parlate Americo-Italianie." In *Atti di convegni Lincei*, 195–218. Rome: Accademia Nazionale dei Lincei, 1985.

Barolini, Helen. "Becoming a Literary Person Out of Context." *Massachusetts Review* 27.2 (1986):262–74.

———. "A Circular Journey." *Texas Quarterly* 21.2 (1978):109–26.

———. *Festa: Recipes and Recollections*. New York: Harcourt, 1988.

———. "The Finer Things in Life." *Arizona Quarterly* 29.1 (1973):26–36.

———. Introduction to *The Dream Book: An Anthology of Writings by Italian-American Women*, ed. Helen Barolini, 3–56. New York: Schocken Books, 1985.

———. *Love in the Middle Ages*. New York: William Morrow, 1986.

———. Preface to *The Dream Book*. New York: Schocken Books, 1985.

———. *Umbertina*. New York: Seaview, 1979.

Barthes, Roland. 1950. *Mythologies*. Trans. Annette Lavers. New York: Hill and Wang, 1987.

———. "Science versus Literature." In *Introduction to Structuralism*, ed. M. Lane, 410–16. New York: Basic Books, 1970.

Barzini, Luigi. *From Caesar to the Mafia*. 1971. Reprint. New York: Bantam Books, 1972.

Beach, Joseph Warren. *American Fiction: 1920–1940*. New York: Macmillan, 1942.

Bevilacqua, Winifred Farrant. "Rosa: The Life of an Italian Immigrant—The Oral History Memoir of a Working-Class Woman." In *Italy and Italians in America. Rivista di studi anglo-americani* 3.4–5 (1984–85):545–55.

Bidney, David. "Vico's New Science of Myth." In *Giambattista Vico, an International Symposium*, ed. Giorgio Tagliacozzo, 259–67. Baltimore: Johns Hopkins University Press, 1969.

Boelhower, William. *Immigrant Autobiography in the United States: Four Versions of the Italian American Self*. Verona: Essedue Edizioni, 1982.

——. *Through a Glass Darkly: Ethnic Semiosis in American Literature*. 1984. Reprint. New York: Oxford University Press, 1987.

Bona, Mary Jo. "Broken Images, Broken Lives: Carmolina's Journey in Tina DeRosa's *Paper Fish*." *MELUS* 14.3–4 (1987):87–106.

——. "Claiming a Tradition: Italian American Women Writers." Ph.D. diss., University of Wisconsin, 1989.

——. "Mari Tomasi's *Like Lesser Gods* and the Making of an Ethnic *Bildungsroman*." *Voices in Italian Americana* 1.1 (1990):15–34.

——, ed. *The Voices We Carry*. Montreal: Guernica, 1994.

Bruce-Novoa, Juan. *Chicano Authors: Inquiry by Interview*. Austin: University of Texas Press, 1980.

——. *Chicano Poetry, a Response to Chaos*. Austin: University of Texas Press, 1982.

Buchler, Justus, ed. *Philosophical Writings of Peirce*. New York: Dover, 1955.

Buhle, Paul M. *A Dreamer's Paradise Lost: Louis C. Fraina/Lewis Corey (1892–1953) and the Decline of Radicalism in the United States*. Atlantic Highlands, N.J.: Humanities Press International, 1995.

Burgess, Anthony. "Alien. Poems. (1964–1970)." *Misure critiche. Su/Per Rimanelli: Studi e Testimonianze* 17–18.65–67 (1987–88):244–5.

Buttitta, Ignazio. "The Ass." Trans. Justin Vitiello. In *First and Most Recent Poems*, ed. M. Puglisi. Turin: Gruppo Editoriale Forma, 1983.

Byrne, Jack. "Sorrentino's *Steelwork*: Expanding Eddy Beshary's 'Annual Listing' (or) Beyond 'Besharyism.'" *Review of Contemporary Fiction* 1 (Spring 1981):171–89.

Cammett, John M., ed. *The Italian American Novel*: Proceedings of the Second Annual American Italian Historical Association Conference. Staten Island, N.Y.: American Italian Historical Association, 1969.

Caponegro, Mary. *The Star Café*. New York: W. W. Norton, 1991.

——. *Tales from the Next Village*. Providence, R.I.: Lost Roads Publishers, 1985.

Caroli, Betty Boyd. "Italian Women in America: Sources for Study." *Italian Americana* 2.2 (1976):242–51.

Casciato, Art. "The Bricklayer as Bricoleur: Pietro di Donato and the Cultural Politics of the Popular Front." *Voices in Italian Americana* 2.2 (1991): 67–76.

Calvino, Italo. *Fiabe Italiane*. Turin: Giulio Einaudi, 1956.

Cavaluzzi, Anthony. "'Flesh and Soul': Religion in Di Donato's *Naked Author.*" *Voices in Italian Americana* 2.2 (1991):59–66.

Chamberlain, John. Review of *Wait until Spring, Bandini. Scribner's* 104.6 (1938):69–70.

Clifford, James. "Introduction: Partial Truths." In *Writing Culture: The Poetics and Politics of Ethnography*, ed. James Clifford and George E. Marcus, 1–26. Berkeley: University of California Press, 1986.

———. *The Predicament of Culture: Twentieth-Century Ethnography, Literature, and Art.* Cambridge: Harvard University Press, 1988.

Cooney, Seamus, ed. *John Fante: Selected Letters 1932–1981.* Santa Rosa, Calif.: Black Sparrow, 1991.

Cordasco, Francesco. "The *Risorgimento* of Italian-American Studies." *Journal of Ethnic Studies* 2.4 (1975):104–12.

Daly, Robert. "Liminality and Fiction in Cooper, Hawthorne, Cather and Fitzgerald." In *Victor Turner and the Construction of Cultural Criticism*, ed. Kathleen M. Ashley, 70–85. Bloomington: Indiana University Press, 1990.

D'Angelo, Pascal. *Son of Italy.* New York: Macmillan, 1924.

Dante. *The Banquet.* Trans. Christopher Ryan. Saratoga, Calif.: Anna Libri, 1989.

Dearborn, Mary V. *Pocohantas's Daughters: Gender and Ethnicity in American Culture.* New York: Oxford University Press, 1986.

DeLillo, Don. *Americana.* 1971. Reprint. New York: Penguin, 1989.

———. "The Angel Esmeralda." *Esquire* (May 1994): 100–9.

———. "Baghdad Towers West." *Epoch* 17 (1968):195–217.

———. "Coming Sun. Mon. Tues." *Kenyon Review* 28.3 (1966):378–94.

———. *End Zone.* 1972. Reprint. New York: Penguin, 1986.

———. *Great Jones Street.* New York: Houghton Mifflin, 1973.

———. "In the Men's Room of the Sixteenth Century." *Esquire* (December 1971):174.

———. *Libra.* New York: Viking, 1988.

———. *Mao II.* New York: Penguin, 1991.

———. *Pafko at the Wall. Harper's* (October 1992):35–70.

———. *Players.* New York: Alfred A. Knopf, 1977.

———. *Ratner's Star.* New York: Houghton Mifflin, 1976.

———. "Spaghetti and Meatballs." *Epoch* 14 (1965):244–50.

———. "Take the 'A' Train." *Epoch* 12 (1962):9–25.

DeRosa, Tina. *Father to the Migrants.* Darien, Ill.: Insider Publications, 1989.

———. "An Italian-American Woman Speaks Out." *Attenzione* (May 1980):38–9.

———. *Paper Fish.* 1980. Reprint. New York: The Feminist Press, 1996.

DeVries, Rachel Guido. *Tender Warriors.* Ithaca, N.Y.: Firebrand Books, 1986.

Di Donato, Pietro. "The American Gospels." Unpublished MS, 1989.

———. *Christ in Concrete.* 1939. Reprint. Indianapolis, Ind.: Bobbs-Merrill, 1966.

———. *Immigrant Saint: The Life of Mother Cabrini.* 1960. Reprint. New York: St. Martin's Press, 1991.

———. "The Last Judgement." *VIA* 2.2 (1991):23–43.

———. *Naked Author.* New York: Phaedra, 1970.

———. *The Penitent.* New York: Prentice-Hall, 1962.

———. Speech at the University of Illinois, Chicago, 1978.

———. *This Woman.* New York: Ballantine Books, 1958.

———. *Three Circles of Light.* New York: Julian Messner, 1960.

Diomede, Matthew. *Pietro Di Donato, the Master Builder.* Cranbury, N.J.: Associated University Presses, 1995.

Di Prima, Diane. *Memoirs of a Beatnik.* 1969. Reprint. San Francisco: Last Gasp Press, 1988.

———. *Recollections of My Life as a Woman.* New York: Viking, 1996.

"Drive for Law to Deport 6,000,000 Aliens Will Be Organized All over the Contry." *New York Times,* June 23, 1935, 1.

Dworkin, Ronald. "Views." *Listener,* August 24, 1972, 233–4.

Eder, Richard. Review of Mary Caponegro, *The Star Café.* "This Is Not a Book Review." *Los Angeles Times Book Review,* July 1, 1990, 3.

Esposito, Michael D. "The Evolution of Pietro Di Donato's Perceptions of Italian Americans." In *The Italian Americans through the Generations,* ed. Rocco Caporale, 176–84. Proceedings of the 15th Annual Conference of the American Italian Historical Association. Staten Island, N.Y.: American Italian Historical Association, 1986.

———. "Pietro Di Donato Reevaluated." *italian americana* 6.2 (1980): 179–92.

———. "The Travil of Pietro Di Donato." *MELUS* 7.2 (1980):47–60.

Ets, Marie Hall. *Rosa: The Life of an Italian Immigrant.* Minneapolis: University of Minnesota Press, 1970.

Falassi, Alessandro. *Folklore by the Fireside: Text and Context of the Tuscan Veglia.* Austin: University of Texas Press, 1980.

Fante, John. *Ask the Dust.* 1939. Reprint. Santa Barbara, Calif.: Black Sparrow, 1980.

———. *1933 Was a Bad Year.* Santa Barbara, Calif.: Black Sparrow, 1985.

———. *Prologue to Ask the Dust.* Santa Rosa, Calif.: Black Sparrow, 1990.

———. *The Road to Los Angeles.* Santa Barbara, Calif.: Black Sparrow, 1985.

———. *Wait until Spring, Bandini.* 1938. Reprint. Santa Barbara, Calif.: Black Sparrow, 1983.

———. *The Wine of Youth: Selected Stories.* Santa Barbara, Calif.: Black Sparrow, 1985.

Farrell, James T. "The End of a Literary Decade." In *Literature at the Barricades: The American Writer in the 1930s,* ed. Ralph Bogardus and Fred Hobson, 204–210. University: University of Alabama Press, 1982.

Felski, Rita. "The Novel of Self-Discovery: Necessary Fiction?" *Southern Review* 19.2 (1980):131–48.

Ferraro, Thomas J. "Blood in the Marketplace: The Business of Family in the *Godfather* Narratives." In *The Invention of Ethnicity,* ed. Werner Sollors, 176–207. New York: Oxford University Press, 1989.

———. *Ethnic Passages: Literary Immigrants in Twentieth Century American Literature.* University of Chicago Press, 1993.

Fischer, Michael J. "Ethnicity and the Post-Modern Arts of Memory. In *Writing Culture: The Poetics and Politics of Ethnography*, ed. James Clifford and George E. Marcus, 194–233. Berkeley: University of California Press, 1986.

Fraina, Louis. "Human Values in Literature and Revolution." *Story* 8 (May 1936):4.

———. "Socialism and the Catholic Church." *Daily People*, November 5, 1911, 5.

Franklin, Benjamin. *Autobiography.* Ed. Max Farrand. Berkeley: University of California Press, 1949.

French, Warren. *The Social Novel at the End of an Era.* Carbondale: Southern Illinois University Press, 1966.

———, ed. *The Thirties: Fiction, Poetry, Drama.* Deland, Fla.: Everett Edwards, 1967.

Gambino, Richard. *Blood of My Blood.* 1973. Reprint. New York: Anchor, 1975.

Gans, Herbert J. "Symbolic Ethnicity: The Future of Ethnic Groups and Cultures in America." In *On the Making of Americans: Essays in Honor of David Riesman*, ed. Herbert J. Gans et al., 193–220. Philadelphia: University of Pennsylvania Press, 1979.

Gardaphé, Fred L. *Dagoes Read: Tradition and the Italian/American Writer.* Toronto: Guernica Editions, 1996.

———. "From Oral Tradition to Written Word: Toward an Ethnograpically Based Literary Criticism." In *From the Margin: Writings in Italian Americana*, ed. Anthony Tamburri et al., 294–306. West Lafayette, Ind.: Purdue University Press, 1991.

———. "Giose Rimanelli: New Directions of a Literary Missionary." *Misure critiche. Su/Per Rimanelli: Studi e Testimonianze* 17–18.65–67 (1987–88):235–43.

———. "An Interview with Tina DeRosa." *Fra Noi* 24 (May 1985):23.

———. Introduction to *Christ in Concrete*, ix–xviii. New York: Signet, 1993.

———. "(In)visibility: Cultural Representation in the Criticism of Frank Lentricchia." *Differentia* 6–7 (Spring–Summer 1994):201–18.

———. "Italian/American Literary Responses to Fascism." In *Romance Languages Annual*, ed. Jeanette Beer, Charles Ganelin, and Ben Lawton, 254–9. West Lafayette, Ind.: Purdue University Research Foundation, 1993.

———. *The Italian-American Writer: An Essay Annotated Checklist.* Spencertown, N.Y.: Forkroads Press, 1995.

———. "Lo scrittore Italo-Americano è ancora un emigrante." *Bolletino della Fondazione Rimanelli* (1987):4.

———. "My House Is Not Your House: Jerre Mangione and Italian/American Autobiography." In *American Lives*, ed. James Robert Payne, 139–77. Knoxville: University of Tennessee Press, 1992.

———. "Parini's *Patch Boys* Mines Italian American Heritage." *Fra Noi* 26 (April 1987): 37–40.

———. Review of *Italian-American Poetry*, by Ferdinando Alfonsi. *Italica* 70.2 (1993): 219–21.

———. "Visibility or Invisibility: The Postmodern Prerogative in the Italian/American Narrative." *Almanacco* 2.1 (1992):24–33.

Gardaphé, Fred L., Anthony J. Tamburri, and Paul Giordano. Introduction to *From the*

Margin: Writings in Italian Americana, 1–11. West Lafayette, Ind.: Purdue University Press, 1991.

Garside, E. B. Review of *Christ in Concrete. Atlantic* (1939):292.

——. "John Fante vs. John Selby." Review. *Atlantic* (1939):292.

Gates, Henry Louis, Jr. "Criticism in the Jungle." In *Black Literature and Literary Theory*, ed. Gates, 1–24. New York: Methuen, 1984.

——. *The Signifying Monkey.* New York: Oxford University Press, 1988.

"Gay Talese, 1932–." *Contemporary Literary Criticism*, vol. 37, ed. Daniel G. Marowski, 390–405. Detroit: Gale Research Company, 1986.

Geertz, Clifford. "Blurred Genres: The Refiguration of Social Thought." *American Scholar* 49 (1980):165–79.

——. *The Interpretation of Cultures.* New York: Basic Books, 1973.

——. *Local Knowledge.* New York: Basic Books, 1983.

Geismar, Maxwell. *Writers in Crisis: The American Novel: 1925–1940.* London: Secker and Warburg, 1947.

Gramsci, Antonio. *Quaderni del carcere.* 4 vols. Ed. Valentino Gerratana. Turin: Giulio Einaudi Editore, 1975.

——. "The Southern Question." In *The Modern Prince and Other Writings*, 28–51. New York: International Publishers, 1957.

Green, Rose Basile. *The Italian-American Novel: A Document of the Interaction of Two Cultures.* Cranbury, N.J.: Associated University Presses, 1974.

Greenblatt, Stephen. *Renaissance Self-Fashioning: From More to Shakespeare.* Chicago: University of Chicago Press, 1980.

Gurko, Leo. *The Angry Decade.* New York: Harper and Row, 1968.

Gusdorf, Georges. "Conditions and Limits of Autobiography." In *Autobiography: Essays Theoretical and Critical*, ed. James Olney, 28–48. Princeton: Princeton University Press, 1980.

Hamill, Pete. "Bonanno and Son." *Washington Post Book World*, November 7, 1971, 4.

Hansen, M. L. "The Third Generation in America." *Commentary* 14.5 (1952):492–500.

Hart, Henry, ed. *American Writers' Congress.* New York: International Publishers, 1935.

——, ed. *The Writer in a Changing World.* New York: Equinox Cooperative Press, 1937.

Hendin, Josephine Gattuso. *The Right Thing to Do.* Boston: David R. Godine, 1988.

——. *Vulnerable People: A View of American Fiction since 1945.* New York: Oxford University Press, 1978.

Hicks, D. Emily. *Border Writing: The Multidimensional Text.* Minneapolis: University of Minnesota Press, 1991.

Holte, James Craig. "Benjamin Franklin and Italian-American Narratives." *MELUS* 5.4 (1978): 99–102.

——. *The Ethnic I: A Sourcebook for Ethnic American Autobiography.* New York: Greenwood Press, 1988.

——. "The Representative Voice: Autobiography and the Ethnic Experience." *MELUS* 9.2 (1982):25–46.

Homberger, Eric. *American Writers and Radical Politics, 1900–39*. New York: St. Martin's Press, 1986.

Hutcheon, Linda. *A Poetics of Postmodernism: History, Theory, Fiction*. New York: Routledge, 1988.

——. *The Politics of Postmodernism*. New York: Routledge, 1989.

Jameson, Fredric. "Postmodernism and Consumer Society." In *The Anti-Aesthetic: Essays on Postmodern Culture*, ed. Hal. Foster, 111–25. Seattle: Bay Press, 1983.

Kazin, Alfred. *On Native Ground*. New York: Harcourt Brace Jovanovich, 1942.

Kirschenbaum, Blossom. "Mary Caponegro: Prize-Winning American Writer in Rome." In *"Prix de Rome": The Rome Prize in Literature, 1952–1992*. New York: Peter Lang, forthcoming.

Klein, Marcus. *Foreigners: The Making of American Literature, 1900–1940*. Chicago: University of Chicago Press, 1981.

Kolb, Harold. "Defining the Canon." In *Redefining American Literature History*, ed. A. LaVonne Brown Ruoff and Jerry Ward, 35–51. New York: MLA, 1991.

Krupat, Arnold. *The Voice in the Margin*. Berkeley: University of California Press, 1989.

La Gumina, Salvatore, ed. "The Establishment's Solution to the 'Foreign Problem' (1914–1930)." In *WOP!: A Documentary History of Anti-Italian Discrimination in the United States*, 181–248. San Francisco: Straight Arrow Books, 1973.

Lauter, Paul. "Caste, Class, Canon." In *A Gift of Tongues: Critical Challenges in Contemporary American Poetry*, ed. Marie Harris and Kathleen Aguero, 57–82. Athens: University of Georgia Press, 1987.

LeClair. Tom. *In the Loop: Don DeLillo and the Systems Novel*. Champaign: University of Illinois Press, 1987.

LeClair, Tom, and Larry McCaffery. "An Interview with Don DeLillo." In *Anything Can Happen*, 80–90. Urbana: University of Illinois Press, 1983.

Lentricchia, Frank. "The American Writer as Bad Citizen." In *Introducing Don DeLillo*, ed. Lentricchia, 1–6. Durham: Duke University Press, 1991.

——. *Ariel and the Police*. Madison: University of Wisconsin Press, 1988.

——. *The Edge of Night*. New York: Random House, 1994.

——. Introduction to *New Essays on White Noise*, ed. Lentricchia, 1–14. New York: Cambridge University Press, 1991.

——. "*Libra* as Postmodern Critique." In *Introducing Don DeLillo*, ed. Lentricchia, 193–215. Durham: Duke University Press, 1991.

——. "Luigi Ventura and the Origins of Italian-American Fiction." *italian americana* 1.2 (1974):189–95.

——. "My Kinsman, T. S. Eliot." *Raritan* 11.4 (1992):1–22.

——. Review of John J. Soldo, *Delano in America & Other Early Poems*. *italian americana* 1.1 (1974):124–5.

——. "Tales of the Electronic Tribe." In *New Essays on White Noise*, ed. Lentricchia, 87–113. New York: Cambridge University Press, 1991.

Leonardi, Susan J. "Recipes for Reading: Summer Pasta, Lobster à la Riseholme, and Key Lime Pie." *PMLA* 104 (1989):340–7.

Ling, Amy. *Between Worlds: Women Writers of Chinese Ancestry.* New York: Pergamon Press, 1990.

Lord, Eliot, John J. D. Trenor, and Samuel J. Barrows. *The Italian in America.* New York: B. F. Buck, 1905.

Lounsberry, Barbara. *The Art of Fact: Contemporary Artists of Nonfiction.* New York: Greenwood Press, 1990.

Luccock, Halford E. *American Mirror: Social, Ethical and Religious Aspects of American Literature, 1930–1940.* New York: Macmillan, 1940.

Madden, David. *Proletarian Writers of the Thirties.* Carbondale: Southern Illinois University Press, 1968.

Maglione, Connie, and Carmen Fiore. *Voices of the Daughters.* Princeton, N.J.: Townhouse Publishing, 1989.

Malpezzi, Frances, and William Clements. *Italian-American Folklore.* Little Rock, Ark.: August House, 1992.

Mangione, Jerre. "Acrobat to Il Duce." Review of *Better Think Twice about It* and *The Outcast,* by Luigi Pirandello. *New Republic,* August 28, 1935, 82–3.

——. *America Is Also Italian.* New York: G. P. Putnam's Sons, 1969.

——. "Comments." In *Contemporary Novelists,* 4th ed., ed. D. L. Kirkpatrick, 570–2. New York: St. Martin's Press, 1986.

——. "A Double Life: The Fate of the Urban Ethnic." In *Literature and the Urban Experience,* ed. Michael C. Jaye and Ann Chalmers Watts, 169–83. New Brunswick, N.J.: Rutgers University Press, 1981.

——. *The Dream and the Deal: The Federal Writers' Project 1935–1943.* 1972. Reprint. Philadelphia: University of Pennsylvania Press, 1983.

——. *An Ethnic at Large: A Memoir of America in the Thirties and Forties.* 1978. Reprint. Philadelphia: University of Pennsylvania Press, 1983.

—— [Pseud. Mario Michele]. "Fontamara Revisited." *New Republic,* May 26, 1937, 69–71.

——. "Happy Days in Fascist Italy." Review of *Fontamara,* by Ignazio Silone. *New Masses,* October 2, 1934, 37–8.

——. "Little Italy." Review of *Christ in Concrete. New Republic,* August 30, 1939, 111–12.

——. *Mount Allegro.* 1943. Reprint. New York: Harper and Row, 1989.

——. *Mussolini's March on Rome.* New York: Franklin Watts, 1975.

——. *Night Search.* New York: Crown Publishing, 1965.

—— [Pseud. Jay Gerlando]. "Pirandello Didn't Know Him." Review of *Mr. Aristotle,* by Ignazio Silone. *New Masses,* November 12, 1935, 23–24.

——. Review of *The Grand Gennaro. New Republic,* October 23, 1935, 313.

——. *The Ship and the Flame.* New York: A. A. Wyn, 1948.

Mangione, Jerre, and Ben Morreale. *La Storia.* New York: Harper-Collins, 1992.

Marcus, George E., and Michael M. J. Fischer. *Anthropology as Cultural Critique: An Experimental Moment in the Human Sciences.* Chicago: University of Chicago Press, 1986.

Maso, Carole. *The Art Lover.* San Francisco: North Point Press, 1990.

——. *Ava.* Normal, Ill.: Dalkey Archive Press, 1993.

——. *Ghost Dance.* San Francisco: North Point Press, 1986.

Mathias, Elizabeth, and Richard Raspa. *Italian Folktales in America: The Verbal Art of an Immigrant Woman.* Detroit: Wayne State University Press, 1985.

Mazzuchelli, Samuel. *The Memoirs of Father Samuel Mazzuchelli, O.P.* Chicago: Priory Press, 1967.

Melling, Philip H. "Samples of Horizon: Picaresque Patterns in the Thirties." In *Nothing Else to Fear: New Perspectives on America in the Thirties,* ed. Stephen Baskerville and Ralph Willett, 104–31. Dover, N.H.: Manchester University Press, 1985.

Messenger, Christian. "The Authority of the Signifier: Barthes and Puzo's *The Godfather.*" Unpublished essay, 1992.

Millgate, Michael. *American Social Fiction: James to Cozzens.* New York: Barnes and Noble, 1964.

Molesworth, Charles. "Don DeLillo's Perfect Starry Night." In *Introducing Don DeLillo,* ed. Frank Lentricchia, 143–56. Durham: Duke University Press, 1991.

Mooney, James. *The Ghost-Dance Religion and the Sioux Outbreak of 1890.* 1896. Reprint. Chicago: University of Chicago Press, 1965.

Moreau, Michael, ed. *Fante/Mencken: A Personal Correspondence, 1930–1952.* Santa Rosa, Calif.: Black Sparrow, 1989.

Morgan, L. H. *Researches in the Lines of Human Progress from Savagery through Barbarism to Civilization.* New York: Henry Holt, 1877.

——. *Systems of Consanguinity and Affinity of the Human Family.* Washington, D.C.: Smithsonian Institution, 1870.

Morreale, Ben. *A Few Virtuous Men.* Montreal: Tundra Books, 1973.

——. "Jerre Mangione: The Sicilian Sources." *italian americana* 7.1 (1981): 5–17.

——. "Mangione and the Yearning for Home." *Fra Noi* 25 (November 1986):41.

——. *Monday Tuesday . . . Never Come Sunday.* Plattsburgh, N.Y.: Tundra Books, 1977.

Moss, Leonard. "The Family in Southern Italy: Yesterday and Today." In *The United States and Italy: The First Two Hundred Years,* ed. Humbert S. Nelli, 1–12. New York: American Italian Historical Association, 1976.

Mulas, Franco. "The Ethnic Language of Pietro Di Donato's *Christ in Concrete.*" In *From the Margin: Writings in Italian Americana,* ed. Anthony J. Tamburri, Paolo Giordano, and Fred L. Gardaphé, 307–15. West Lafayette, Ind.: Purdue University Press, 1992.

——. *Le poesie di Pascal D'Angelo.* Sassari: Università degli Studi di Sassari, 1989.

Napolitano, Louise. *An American Story: Pietro di Donato's "Christ in Concrete."* New York: Peter Lang, 1995.

O'Brien, John. "An Interview with Gilbert Sorrentino." *Review of Contemporary Fiction* 1.1 (1981):5–27.

Olney, James. *Metaphors of Self: The Meaning of Autobiography.* Princeton: Princeton University Press, 1972.

Ong, Walter. *Orality and Literacy.* New York: Methuen, 1982.

Orsini, Daniel. "Rehabilitating Di Donato, a Phonocentric Novelist." In *The Melting Pot and Beyond: Italian Americans in the Year 2000*, ed. Jerome Krase and William Egelman, 191–205. Proceedings of the 18th Annual Conference of the American Italian Historical Association. Staten Island, N.Y.: American Italian Historical Association, 1987.

Orth, Samuel P. *Our Foreigners*. New Haven: Yale University Press, 1920.

Paglia, Camille. *Sexual Personae*. New York: Vintage, 1991.

Panunzio, Constantine. "Italian Americans, Fascism, and the War." *Yale Review* 31 (June 1942):771–82.

———. *The Soul of an Immigrant*. New York: Macmillan, 1921.

Pastore, Judith Laurence. "Marriage American Style: Don DeLillo's Domestic Satire." *Voices in Italian Americana* 1.2 (1990):1–19.

———. "Pirandello's Influence on American Writers: Don DeLillo's *The Day Room*." *Italian Culture* 8 (1990):431–47.

Patti, Samuel J. "Autobiography: The Roots of the Italian-American Narrative." *Annali d'Italianistica* 4 (1986):243–8.

Peragallo, Olga. *Italian-American Authors and Their Contribution to American Literature*. New York: S. F. Vanni, 1949.

Puzo, Mario. *Dark Arena*. 1953. Reprint. New York: Dell, 1969.

———. *Fools Die*. New York: Signet, 1978.

———. *The Fortunate Pilgrim*. New York: Atheneum, 1964.

———. *The Godfather*. 1969. Reprint. New York: Fawcett Crest, 1970.

———. *The Godfather Papers and Other Confessions*. New York: Fawcett, 1972.

———. *The Sicilian*. New York: Linden Press, 1984.

Reilly, John. "Criticism of Ethnic Literature: Seeing the Whole." *MELUS* 5.1 (1978): 2–13.

———. "Literary Versions of Ethnic History from Upstate New York." In *Upstate Literature: Essays in Memory of Thomas F. O'Donnell*, ed. Frank Bergmann, 183–200. Syracuse: Syracuse University Press, 1985.

Rideout, Walter. *The Radical Novel in the United States, 1900–1954*. Cambridge: Harvard University Press, 1956.

Rimanelli, Giose. *Benedetta in Guysterland*. Montreal: Guernica, 1993.

———. *The Day of the Lion*. Trans. Ben Johnson, Jr. New York: Random House, 1954.

———. *Italian Literature: Roots and Branches*. New Haven: Yale University Press, 1975.

———. *Modern Canadian Stories*. Toronto: Ryerson Press, 1966.

———. *Original Sin*. Trans. Ben Johnson, Jr. New York: Random House, 1957.

———. *Peccato originale*. Milan: Mondadori, 1954.

———. *Tiro al piccione*. Milan: Mondadori, 1953. Reprint. Turin: Einaudi, 1991.

———. *Tragica America*. Genoa: Immordino, 1968.

———. *Una posizione sociale*. Florence: Vallechi, 1959.

Ruoff, A. LaVonne Brown. *American Indian Literatures: An Introduction, Bibliographic Review and Selected Bibliography*. New York: MLA, 1990.

Ruoff, A. LaVonne Brown, and Jerry W. Ward, eds. *Redefining American Literary History*. New York: MLA, 1990.

Russo, John Paul. "The Choice of Gilbert Sorrentino." In *From the Margin: Writings in Italian Americana*, ed. Anthony Tamburri et al., 338–56. West Lafayette, Ind.: Purdue University Press, 1991.

———. "The Poetics of Gilbert Sorrentino." *Rivista di studi anglo-americani* 3.4–5 (1984–85):281–303.

Said, Edward. *The World, the Text, and the Critic*. Cambridge, Mass.: Harvard University Press, 1983.

Saldívar, Ramón. *Chicano Narrative: The Dialectics of Difference*. Madison: University of Wisconsin Press, 1990.

Salusinszky, Imre. "Frank Lentricchia." In *Criticism in Society*, 177–206. New York: Methuen, 1987.

Salzman, Jack, and Barry Wallenstein, eds. *Years of Protest: A Collection of American Writings of the 1930s*. New York: Pegasus, 1967.

Segale, Sister Blandina. *At the End of the Santa Fe Trail*. 1912. Reprint. Milwaukee: Bruce Publishers, 1948.

Sheed, Wilfrid. "Everybody's Mafia." *New York Review of Books*, July 20, 1972, 23–5.

Sheppard, R. Z. "Second Banana." *Time*, October, 4, 1971, 83–4.

Sifakis, Carl. *The Mafia Encyclopedia*. New York: Facts on File Publications, 1987.

Sinicropi, Giovanni. "Christ in Concrete." *italian americana* 3.2 (1977):175–83.

Sollors, Werner. *Beyond Ethnicity: Consent and Descent in American Culture*. New York: Oxford University Press, 1986.

Sorrentino, Gilbert. *Aberration of Starlight*. 1980. Reprint. New York: Penguin, 1981.

———. *Blue Pastoral*. San Francisco: North Point Press, 1983.

———. *Crystal Vision*. 1981. Reprint. New York: Penguin, 1982.

———. *Imaginative Qualities of Actual Things*. 1971. Reprint. Elmwood Park, Ill.: Dalkey Archive Press, 1991.

———. *Mulligan Stew*. New York: Grove Press, 1979.

———. *The Sky Changes*. 1966. Reprint. San Francisco: North Point Press, 1986.

———. *Something Said*. San Francisco: North Point Press, 1984.

———. *Splendide-Hôtel*. 1973. Elmwood Park, Ill.: Dalkey Archive Press, 1984.

———. *Steelwork*. 1970. Reprint. Elmwood Park, Ill.: Dalkey Archive Press, 1992.

Stefanile, Felix. "The Dance at Saint Gabriels." In *From the Margin: Writings in Italian Americana*, ed. Anthony J. Tamburri et al., 158. West Lafayette, Ind.: Purdue University Press, 1991.

———. "Stone." In *A Suit of Four: A. L. Lazarus, Barriss Mills, Felix Stefanile and Bruce Woodford*, 44–7. West Lafayette, Ind.: Purdue University Studies, 1973.

Swados, Harvey, ed. *The American Writer and the Great Depression*. Indianapolis, Ind.: Bobbs-Merrill, 1966.

Talese, Gay. *Honor Thy Father*. New York: Fawcett Crest, 1971.

———. "Image of the Mafia." *New York Times*, October 5, 1971, 41.

------. "Where Are the Italian-American Novelists?" *New York Times Book Review*, March 14, 1993. 1.

Tamburri, Anthony Julian. "Giose Rimanelli's *Benedetta in Guysterland:* A 'Liquid' Novel of Questionable Textual Boundaries." *World Literature Today* 68.3 (1994): 473–78.

------. "In (Re)cognition of the Italian/American Writer: And Categories." *Differentia* 6–7 (Spring–Summer 1994):9–32.

------. *To Hyphenate or Not to Hyphenate.* Montreal: Guernica, 1991.

------. "*Umbertina*: The Italian/American Woman's Experience." In *From the Margin: Writings in Italian Americana*, ed. Anthony J. Tamburri et al., 357–73. West Lafayette, Ind.: Purdue University Press, 1991.

Tamburri, Anthony Julian, Paolo A. Giordano, and Fred L. Gardaphé, eds. *From the Margin: Writings in Italian Americana.* West Lafayette, Ind.: Purdue University Press, 1991.

Torgovnick, Marianna. "*The Godfather* as the World's Most Typical Novel." *South Atlantic Quarterly* 87.2 (1988):329–53.

Tusiani, Joseph *Gente Mia.* Stone Park, Ill.: Italian Cultural Center, 1978.

Tyler, Stephen. "Post-Modern Ethnography: From Document of the Occult to Occult Document." In *Writing Culture: The Poetics and Politics of Ethnography*, ed. James Clifford and George E. Marcus, 122–40. Berkeley: University of California Press, 1986.

Valerio, Anthony. "The Last Godfather." *VIA* 1.1 (1990):99–102.

------. *Valentino and the Great Italians.* New York: Freundlich Books, 1986.

Vecoli, Rudolph. "The Coming of Age of the Italian Americans: 1945–1974." *Ethnicity* 5 (1978):119–47.

------. "The Italian-American Literary Subculture: An Historical and Sociological Analysis." In *The Italian American Novel*, ed. John M. Cammett, 6–10. Proceedings of the Second Annual American Italian Historical Association Conference. Staten Island, N.Y.: American Italian Historical Association, 1969.

Verene, Donald Philip. *The New Art of Autobiography: An Essay on "The Life of Giambattista Vico Written by Himself."* New York: Oxford University Press, 1991.

Vico, Giambattista. *The New Science.* 1948. Reprint. Trans. Thomas Goddard Bergin and Max Harold Fisch. New York: Columbia University Press, 1968.

Viscusi, Robert. "Breaking the Silence: Strategic Imperatives for Italian American Culture." *VIA* 1.1 (1990):1–14.

------. "*Il caso della casa*: Stories of Houses in Italian America." In *The Family and Community Life of Italian Americans*, ed. Richard J. Juliani, 1–10. Proceedings of the 13th Annual Conference of the American Italian Historical Association. Staten Island, N.Y.: American Italian Historical Association, 1983.

------. "Circles of the Cyclopes: Schemes of Recognition in Italian American Discourse." In *Italian Americans: New Perspectives in Italian Immigration and Ethnicity*, ed. Lydio Tomasi, 209–19. Staten Island, N.Y.: Center for Migration Studies, 1986.

———. "Debate in the Dark: Love in Italian-American Fiction." In *American Declarations of Love*, ed. Ann Massa, 155–763. New York: St. Martin's Press, 1990.

———. "*De Vulgari Eloquentia*: An Approach to the Language of Italian American Fiction." *Yale Italian Studies* 1 (Winter 1981:):21–38.

———. "A Literature Considering Itself: The Allegory of Italian America." In *From the Margin: Writings in Italian Americana*, ed. Anthony J. Tamburri et al., 265–81. West Lafayette, Ind.: Purdue University Press, 1991.

———. "Narrative and Nothing." *Differentia* 6–7 (Spring–Summer 1994):77–99.

———. " 'The Semiology of Semen': Questioning the Father." In *The Italian Americans through the Generations*, ed. Rocco Caporale, 185–95. Proceedings of the 15th Annual Conference of the American Italian Historical Association. Staten Island, N.Y.: American Italian Historical Association, 1986.

Vizenor, Gerald. "Trickster Discourse." In *Narrative Chance: Postmodern Discourse on Native American Literatures*, ed. Vizenor. Albuquerque: University of New Mexico Press, 1989.

Von Huene–Greenberg, Dorothee. "A *MELUS* Interview: Pietro Di Donato." *MELUS* 14.3–4 (1987):33–52.

Wald, Alan. "Theorizing Culture Difference: A Critique of the 'Ethnicity School.' " *MELUS* 14.2 (1987):21–34.

White, Hayden. "The Tropics of History: The Deep Structure of the *New Science*." In *Tropics of Discourse: Essays in Cultural Criticism*, 197–217. Baltimore: Johns Hopkins University Press, 1978.

Young, Donald. *Research Memorandum on Minority Peoples in the Depression*. 1937. Reprint. New York: Arno Press, 1972.

Index

Fred L. Gardaphé is Professor of English at Columbia College in Chicago, where he teaches writing, American literature, and Italian American culture. He is an associate editor of the newspaper *Fra Noi* and a coeditor of *Voices in Italian Americana* and has published fiction, essays, and critical articles in local and national publications. His books include *Dagoes Read: Tradition and the Italian/American Writer* (1996) and *The Italian-American Writer: An Essay and Annotated Checklist* (1995). He is a coeditor of *From the Margin: Writings in Italian Americana* and the editor of *New Chicago Stories.* His reviews of Italian American literature have appeared regularly in *Fra Noi* since 1984, in the *Philadelphia Inquirer*, and in scholarly journals.

He was recently elected to the National Book Critics Circle and has been vice president of the American Italian Historical Association since 1993. He has also written two one-act plays: "Vinegar and Oil" (produced by Chicago's ItalianAmerican Theater Company in 1987) and "Imported from Italy" (produced by Zebra Crossing Theater in 1991). His short story "Morra, Amore" won second prize in the 1987 Unico literary contest.

Library of Congress Cataloging-in-Publication Data

Gardaphé, Fred L.

Italian signs, American streets : the evolution of Italian

American narrative / Fred L. Garaphé.

p.   cm. — (New Americanists)

Includes bibliographical references and index.

ISBN 0-8223-1730-3 (alk. paper). —

ISBN 0-8223-1739-7 (pbk. : alk. paper)

1. American literature — Italian American authors — History and

criticism.   2. American literature — 20th century — History and

criticism.   3. Italian Americans — Biography — History and criticism.

4. Italian Americans — Intellectual life.   5. Italian Americans in

literature.   6. Ethnic groups in literature.   7. Narration

(Rhetoric)   8. Autobiography.   I. Title.   II. Series.

PS153.18G37   1996

810.9'851 — dc20   95-40678

CIP